Dreaming Equality

Dreaming Equality

Color, Race, and Racism in Urban Brazil

ROBIN E. SHERIFF

RUTGERS UNIVERSITY PRESS
New Brunswick, New Jersey, and London

Library of Congress Cataloging-in-Publication Data

Sheriff, Robin E., 1959–
Dreaming equality : color, race, and racism in urban Brazil / Robin E. Sheriff.
p. cm.
Includes bibliographical references and index.
ISBN 0-8135-2999-9 (cloth : alk. paper)—ISBN 0-8135-3000-8 (pbk. : alk. paper)
1. Blacks—Brazil—Rio de Janeiro—Social conditions. 2. Racism—Brazil—Rio de
Janeiro. 3. Blacks—Brazil—Rio de Janeiro—Attitudes. 4. Blacks—Civil rights—
Brazil—Rio de Janeiro 5. Whites—Brazil—Rio de Janeiro—Attitudes. 6. Middle
class—Brazil—Rio de Janeiro—Attitudes. 7. Rio de Janeiro (Brazil)—Race relations.
I. Title.

F 2646.9.N4 S44 2001
305.896′08153—dc21
2001019294

British Cataloging-in-Publication data for this book is available from the British
Library

Manufactured in the United States of America

For Irene and Dica, grandmothers by blood and spirit

Contents

Acknowledgments *ix*

	Introduction	*1*
Chapter 1	The Hill	*13*
Chapter 2	Talk: Discourses on Color and Race	*29*
Chapter 3	Silence: Racism and Cultural Censorship	*59*
Chapter 4	Narratives: Racism on the Asphalt	*84*
Chapter 5	Narratives: Racism at Home	*118*
Chapter 6	Whiteness: Middle-Class Discourses	*150*
Chapter 7	Blackness: Militant Discourses	*185*
Chapter 8	Conclusion: Dreaming	*218*
	Epilogue	*225*

Notes   *235*
References   *243*
Index   *255*

Acknowledgments

I owe the deepest debt to the people of Morro do Sangue Bom, who, despite the insecurity and hardship in which they lived, gave me friendship, shelter, and protection. People on the asphalt, as I was told, "might starve to death before they would go and ask a neighbor for an egg"; but on the hill, I was to understand, it was not independence but the practice of *confiança*, or trust, that not only held body and soul together but also communicated a larger faith in the things that really matter. They understand, I hope, that my permanent debt to them is not a burden but one of many gifts that I tightly hold.

Over the years it has taken me to learn anthropology, I have leaned on many in the United States as well. I would like to thank those who helped me get by: Wendy Barron, Sanjib Baruah, Mario Bick, John Burdick, Arthur Chandler, Olivier Conan, Ros Daly, David Hartheimer, Audrey Heffernan, Jerry Jenkins, Laura Kittross, Lisa Krueger, Gene Mederos, Maureen O'Dougherty, Michael Putnam, Daphne Ross, Gerry Ross, Jane Ross, Glenda Ruby, Lisa Schnall, Joseph Shohan, Beata Vidacs, my parents, Edwin Sheriff and Patricia Sheriff, and my grandmother, Irene McNarney. For getting me home in one piece, I extend special thanks to Audrey Heffernan.

I owe a debt to Mario Bick, who introduced me to both anthropology and Brazilianist studies. My commitment to the discipline of anthropology through difficult and sometimes fearsome circumstances is due, in large measure, to his encouragement. Over many years, I have benefited from the tricksterish wit and uncommonly good sense of Vincent Crapanzano. His support has allowed me to trust my own voice with a degree of grit that I would not otherwise have. His vision of the possibilities within anthropology and his respect for the abiding mystery of the worlds in which we practice it have profoundly influenced my own approach to our discipline.

I have been blessed before, during, and after my fieldwork with the support and insights of a number of Brazilianist colleagues in the United States. I would like to thank Cristiana Bastos, Diana Brown, John Burdick, Sue Anne Caulfield, Donna Goldstein, Daniel Gross, Lindsay Hale, Sara Nelson, Maureen O'Dougherty, Ben Penglase, and France Winddance Twine. I have, in addition, benefited from wide-ranging discussions with non-Brazilianist colleagues, especially August Carbonella, Elizabeth Chin, Carmen Ferradas, Jonathan Hearn, Aisha Khan, Chris Leonard, Patricia Musante, Alyson Purpura, and Beata Vidacs.

I would like to thank the faculty, staff, and visiting fellows of the Race and Ethnicity Program of the Institute of Philosophy and Social Sciences, Federal University of Rio de Janeiro, for their invitation to participate in their fellowship program for visiting scholars. I especially benefited from lively late-night debates with Vincent Crapanzano, Olivia da Cunha, Peter Fry, Yvonne Maggie, Guy Massart, Claudia Rezende, and Livio Sansone. Over many years, Peter Fry has offered shelter and good meals while challenging my thinking in many significant ways; he has saved me from too rigid an understanding of Brazil. I would also like to thank Gilberto Velho, who served as my field advisor during the period of my research, and Carlos Hasenbalg, whose work and support have allowed me to keep my footing in a particularly controversial field. At Florida International University, I extend my thanks to Janet Chernela, Peter Craumer, Stephen Fjellman, Jean Muteba Rahier, Ken Rogerson, and Richard Tardanico.

Several institutions have generously supported various stages of my research and writing. A U.S. Department of Education Title VI Language Study Grant funded language training in Rio, and a grant from the Department of Anthropology at the Graduate Center of the City University of New York (CUNY) allowed me to pursue preliminary research in Rio. My fieldwork was generously supported by a grant from the Wenner-Gren Foundation for Anthropological Research, and a critical period of analysis and writing was supported by a Leonard Silk Dissertation Fellowship, administered by CUNY. A Richard C. Wade Prize, also administered by CUNY, provided critical assistance and moral support during the later phases of writing.

Finally, I would like to thank those who read and provided many perceptive and provocative comments on earlier drafts of the book: Vincent Crapanzano, Donna Goldstein, Carlos Hasenbalg, Yolanda Moses, and Jane Schneider. Their assistance and encouragement have been invaluable. David Myers, editor extraordinaire at Rutgers University Press, has been unstinting in his support and exceptionally wise counsel. Thanks are also due to Karen Johnson, for eagle-eyed copyediting. Finally, I extend many thanks to Elaine Heffernan, good listener, great artist, who produced the artwork for this book. Any errors that remain are, of course, entirely my own.

Dreaming Equality

Being invisible and without substance, a disembodied voice, as it were, what else could I do? What else but try to tell you what was really happening when your eyes were looking through? And it is this which frightens me: Who knows but that, on the lower frequencies, I speak for you?

— RALPH ELLISON

Introduction

*Twilight began while I was some miles in the woods, and a
sensation of fear crept over me from recollections of stories
of runaway slaves robbing stray wanderers after nightfall.
Having no stick, I stepped aside at an angle of the path,
and cut one from a paineira tree. While removing the spines
with a knife, a tall Negro with an ominous-looking staff
burst suddenly on me. He stood, gazed, passed on, and
anon returned with club upraised. I tried to look bold, and
asked what he wanted. He understood not the words, but
comprehended my wants. Seeing I had got a poor branch—
one not worth dressing, and whose prickles had drawn blood
from my fingers—with a smile he drew near and offered me
his. I hesitated, when he gently put it in my hand and went
on his way. Ashamed of my suspicions, I called after him,
and with difficulty got the kind-hearted man to accept a
slight acknowledgment of his good will. It was dark when I
arrived in the artificial world below.*
—THOMAS EWBANK, *Life in Brazil*

THE ABOVE PASSAGE was written by Thomas Ewbank, an English gentleman
traveler who sojourned in the city of Rio de Janeiro in the early 1850s, more
than thirty years before the abolition of slavery in Brazil. On the occasion
Ewbank describes, he had hiked alone and unarmed into the dense tropical
forests of Santa Teresa, a mounded series of steeply rising and nearly inacces-
sible hills, to make sketches of the vistas there, which then, as today, offered
unparalleled views of the "artificial world" below.

It is small wonder that both Ewbank and the "kind-hearted man" whom
he met in the darkening woods sought, though for very different reasons, to
escape from that world and to view it from afar. It was, by all accounts, one of

enormous suffering, cruelty, voluptuous lethargy, absurd pageantry, and easy death. Foreign travelers who wrote about Rio were impressed not only by the natural splendors of the wilderness that hemmed the city but by the human bodies that clogged its elite parlors or, alternatively, those that ran, limped, and collapsed—and certainly despaired—along its narrow, muddy, and stinking streets.

"It is a principle with them to sit and rest as much as possible," one traveler wrote of Rio's listless elite. "With this view of life, they eat, sleep, keep their temper and grow fat. Calm and composed, quiet and noiseless" (Stewart 1856, 274) the bodies of the wealthy were pale and "very corpulent, from their living well and taking little exercise" (Gardner 1970, 4). Exceptions were made on holidays and Sundays when "in their best dresses, and in formal procession of two and two" (Gardner, 295) "some of the fattest ladies and gentlemen" (Ewbank 1856, 274) were to be seen promenading in Rio's majestic parks and going to and from worship, followed by a retinue of liveried but barefoot house slaves. "I would . . . implore them to think," one writer remarked, "of the evil slavery brings, not only to the Negroes but to themselves, not only to themselves but to their families and their posterity" (Graham 1824, 228).

Not far from these pampered settings, Rio's auction houses sold "crockery-ware, old books, shoes, pickles, etc." as well as "living beings." "They were of every shade, from deep Angola jet to white or nearly white" (Ewbank 1856, 282, 283). "Rows of young creatures were sitting," another writer observed, "their heads shaved, their bodies emaciated, and the marks of recent itch upon their skins" (Graham 1824, 227). The "anguish" of mothers who were "brought out, exposed, examined, and disposed of" was matched by weeping children, "obviously dreading to be torn away" (Ewbank 1856, 283). Others lay wasting from disease, hunger, and a gruesome journey across the Atlantic or the countryside, "evidently too sick to sit up" (Graham 1824, 227). Meanwhile, throughout the streets of the city, "coffee-bag carriers, their naked bodies reeking with oily sweat," arrived from the outlying plantations, bearing on their backs their masters' exportable products, while others, "tugging and hauling and pushing over the rough pavements heavily laden trucks and carts," transported for their urban masters "an overload for an equal number of mules or horses" (Stewart 1856, 72). Those who rebelled were submitted to the "heaviest and cruelest instruments of torture . . . doubling the bodies of the victims into the most painful and unnatural positions" (Ewbank 1856, 438).

Suicide among the enslaved was rife, and many of those who fled from forced toil had, in fact, "reached the spirit land" (Ewbank 1856, 281). While the swollen wealthy dined on the best that the bustling city and fertile countryside could offer, slaves stuffed themselves with dirt (Koster 1817, 213) and were buried in shallow graves in the woods or simply thrown upon the wide, crescent-shaped beaches where dogs did "their work of abomination" (Graham 1824, 111).

Some, evidently, escaped from this fate and fled to the wilderness of Santa Teresa, the dense forest high above the city where Ewbank lost his way. There, they "harbor[ed] . . . and prowl[ed] for means to live" and slaked their thirst from the legendary waters of the Mae d'Agua River (Ewbank 1856, 428). They would have done so at, or close to, the site of the present-day community that I call Morro do Sangue Bom, a shantytown that clings precariously to the awkward tilt of Santa Teresa's highest peak.[1]

Those who now live in Morro do Sangue Bom, most of whom are descendants of both urban and rural *cativos*, or captives, tell the tale that their hillside community was built upon the bones of slaves. My nine-year-old friend, Tiago, one of the first to tell me this simple and unembellished story, only shivered and said, "Who knows?" when I asked him if the garbage-strewn, windswept plateau on which we had gone walking might be haunted. Even now, Morro do Sangue Bom, despite its location in one of the world's most densely populated cities, abuts a massive tropical forest. As Tiago's elders knew, vicious gangsters and death squads sometimes dumped the bodies of their victims in the woods nearby. It was the violence and injustice in the world of the living rather than the spirits of the dead that most preoccupied the people of Morro do Sangue Bom.

The story may well be apocryphal. When I searched through various archives, looking for forgotten tales of Santa Teresa, I could find nothing that hinted at a cemetery of slaves. Given the careless lassitude with which deceased captives were apparently laid to their final rest, I had difficulty imagining that their masters would have had them carried so far, high into a place that held fear for so many. I like to believe that the rumored dead who lay underneath the soil of Morro do Sangue Bom were *quilombolas*, escaped slaves, who, while not entirely free, would have worked and lived for themselves and for each other, and buried their own with feeling and respect.

Outsiders still fear the *morros*, or hillside shantytowns, of Santa Teresa, populated as they supposedly are by what the district's middle-class residents are apt to call *marginais*, or criminals. Like the man that Ewbank met in the woods, most of the people who are found there are grossly misjudged. Imagined from the outside as a den of thieves and dope peddlers, from the inside, Morro do Sangue Bom, and other communities like it, are working-class neighborhoods whose marginality is given less by the few criminals who practice their trades there than by poverty and racism. The bones of history, as the story of the slave cemetery suggests, are partly buried but still close to the surface of everyday life. "Slavery has not ended," Daniel, Tiago's father, told me. "They used to beat us with the whip. Now they beat us with hunger." Although Daniel repeated this observation several times during the twenty months that I lived in Morro do Sangue Bom—usually after his wealthy clients failed to pay him for his labor—neither slavery nor racism were frequent topics of conversation there. This is one of the greatest puzzles of Brazil, what drew me to conduct ethnographic research in a *favela*, or shantytown, in Rio de Janeiro: although racism is abundantly evident in Brazil's bifurcated social structure, in the interactions that constitute everyday life for Brazilians of African descent, and in the derogatory ways that blackness is figured in speech, Brazil is renown throughout the world as a "racial democracy." Neither Daniel nor his young son Tiago were deceived by this notion, but as a nationalist ideology, a cultural myth, and as a dream of how things ought to be, the force of *democracia racial* (racial democracy) is strong enough to muffle the impulse to talk—spontaneously, freely, explicitly—about the wounds of racism.

This book is about the ways in which a variety of urban Brazilians—particularly those of African descent—struggle with the meanings of skin color, race, and racism. These meanings lie at the center of Brazilian culture—culture conceived not as a monolithic product of uniform beliefs and practices, but as a site of contradiction, inequality, and discordance. *Dreaming Equality* approaches the ideology of racial democracy from the perspective of those who live in the shadow of its promises while experiencing its deceptions and betrayals.

Racial Democracy: Myth and Dream

Although the racial democracy thesis is far more than a literary construction, its codification is usually attributed to Gilberto Freyre, Brazil's preeminent sociologist, historian, and novelist. First published in 1933, his best-known work, *Casa Grande e Senzala* (translated into English as *The Masters and the Slaves*, 1986), is arguably among the great masterpieces of Latin American literature. Throughout his long career, Freyre sought to construct what he called an "intimate history" of Brazil, and he defined that history as the product, above all, of the collision between, and blending of, European, Amerindian, and African cultures. Under the tutelage of Franz Boas at Columbia University, Freyre challenged the racist theories then current in Brazil and elsewhere, and through an artful mixture of historical research, more or less casual observation, literary musing, and voluptuous prose, he defended the African contribution to Brazil's culture and reconstituted the country as a *democracia racial*, or racial democracy.

Largely because the Moors of Africa had once conquered and ruled the Portuguese, Freyre argued, those who settled Brazil were, unlike their English counterparts to the north, relatively free of most onerous and distancing forms of racial prejudice. What Freyre typically described as a "lubricious" (if sometimes sadomasochistic) eroticism between Brazilian masters and their slaves was called to serve as both a metonym of and a metaphor for the uniquely harmonious and sensuous character of the nation.

Although Freyre wrote that he had "no pedagogic intention" (1986, lix) in writing *Casa Grande e Senzala* and confessed that much of it was based on "highly personal intuitions," the book continues to serve as a kind of master narrative of Brazilian culture, particularly in the tangled area of race relations. In the 1930s, Freyre clearly had his finger on the pulse of public discourses of self-representation in Brazil. His intuitions were widely shared, and they remain compelling, for many Brazilians still echo the tropes of racial mixture, hybridity, and harmony. Middle-class Brazilians, particularly, insist that racialized prejudice and discrimination pale beside the sentiments and behavior that produced and are produced by *mestiçagem*, or miscegenation. Freyre codified a dream that is at once an intimate and a distinctly communal and nationalistic one. In arguing that his country had avoided the race problem through an easy-going color-blind fraternity, Freyre asserted the existence of an abiding moral superiority among Brazilians. This assertion has, if anything, grown more poignant, though chimerical, in the decades since his masterpiece was published.

Although a number of North American scholars supported the racial democracy thesis during the post–World War II years, it has been under considerable attack since at least the 1970s.[2] Brazil is, as many have pointed out, a land of striking contrasts, and these contrasts are nowhere more evident than in what people in Morro do Sangue Bom call *poder acquisitiva*, or purchasing power. Santa Teresa is typical of other Rio neighborhoods, and indeed typical of other Brazilian cities, in its intimate juxtaposition of wealth and poverty. Turn-of-the-century mansions and luxury high-rise apartment buildings face off against nearly a dozen crowded, rat-infested favelas. Those on both sides of the economic divide have views of one another across the hilly terrain of the district, and no one there, or elsewhere in Brazil, disputes the fact that the country has one of the most unequal distributions of wealth in the world. The debate on racial democracy has thus centered, to a significant degree, on what role racial identity plays, if any, in the structuring of this inequality.[3] Middle-class white residents of Santa Teresa—many of whom live close to but have never visited Morro do Sangue Bom—forcefully articulate the mainstream view that it is the disadvantages of class, and not race or color, that obstruct the mobility of their less fortunate neighbors. This insistence that racialized prejudice and discrimination are relatively mild or even non-existent in Brazil has remained one of the most durable features of democracia racial—despite the spate of research that demonstrates that modern racist practices have, if anything, tightened the noose of racialized inequality as Brazil has moved from a largely agrarian to an industrialized, globally linked economy.

In 1988, one hundred years after the abolition of slavery in Brazil, the newsmagazine *Veja* broke the customary silence the media observes on the topic of racism by citing some of the conclusions of this research: "One hundred years after abolition, there are in Brazil two distinct citizenships—the white and the black. It is not only a question of color but of the quality of life. The black man, when he is born, has a thirty percent less chance of completing five years of age. As he grows up, his chances of leaving school before learning to read are double [those of whites]. When he dies, he ends a life whose expectancy is 50 years. If he were white, he would have a life expectancy of 63 years" (*Veja* 1988).

Brazilians of African descent lag far behind their white counterparts in all of the relevant measures of economic well-being and quality of life: infant mortality, health, education, employment, occupation, income, and life expectancy. Even when they apparently start off with equal socioeconomic advantages, demographic research suggests, nonwhite sons have access to fewer opportunities to reproduce or maintain the status achievements of their fathers (Hasenbalg 1985). In such an environment, black Brazilians rarely have access to higher education, and when they do, racism apparently still dogs their efforts to raise their socioeconomic status. As Hasenbalg has noted, "the mean income of non-whites with college education is smaller than that of whites with junior high school education" (1985, 39).[4] Color itself, and not merely the disadvantage of class, structures the processes by which Brazilians of African descent are systematically denied access to the opportunities to pursue trajectories of upward mobility. Despite hard work, people of color, such as those in Morro do Sangue Bom, are mired in what they call misery and hunger. Even if Tiago's father, Daniel, engaged in a bit of hyperbole when he said, "Slavery has not ended," he undoubtedly had a point: most black Brazilian families remain at the bottom of the socioeconomic ladder.

The questions I brought to my research in Rio de Janeiro were relatively simple ones, yet they have not been addressed during a half-century of research on the issue of race in Brazil.[5] What lies, culturally speaking, between the mainstream nationalist belief in democracia racial and the stark reality of racialized oppression? How do poor urban Brazilians of African descent perceive, experience, and interpret racism in a country where its very existence tends to be publicly denied? Given this public denial, how is racism talked about in the privacy of the family and the community—or is it even talked about at all? I had even more basic, underlying questions: What is the meaning of "race" for people such as those in Morro do Sangue Bom? Is it largely irrelevant—as many Brazilians are apt to claim when speaking in the idioms of democracia racial—or is it fundamental to one's identity, given its significance in determining one's chances in life?

As a nationalist ideology—a story, really, about how people of different colors do, or ought to, relate to one another—democracia racial affects the beliefs, actions, and talk of all Brazilians. Different groups, however, have divergent approaches to the issue, differing levels and types of investment in the story, and different bases of experience from which to judge its meaning and truth value. Democracia racial is, I believe, best defined as a set of discourses—patterned ways of talking about issues related to color, race, class, equality, and inequality. Both descriptive and prescriptive statements about history, identity, consciousness, family, community, nation, and love permeate these discourses and place them at the center of Brazilian culture and beliefs about national character.

To suggest that democracia racial is little more than an elite conspiracy is certainly to misjudge its tentacular reach and its power to organize sentiments as well as public discourses. At the same time, however, there is a mainstream set of cultural understandings, an epicenter of power, as it were, from which the core statements of democracia racial radiate. The overwhelmingly white Brazilian middle class—who are in many critical cultural senses dominant without necessarily representing a true economic or political elite—occupy this epicenter. Because I wanted to document democracia racial as something more tangible than an abstract nationalist ideology—to locate it, literally, within the mouths of speaking subjects—I sought out the views, opinions, and experiences of middle-class white people who live close to Morro do Sangue Bom.

Although I have organized this ethnography primarily around the experiences, understandings, and talk of people in Morro do Sangue Bom and have set the words of their middle-class neighbors in the background, it is critical to remember that these middle-class words represent, in sociopolitical and cultural terms, something more like a foreground. Just as it is one of the privileges of dominance to remain relatively unmoved by, or even ignorant of, the van-

tage points of those who are less free to speak their minds, so the onus of marginality expresses itself through the constant measuring of oneself and one's
words against a powerful standard.

There is, of course, a radical and systematic critique of democracia racial;
it is articulated by the militants in Brazil's black movement. Because the
movement, a small and fractionated one, has not yet succeeded in achieving
high visibility among either middle-class whites or poor Brazilians of African
descent, its discourses remain on the periphery. Nevertheless, my interviews
with many of Rio's more active black militants provide a valuable counterpoint and a commentary on those I conducted in Morro do Sangue Bom and
Santa Teresa. Moreover, as recent research suggests, militant critiques of
democracia racial and publicly articulated concepts of black consciousness
may be gradually achieving increasing salience.[6] The cultural meanings of
democracia racial are likely to become more complex, more compromised and
more loudly contested in the coming years.

This ethnography is thus an attempt to document the range of contemporary understandings of democracia racial—and the manner in which they
are articulated by those in different and distant social locations—while focusing particularly on those that are the least recognized, the least heard, and the
least understood within Rio de Janeiro's public, sociopolitical landscape.

Racism, as so many scholars have cogently demonstrated, is fundamentally rooted in processual class structures, historically shifting modes of production, distribution, and consumption, and, increasingly, in the unequal
exchanges that tie local political economies to the global processes of capitalism. It is, once again, the gap that lies between these material structures of
racism in Brazil and the cultural meanings of democracia racial with which I
am most concerned. People in Morro do Sangue Bom and similar communities construct their daily lives within this gap. Their thoughtful reflections on
the contradictions under which they labor—in frankly emotional as well as
directly physical terms—provide a great deal of insight into the symbolic, cultural, and discursive arenas in which racialized power is manifest in Brazil.
Directly following my informants in Morro do Sangue Bom, I emphasize what
might be called the moral dimension of racism, a dimension that, while
invoked in all discussions of domination, emerges most clearly and explicitly
not in those discussions that focus on the disembodied structures through
which power is distributed but in those that describe, ponder, and interpret
what is often dismissed as subjective experience.

My attention is primarily directed toward discourse and its role in constructing cultural meaning and experience. In this book, I conceptualize discourse both as a method and focus of study and as a complex and fluid—and,

at the same time, thoroughly commonsense—unit of analysis. While my understanding of the larger significance and functions of discourse is certainly informed by writers who emphasize the intersection of language use and power, I am more directly concerned with a set of questions that elucidate the play of discourse in ethnographically grounded contexts: the ways in which my informants talked about, alluded to, invoked and/or avoided color, race, and racism in everyday speech; how they characterized and accounted for their own talk and their silence, as well as the talk and silence of others; and how they articulated their understandings of, and described their encounters with, racism.[7]

My understanding of the cultural significance of talk continually meshed with that of my informants, who constantly engaged in metadiscursive commentary—talk about talk—and who referred, over and over again, to the discursive dimension of racialized identities and racism. Although these commentaries and references took different shapes (and were directed toward differently imagined audiences) within the three groups that I listened to—people in Morro do Sangue Bom, their white middle-class neighbors, and black militants based in Rio—they all circled around the notion that the ways in which Brazilians talk and do not talk to each other define, no less than the material structures in which talk is embedded, the peculiar and contested character of racialized inequality in Brazil. While all ethnographies are inherently collaborative projects, I have tried, perhaps to a greater than usual degree, to preserve, or at least to represent, the authority of my informants.[8]

Chapter 1 describes the community of Morro do Sangue Bom, provides a chronology of my fieldwork, and introduces a number of the people who became, in many cases, friends as well as informants. In order to enhance narrative continuity, these same people are quoted in the chapters that follow. Although favelas are imagined by those who have never visited one to be fearsome, brutish places, they can be, during distinct historical moments at least, havens of *união*, or union, where social networks are extremely dense and neighbors look out for one another. Morro do Sangue Bom was such a place during most of the twenty months that I lived there. However, as I describe in an epilogue, it later fell prey to gang warfare and social collapse.

Chapter 2 focuses on the language in which color and race are constructed. Given the scores of words that refer to color, as well as the debates about who is and who is not "black" in Brazil, this linguistic groundwork is critical to understanding how people in Morro do Sangue Bom think of themselves in terms of color and racial identity. I challenge conventional understandings of racial categories and racial classification in Brazil by describing the ways in which my informants actually use the Brazilian race-color lexicon in natural settings. Contrary to the conventional notion that Brazilians see race as a fluid continuum, people in Morro do Sangue Bom insist that "if you don't pass for white, you are black." This fact has significant cultural and political implications.

Chapter 3 presents an analysis of the pervasive silence surrounding the issue of racism in Morro do Sangue Bom and elsewhere in Brazil. This silence has been interpreted as acquiescence to the claims of democracia racial, but as I demonstrate in the fourth and fifth chapters, my informants provided many accounts of personal encounters with racism for the benefit of my research. I thus argue that the silence surrounding the subject of racism represents a form of cultural censorship, and I focus on the ways in which people in Morro do Sangue Bom both recognize and account for their own silence. This chapter includes an analysis of the legend of Escrava Anastácia, a popular saint. I argue that she symbolically represents racialized oppression in Brazil and the cultural censorship that hinders its exposure.

Chapters 4 and 5 focus on narratives of racism that were produced in interviews with people in Morro do Sangue Bom. Chapter 4 concerns the ways in which my informants describe encounters with racism, encounters that occur on what they call the *asfalto*, or asphalt, of the city's public arenas as well as in the private homes where domestic servants perform their labor. Chapter 5 presents narratives of racism that occurs closer to home—within the community of Morro do Sangue Bom itself and/or within families and between individuals. The ways in which these different types of narratives are related are critical because they illustrate the cultural shape of racism as it is experienced in a world in which its significance tends to be publicly denied.

Chapter 6 focuses on the social worlds and discourses of middle-class whites who live close to Morro do Sangue Bom. It illustrates, in very direct terms, the tone and durability of dominant understandings of the meanings of race and racism in Brazil. Although my middle-class white informants did not categorically deny the existence of racism in their country, they qualified it through narrative strategies that directly align themselves with the more conservative features of democracia racial. In larger terms, I intend this chapter as an ethnographic contribution to the recent scholarly concern with the social and cultural construction of whiteness.

Chapter 7 focuses on the militants involved in Brazil's emergent black movement. Although people in Morro do Sangue Bom remain largely unaware of the existence of this movement, my description and quotation of activist discourse spells out the larger cultural arena in which the meanings associated with color, race, and racism are contested, and it offers additional insights into the complexities involved in the construction of racialized identities in Brazil.

The eighth and final chapter is frankly provisional. A brief discussion of the larger meanings and contradictory functions attached to the ideology of democracia racial is followed by an exclusive consideration of its mystificatory character. Recent scholars have tended to misjudge the extent to which democracia racial also represents—for Brazilians of all colors and social classes—a passionately embraced dream. Racism in Brazil, no matter how fruitfully we may locate it within global continuities, remains culturally distinct.

The epilogue describes the historical events that surrounded the destruction of community in Morro do Sangue Bom and some of the personal responses to, and consequences of, its aftermath.

A Note on Translation, Quotation, and Terminology

Carioca, or Rio, Portuguese is known for its informality and, among those of the working classes especially, for its inattention to what lettered people call correct grammar (Koike 1992). The conversations I had with my informants were, like nearly all conversations, full of half-uttered starts and stops, repair work, small leaps in which words seemed to be left out, laughter, and emphatic outbursts. It is a habit among some Cariocas, or Rio natives, to tell first the major outlines of a story and its narrative climax, and then to retell it twice more with added details, especially those related to emotional response. Although some of my informants noticed this habit in others and were annoyed by it, it was a particularly felicitous one for a foreign researcher.

In my translations, I have favored a more literal style, rather than substitutions in what could arguably be considered a more equivalent, colloquial, and informal English. (I make exceptions with certain Portuguese expletives, which, if translated literally, would call more attention to themselves than they did in the original conversations.) Whatever stylistic nuance may be lost in such an approach is, I believe, compensated by attention to accuracy and both cultural and conversational context. In cases where the meaning and/or the narrative flow of the original Portuguese is unclear in its direct English translation, I have enclosed grammatically suggested but unspoken words in brackets. Ellipses indicate unclear speech, excessive repetition, tangential asides, or, in a few cases, my edited arrangement of thrice-told stories or viewpoints. In some cases I have, for the sake of clarity, used verb tense more consistently than it was used in the original Portuguese.

Most of my quotations are taken directly from audiotapes and are thus verbatim or, as a result of the modifications described above, nearly verbatim.

There are exceptions, however, for in some cases, comments and conversations have been reconstructed from highly detailed field notes.

Throughout this book, when I use the term "race" or other terms related to it (e.g., "mixed race," "racial traits," "black blood"), I refer, specifically, to my informants' local, cultural understandings or, more generally, to broader cultural, ideological, and historical constructions. Along with the vast majority of contemporary anthropologists, I reject the notion that race represents a valid biological or scientific category. The concept of race is always and everywhere a distinctly cultural rather than natural category.

I have followed the standard social scientific practice of using pseudonyms for both my primary research site and all of the informants whom I quote or describe—including those black militants who are arguably public figures. I have not, however, produced composite portraits or otherwise garbled my data.

Chapter 1   The Hill

From Africa to Rio

It has been estimated that in the course of the transatlantic slave trade, three and a half million Africans were sequestered in Brazil—more than in any other country in the world (Curtin 1969). The transport of Tiago's African ancestors to Brazil began in the late sixteenth century and continued openly until 1850, when Brazilian authorities submitted to British pressures to abolish the trade. After that year, slave merchants, most of them Portuguese, set anchor outside of the major ports and continued a reduced, clandestine traffic. The internal trade in Africans and the Brazilian-born sons and daughters of Africans increased.

The enslaved, like their counterparts in the United States and the Caribbean, were primarily from diverse ethnic groups in West Africa and southwest Africa, although Mozambicans arrived in the nineteenth century. Some were from Islamicized groups such as the Hausa; they commanded written Arabic and were often more literate than their masters. The slave population was internally divided, not only in terms of differences, and at times oppositions, between Brazilian-born and African captives but in terms of ethnicity and religion, both of which played a role in some of the most dramatic slave uprisings, particularly in northeastern Brazil (Reis 1988). Within the religious arena, the practices of the Nago, or Yoruba, people emerged as the predominant national influence, as is evidenced by the contemporary popularity of Candomblé and Umbanda, both of which are spirit-possession religions. The continuing vitality and reinterpretation of Brazilian syncretistic traditions which originated, in part, in an amalgam of African traditions is attributed to the constant influx of Africans into the colony and to the relative lack of con-

trol that Brazilian slave owners were able to exercise over the cultural practices of slaves (Harris 1964).[1]

As the soils of the sugar-producing region in the north of the country
became exhausted in the early nineteenth century, the bulk of the slave population shifted southwards, to labor on coffee plantations in the states of São
Paulo, Rio de Janeiro, and Minas Gerais and in the soon-to-be-depleted mines
of the latter state. By the early 1870s, the state of Rio de Janeiro had the
largest slave population within the country, at approximately three hundred
thousand (Graham 1970, 436; see also Klein 1971; Russell-Wood 1982; Stein
1957). Free people of color were by then numerous. During the same period,
approximately 38 percent of all people of color in the countryside of the state
of Rio de Janeiro were freedmen; in the city of Rio, approximately 60 percent
were freedmen (Klein 1969, 36).

In the waning years of the nineteenth century, a combination of declin-
ing profits among plantation owners; increasing abolitionist fervor (much of it
centered in Rio de Janeiro) (Conrad 1972; Toplin 1975); the increasing use,
by escaped and physically abused slaves, of the legal intercession of the courts
(Chalhoub 1990; Andrews 1991); and, significantly, the factor of slave rebellions, and the fear of rebellions (Moura 1981; Reis and Silva 1989), led to a
series of half measures by which increasing numbers of slaves were or would be
liberated. Slavery was finally abolished completely in 1888, making Brazil the
last New World country to do so.

Convinced that newly liberated plantation workers would no longer
work for their former masters, planters and politicians convened to recruit
labor, mostly from Europe, through subsidized immigration (Andrews 1991;
Skidmore 1993a). This helped to set the stage for a competitive labor market,
first in rural and then in urban areas, in which Brazilians of African descent
were relegated to the bottom of the labor hierarchy. Although some former
slaves and their families quickly left the plantations where they lived and
worked at the time of abolition, others remained.

For newly liberated agricultural workers, abolition would have produced
few immediate changes in the way they lived and labored. The same was also
true for Rio's urbanized former slaves, many of whom would have been, during
the "time of captivity," what were called *negros de ganho,* slaves who were
hired out by their masters to perform skilled and semiskilled labor as well as
the most menial tasks of maintaining the urban households of the relatively
well-to-do (Graham 1988).

Capitalist formation, industrialization, bureaucratization, urbanization,
and the new forms of class consolidation they generated came earlier to
Brazil's southeastern region—of which Rio de Janeiro is a part—than to the

middle and northern regions of the country. In 1930, world prices for Brazil's agricultural products fell sharply and initiated increased investment in the industrial sector as well as a steady flow of rural workers into the major cities. Some would have been incorporated into the growing industrial working class while others would have pursued livelihoods through the secondary urban economy. For urban women of color, the performance of domestic servitude was a constant throughout the late nineteenth and twentieth centuries. In urban areas such as Rio de Janeiro (where most of Brazil's population is now concentrated), low-paying manual labor still remains the most frequent means by which poor Brazilians of African descent cobble together a livelihood.

Rio's Hillside Shantytowns

It was particularly during the decade of the 1930s that many of Rio's oldest *favelas,* or hillside shantytowns, were first settled. Precise dates are unclear, but this was the period during which Morro do Sangue Bom became a recognized and named community (Prefeitura da Cidade do Rio de Janeiro 1990). Whether the first settlers arrived before abolition as escaped slaves or in the early 1930s as poor wage laborers incorporated into the expanding urban economy, many would have been Cariocas, or natives of the city of Rio. Their numbers would have been slowly augmented by immigrants from the Rio countryside, as well as from the states of Minas Gerais and Espirito Santo.

Nearly everyone I knew in Morro do Sangue Bom who was under the age of forty had been born and raised in the community. Some of their parents had been Cariocas, but many were from rural areas; they had arrived in Morro do Sangue Bom as young adults or teenagers during the 1940s and 1950s. Unable to afford even the most substandard rental spaces in the city center, they were part of an ever-expanding population of urban poor who had no alternative but to build first crude shacks, and then small brick or wood houses on the city's hillsides. By 1949, 17 percent of Rio's population lived in such hillside communities. Extremely rustic houses could be built with two or three months' worth of an average poor worker's salary. Among other factors, the relative ease with which the poor housed themselves—albeit in conditions of misery—contributed to the extremely slow growth in wages (Pearse 1961).

Many favelas (whose residents tend to prefer the softer, somewhat euphemistic term *morro,* or hill, to designate their communities) began as illegal squatter communities.[2] Several of Morro do Sangue Bom's older residents told me that their hill had once belonged to a wealthy German family that sought to regain control of the land and to evict its home builders in the early 1940s. Despite the relative isolation of the community and the greater-than-average difficulties it posed in terms of transportation to and from the city center, the residents of Morro do Sangue Bom were desperate to preserve their foothold on the hill. They marched en masse, as the story goes (see also, Prefeitura 1990), to seek the protection and patronage of Dona Darcy, the wife of Brazil's charismatic populist dictator/president, Getulio Vargas. As Brazil had sided with the Allies in the world war that was then raging overseas, Dona Darcy was moved to dispossess the Germans of the land and to donate it, free and clear, to the people of Morro do Sangue Bom.

When I was living in the community between 1990 and 1992, it had a population that I estimated at approximately 5,500. Older adults, including those in their thirties and forties, could recall a time in their childhood when the hill was still bush country. Houses were relatively sparse. Trees, some of them fruit bearing, and small snake-infested gardens lay between them. Its real boom probably occurred as late as the 1960s or even the 1970s, when newcomers from the northeastern states of Paraiba and Bahia arrived, along with a steady trickle of people from both the urban and rural areas of the neighboring state of Minas Gerais. Other families and individuals relocated to Morro do Sangue Bom after originally settling in Rio's more centrally located shantytowns, some of which were razed in the 1960s and 1970s to make room for the city's expanding middle class (see Perlman 1976).

By 1970, there were approximately 300 favelas within the city of Rio de Janeiro. In the same year, 30 percent of those living in favelas were reported to be unemployed. Fifty percent of the employed worked in industry and civil construction, and another 20 percent were engaged in domestic service. More than half of the employed earned only one minimum salary, an amount well under one hundred (U.S.) dollars per month (Nunes 1976). By 1992, it was estimated that Rio de Janeiro had 573 favelas, which housed approximately 18 percent of the city's population (Iplan-Rio 1993).

When the residents of Morro do Sangue Bom recount the history of their community, stories concerning the lack of potable water and electricity are consistently emphasized. Water was not piped onto the hill until the late 1970s. Before that time, I was told, water was fetched about two or three times a week from a natural spring at the edge of the forest about three miles down the road. The able-bodied made these trips after work. Head-toting large metal canisters, they returned after three o'clock in the morning, feeling their way gingerly up the steep hillside, for there was, at that time, no electricity to light their way.

Electricity also arrived in the late 1970s through an arrangement brokered between residents and local political patrons. Morro do Sangue Bom and other communities like it, however, continue to be substandard in terms of infrastructure and public services. While I was there, during frequent heavy rainstorms the hill lost power for hours at a time, and the water supply often, and unpredictably, ran dry. Municipal garbage service was grossly inadequate, with the result that many residents simply threw their household waste onto unoccupied sections of the hill, where it served as a constantly replenished food supply for rats.

The community's largest drainage ditches, which carried both rain water and sewage, remained open and often overflowed onto the busy footpaths until 1991, when they were finally sealed through a combination of municipal funds and local labor. All of these advances were the proud accomplishments of a group of men and women who were directly involved in, or closely associated with, the residents' association, which had been in existence since the early 1970s. Operating within a number of overlapping, local political arenas, such as the citywide federation of favelas, these people had considerable political and bureaucratic savvy (see Gay 1994; Leeds and Leeds 1970; Perlman 1976; Valladares 1978; Zaluar 1985).

Favelas, particularly those in Rio de Janeiro, are often figured in both the national and international news media as Brazil's worst urban nightmare. They have always been associated with crime, immorality, violence, and what many writers have called "promiscuity." Although the late 1980s and 1990s have seen a dramatic increase in violence related to drug trafficking, making middle-class fears seem something like a self-fulfilling prophecy, criminal activity is a much frowned-upon pursuit of a small minority of favela inhabitants. Most of those who purchase the marijuana and cocaine that fuel the drug trade are not *favelados* (slum dwellers) but middle-class people. The frequency with which this fact is overlooked in everyday discourses is mirrored and buttressed by the ways in which writers have figured the supposedly typical favelado for their middle-class readership.

In 1947, for example, one writer asserted that "the children and the adults live in horrible promiscuity, creating addictions of roguery and frequenting literal schools of crime" (Oliveira 1947, 52). Another writer commented that "the favela inhabitant, for the most part, is a good person who works or who wants to work," but he added, "The child, normally, lives in promiscuity and as a product of this environment, grows up beaten down by the bad elements and through their examples, becomes, as time passes, a criminal" (Abujamra 1967, 46). The notion that merely living on a morro, or hillside shantytown, condemned one to moral degeneracy is reflected in more recent publications as well. In 1984, for example, one writer asserted that even the favelado who is law abiding "becomes socially *dangerous* through the potential risks that he exhibits" (Pereira 1984, 12, emphasis in original).

Notably, both the popular and the scholarly literatures that deal with favelas and their inhabitants are remarkably silent on the issues of color, race, and racism—despite the fact that Rio's morros are stereotypically associated with *negros* (blacks) and with blackness. In strictly demographic terms, this association is justified. Through an informal survey, I estimated that at least 75 percent of the residents of Morro do Sangue Bom were of color. When it is argued that demographic realities strongly suggest the existence of de facto residential segregation (Telles 1992), however, many Cariocas remark that there are whites living in favelas also. These whites are themselves stereotypically associated with impoverished and frequently illiterate and unskilled immigrants from Brazil's northeastern states. My research in Morro do Sangue Bom suggests that this is, once again, partly justified, for many of the community's white families are from the state of Paraiba.

Because people of color so obviously predominate in Rio's favelas, people in Morro do Sangue Bom occasionally refer to morros in general as *o lugar dos negros*, or the place of the blacks. Black militants often rhetorically compare the favela to the *senzala*, or slave quarters, of the last century. I would argue that the historically entrenched figuring of favela residents, and the figuring of morros themselves as "exactly like a jungle" (Pereira 1984, 17), engages a dissimulating rhetoric within which notions of race are insidiously projected. Everyday discourses about Rio's hillside communities partake of very tangled notions of class, criminality, and race and the weighty silence that conventionally surrounds the latter issue.

Entering Morro do Sangue Bom

I first entered Morro do Sangue Bom in 1988, the centennial of the abolition of Brazilian slavery. I had been staying in a colleague's apartment in Santa Teresa, and I hoped, during my brief weeks in the country, to settle upon a field site for future ethnographic research into the meanings of color, race, and racism in Rio de Janeiro—a city that remains, despite its considerably tarnished reputation, Brazil's premier cultural capital and tourist destination. I often took Santa Teresa's unpredictable, infrequent, and jammed buses to and from the city. Chugging up the absurd twists and turns of the district's cobblestone streets, the bus sometimes seemed about to tip over the side of the mountain. At these times, my fellow passengers, nearly all of whom were poor workers returning from jobs in the city center, would merrily lean to the side of the bus as if they were righting a wave-tossed sailboat and exclaim in concert, *"Oba!"* (Oops!) In the midst of my breathless anxiety and claustrophobia, I would find myself laughing wholeheartedly, absorbed into a circle in which open smiles and snippets of friendly conversation were exchanged. A majority of these passengers took the bus to the last stop, from whence they would slowly wend their way up a narrow side street to Morro do Sangue Bom.

More than one Brazilian anthropologist told me that my desire to pursue research as a full-time resident in a favela was "simply unrealistic." I decided to ignore the warnings—the precise substance of which was never explicitly spelled out, in any case—after my bus trips in Santa Teresa. By inquiring at a local bar and general goods store, I discovered that Morro do Sangue Bom had a residents' association, and I obtained the name of its president.

No one, it seemed, took special notice of my arrival in the community—those who saw me probably assumed that I was there to purchase a pinch of cocaine—and within moments I found myself about to become lost in an intricate maze of narrow pathways. I approached a woman who was hanging her laundry to dry and asked her where I might find the president of the residents' association. "Oh, that guy," she said, "he's never around. Go look for Jorge, his assistant. He's wearing white today." Seeing my uncertainty, she asked a woman leaning from a window if she had seen Jorge. She gave a shout to one person, who in turn shouted down the hill to another, and soon, breathing heavily from the effort of running up the path, Jorge himself appeared.

A stocky, frenetically animated, dark-skinned man in his late twenties, Jorge shook my hand and invited me into the cool interior of the association's headquarters. I told him that I was a researcher and that I hoped to live for a year or two in a community such as Morro do Sangue Bom. Jorge greeted my proposal with enthusiasm, for, as he insisted, neither book-learning nor tourism would teach me about what he called "the reality of Brazil." I asked him if he might know of a family with whom I could stay for a few days in order to meet people and learn about the community. He promised to speak with his sister.

Later, I met the president of the association, a light-skinned man who insisted on being addressed as "the Doctor." He asserted in a reprimanding and authoritarian manner that I must always speak to him directly, even if I had difficulty in locating him. Jorge, as I must surely understand, was "without culture," ignorant, and thoroughly lacking in the social graces necessary to deal with foreigners such as myself. I had, by then, already made up my mind about Jorge. In one of the most fortuitous decisions I was to make, I resolved to avoid the Doctor whenever possible and to place my complete trust in Jorge. His sensitive counsel, social tact, and what quickly became his warm and protective friendship proved to be unfailing.

Several days later I was slowly climbing the steepest steps of the morro, carrying a new blanket and a fresh chicken, on my way to stay with Joia, Jorge's twin sister, who lived with her husband, Daniel, her two sons, Alberto and Tiago, and her husband's brother, Guilherme. Joia and Daniel had purchased their house from an old woman who, they believed, had spent her infancy in slavery. She had left behind a reproduction of a painting that I could not fail to notice. It depicted the road to heaven, illuminated by crosses, and, to the left of it, the road to infamy, darkened by the symbols of weakness and bad deeds. "Which road do you take?" Joia asked on the afternoon of my arrival. She handed me the first of many *caipirinhas*, made from a sweet concoction of sugar, lime juice, and cane liquor. When I told her that I tried to stick to the middle road, she laughed approvingly and said that she did the same.

Over the space of a week, Joia and I searched for common ground in the stories, jokes, and opinions that we traded. We discovered that we were born only several months apart. I deferred to her much as would a younger sister, however, for she, and later several of her closet female friends—as well as her twin brother, Jorge—would teach me everything I needed to know to live in their community.

During my initial visit on the morro I also spent time with six-year-old Tiago while Joia was off to her job as a domestic servant or doing errands in the city. I asked Tiago to tell me the Portuguese names for countless household items and many other things besides; neither of us seemed to tire of this activity nor of each other's company. In my conversations with Joia, who was then twenty-eight, I learned that she had begun dating her husband, Daniel, when she was fifteen, the same year her mother died. Like so many other couples I later came to know in the community, they had both been born and raised in Morro do Sangue Bom. Their first child, Alberto, was born when Joia was seventeen and Daniel was nineteen.[3]

Daniel worked as an air-conditioner and refrigerator repairman, and although his skill placed him in a more secure position than some of the other men on the morro (who patched together a living through odd-jobbing), his income plummeted during the winter months when his middle-class clients did not use their air conditioners. He usually returned from work at dinnertime and left again soon after to drink beer and socialize with his friends on the hill—a habit that irritated Joia, who, after more than ten years of an occasionally difficult but solid and loving marriage, still craved his company.

Alberto, then twelve, was a somewhat shy adolescent, but he seemed already to have begun to adopt an adult's demeanor. We traded opinions on Brazilian and American music. Guilherme, Daniel's brother and the youngest of eight siblings, most of whom I would come to know, laughed easily, but he often seemed to be observing conversations from the sidelines. During that week, Jorge climbed the steps to his sister's house. He joined with the others in insisting that if I were to live on the hill, I must learn how to use the current slang and to swear. *Palavrões*, or big words, Jorge carefully reminded me just before my departure from Rio, were only to be used among close friends, and even then, only in joking.

An Uneasy Peace

Joia and I exchanged letters over a two-year period until finally I wrote that I would be returning a few days before Christmas in 1990. During my first night of return on the morro, I went with Joia, Daniel, and a number of their friends to a carnival rehearsal in the city. We returned to the hill just after dawn, and Joia led me over a rubble-strewn shortcut to the house of Varena, her closet friend since childhood, where I would stay until I found a place of my own. We paused to catch our breath and watched the sun pop up over the Atlantic. We could see straight down into Rio's glittering south zone, crowded by middle-class and elite apartment buildings, crescent beaches, and the granite mountain, called the Pão de Azucar, that rises abruptly from the sparkling aquamarine bay. People on the morro, as I later learned, never tired of their view, ever-changing and often graced by rainbows.

Later that afternoon, we celebrated Alberto's fifteenth birthday, and while it was a more informal affair than a girl's *festa de quinze*, Christmas, which fell two days later, was, in comparison, a dispirited and dreary day. For some, such as Varena, who missed the husband whom she had angrily ejected from the house three years before, Christmas was, in fact, a tearful time, to be endured quietly and with the help of cheap cane liquor. Varena was also angry with Rosemary, a tall, husky-voiced girl of thirteen who had knocked at her door two months before, asking to be taken in by anyone who would adopt her in exchange for domestic work. Rosemary's parents had died within a month of each other, Varena explained, and she had run away from the orphanage where she was preyed upon by sexually aggressive staff people. Mirroring Varena's sour mood, her fifteen-year-old son, Adair, and eight year-old daughter, Lucinda, remained sullen and withdrawn throughout the holiday. No presents were exchanged.

Christmas passed with very little celebration at Joia and Daniel's house as well. Papai Noel, or Santa Claus, was, in Joia's opinion, "a son of a whore." She had revealed to Tiago that he was a figment of someone else's imagination and that the presents he received were not determined by his goodness but by his parents' meager salaries, which must somehow serve the relentless demands of inflation. When she explained such things, Joia told me with a kind of sad pride, Tiago always said, "It's okay Mom, I don't really need anything."

After several days of soft but ceaseless rain, the community seemed to come alive again on New Year's Eve, which Cariocas, after the French, call the *reveillon*. The community's resident gang, Nova Época, was hosting an enormous party.

Most of Rio's morros have what is called a *boca de fumo*, literally a mouth of smoke, where marijuana and cocaine are sold, much of it to Rio's hip middle class. The bocas are controlled by gangs of *traficantes* (drug traffickers) and, like the larger communities within which they operate, these gangs have their own unique histories. They are built, for the most part, upon complex and shifting negotiations and battles with other gangs and with the police and, sometimes, upon local mythologies and the personal charisma of their *chefes*, or bosses. Delson, a native son of Morro do Sangue Bom, was credited with drumming up a corps of young and fearless men who six years before had expelled, after considerable and graphically recalled bloodshed, the previously incumbent gang.

"Those guys," people said, habitually unwilling to speak the name of the previous gang aloud, "would beat your door in, rape your daughter, and steal whatever they liked." The war had been a dark time, and everyone I knew had a story to tell about how close they, their children, or their friends had come to catching a stray bullet.

The victory, however, was decisive, and Nova Época instituted an entirely different kind of local governance. As the community's de facto leader, Delson dispensed emergency loans, mediated disputes, and regularly hosted dances to which the entire community was invited. He was said to have five wives, a car, a telephone, and, behind the inordinately high walls of his hillside home, a small swimming pool. He owned goats, pigs, and several head of stubborn cattle that roamed the community at will, lending it a pastoral air. Despite his wealth, people said that Delson remained a "simple man," generous and without pretension. Still, no one I knew envied him or wanted to be in his place. However glamorous his possessions and however heroic his achievement in seeming to give the community back to itself, he remained, many implied, a criminal and apart from his people. "It would be best if there were no gangs at all, anywhere," as Joia said, but given the seeming inevitability of their existence, Delson and his men were regarded as by far the lesser of many evil possibilities.

During the first days of my fieldwork, behind the scenes and unbeknownst to me, Jorge had approached Delson on my behalf. He sought and gained permission for me to conduct my research and to live on the hill for as long as I liked. Jorge explained that "no one would mess" with me. Like any resident, I was under the protection of Nova Época, although their presence would most likely remain so discrete, and my security on the hill so complete, that I would never know it.

I learned that I had arrived in Morro do Sangue Bom at a particularly opportune moment, what people called an *época de paz,* or period of peace. I left my windows open and my door unlocked, walked undisturbed up and down the hill at any hour of the day or night, and shed the habits of caution that I had developed in New York City.

Beyond Morro do Sangue Bom, however, another, very different kind of era was congealing around a new and very different kind of gang. Putting down roots in the larger morros of the South Zone, imperialist groups like the Red Command were amassing a collection of automatic weapons said to outstrip in their number and ferocity the combined arsenal of Rio's military and civil police. With conquered territory as far distant as the city of São Paulo, they represented a threat, however distant it seemed during the reveillon of 1991, that Nova Época could hardly hope to hold at bay. Delson's calculated diplomacy, political savvy, and what I imagined must be an ability to bluff his way through the ranks of some of Rio's biggest criminal kingpins were critical not to only to the well-being but to the very survival of the community.

Although such concerns were probably not far from Delson's mind on the night of the reveillon, they would have been suppressed by the streams of people making their way down the hill to the flat, asphalted lot where parties, dances, and pickup games of volleyball and soccer were held. A full moon was rising. Nearly everyone was dressed in white in honor of Yemanjá, the Goddess of the Sea; her festival, staged by both Candomblé and Umbanda devotees, coincided with New Year's Eve. Women had marcelled their hair and put on lipstick, and even Tiago was persuaded to wear shoes instead of his usual rubber sandals. To start the long night of festivities, Nova Época had organized a beauty pageant.[4] First preadolescent girls and then teenagers strutted in bathing suits and homemade dresses up and down a floodlighted catwalk constructed that morning and decorated with palm fronds. They were judged by radio personalities and journalists. Delson and his highest-ranking lieutenants were easily recognizable among the crowd; they carried automatic rifles that were polished to a high shine and slung across their crisply ironed white shirts.

After the New Year, the adults on the hill turned up the volume on their stereos and succeeded in drowning out the American pop music that their teenage children favored with the new Samba tunes that would animate the upcoming carnival. One blindingly bright day followed another, and it was during this period and only during this period that I heard relatively frequent and unelicited allusions to racism. Morro do Sangue Bom had once had an award-winning *bloco*, or carnival parade group, but the municipal funds that had supported it had dried up. A decade before, the Sambodromo, a stadium-sized exhibition center, was built in Rio, and what had once been a famously democratic street festival became a spectacle staged for television cameras and a live, well-heeled, paying audience.

Daniel had been among the most photographed of the Sambodromo's performers, but he could no longer afford the inflationary prices of the costumes, nor could he or anyone else I knew on the hill pay for the entrance tickets, the cheapest of which cost upwards of half of a minimum monthly salary. Samba, as people on the morro correctly argued, had been invented by negros, and middle-class and even wealthy whites had stolen it from them and corrupted its spirit. The floats had become dominated by skinny blonde women who seduced the cameras by imitating voluptuous *mulatas* (brown-skinned women), the traditional muses of carnival (Sheriff 1999). "This is a bad controversy," Joia told me one day when she was showing me her collection of special-edition carnival magazines in which Daniel's photograph appeared for the last time. "It is because they are preferred. They're all white and they have these nice bodies, you know? None of them are dark. It's bad you know, because samba is a black thing, it began with the negros. Look at them, they're all white, very pretty, but can they samba? No, they can't samba at all!"

I thought that such conversations might set the stage for my research, but they were sporadic, and days, and then weeks, would pass before I would hear explicit statements about racism.

One morning at dawn, I was awakened by the drone of a low-flying helicopter, and wrapping a towel around myself, I stood by the window. Bearing an uzi that he waved over the area surrounding Varena's house as if it were a flashlight, a member of the civil police leaned from the helicopter's open door. He was so close to my window that were it not for the whirlpools of dust that stung my eyes, I could have winked at him. Varena stepped quietly into the room and gently pushed me away from the window. "You don't know what this is, do you Beth?" she said, using a nickname for me that Joia had chosen. The muscles in her face were taut and I could see that she was searching for a way to explain. "Yes, I do know," I angrily sputtered, "It's terrorism!"

Varena would later find great humor in my outburst and would regularly repeat it to others, but at the moment, she was solemn and anxious. "They are looking for the guys in Nova Época," she explained. At a symbolic level, as

Varena and everyone on the hill knew, far more was occurring. "They are say-ing, 'Good morning, favela,' " she added sarcastically.

These *batidas*, or police shakedowns, were to happen perhaps half a dozen times during my stay in Morro do Sangue Bom. They marked a breakdown in relations between Delson and the police. He sometimes resisted the increas-ingly inflationary kickbacks that they periodically demanded of him. Al-though these abrupt shifts were no doubt more complicated than my friends' whispered explanations seemed to suggest, not even middle-class people believed that batidas were based on the impersonal strategies of state-sanc-tioned law enforcement.[5] Money, machismo, and personal vendettas worked like a bellows on relationships whose details were best left unknown and, if known, unspoken.

Later that day, I learned that one of Delson's wives and a son had spent the night in jail. The police had also stolen his television and VCR. The story, as it passed through the community grapevine, was accompanied by nervous, muffled laughter. Although Delson and his men were thought of as protectors, they, like all who had voluntarily surrendered their virtue to the spoils of crime, would inevitably have the sword turned against them. Today or tomor-row, people implied, they would come to a bad end.

While I was still living with Varena, the Gulf War exploded, and I stayed glued to the television, which carried excerpts of the CNN coverage. Varena and others tried to disengage me from my preoccupations. I should unplug the television and have a drink, they suggested, because there was no point in making myself nervous over something that was happening on the other side of the world.

One evening Joia ordered me to sit in a chair she had carried into the kitchen and said, "Beth, your country is at war but you need to know that there is a war here also. Right here on the morro." Down in the city, Nova Época had killed a young man who, while a resident of Morro do Sangue Bom, had consorted with a rival gang. Joia feared that the rival gang would retaliate and through a process of escalating vendettas initiate another full-scale war on home territory.

The home-based skirmishes that Joia feared didn't happen—not then, anyway—and the rival gang, small and localized like Nova Época, could hardly muster the threat of groups like the Red Command. I moved into the abruptly abandoned house of the murdered man's sister. Mice nested in my drawers, lizards raced up and down the walls in pursuit of insects, and gallons of muddy rainwater flooded the cement floor at every storm but I finally had the solitude that everyone I knew on the morro sought always to avoid.

Despite the tragedy that preceded my occupation, I stayed there contentedly for many months until my landlord told me that a kinsmen would be moving in to take my place.

I went to look at a tiny airless hovel, a basement, really, with an uneven dirt floor and no electricity or running water. It's owner, Seu Arnaldo, promised to cement, paint, and wire it within a month, and he did so with great efficiency. Tucked into a dark and extremely narrow blind alley between the rear walls of two-story houses, I lost my postcard view of Guanabara Bay. After a time, an affectionate, pregnant cat moved in, cleared the house of mice, and stood sentry against the rats that wandered into my alley. Perhaps because I was childless and distant from my kin—both rather pitiable circumstances in the view of my friends and neighbors—they listened indulgently to my frequent reports on the cat's amusing habits.

I came to know Dona Janete, Seu Arnaldo's wife, and their two sons, the eldest of whom, Jacinto, lived with his family in a nearby house that I came to visit often, forming for the first time, relations that were independent of Joia's and Varena's networks of close friends and kin. I became less jealous of my solitude and divided my time between an expanding number of households, where I might drop in unannounced to eat dinner, trade news and gossip, and watch the *telenovelas,* or soap operas, that occupied the quiet weekday nights of so many on the hill.

In April of 1992, I was approached by two journalists while I was waiting to see the doctor who donated his services to the community on Wednesday mornings. They were from one of the major Rio papers and had heard about me from João, a friend and informant in the black movement. The newspaper article they published about me led to others, which then led to several brief spots on national and international television. My interviews with journalists allowed me to view, from close up, how the major news media might construct the issue.

The television reporters especially were concerned with manufacturing a sensationalist story; I was concerned with making explicit denunciations of racism on national television. The ironies that emerged in my attempts to negotiate with them appeared, by turns, hilarious and disturbing. One broadcast was previewed several times before it was aired. "A middle-class American woman came to Rio and guess where she decided to live?" a newscaster asked with "Hard Copy"–style drama. "In a favela!" All of the reports, regardless of their medium, emphasized my color, and inaccurately at that: I was described, with what seemed an irresistible compulsion, as a "blue-eyed blonde." "You are turning me into Xuxa on the morro," I snarled at one reporter, referring to Brazil's saccharin-tongued, angel-blonde megastar (see

Simpson 1993). I was said, with great drama, to be living *no meio dos negros,* or among the blacks.

Most of the reporters argued with me, some more aggressively than others, about the validity of my claim that systemic racism exists in Brazil. Moments after approaching me, one of the first to arrive, a young woman, said with unconcealed skepticism, "Do you really believe that there is racism in Brazil?" Others treated my summation of my informants' perceptions of racism dismissively and insisted, in a thoroughly conventionalized manner, that prejudice and discrimination in Brazil are based entirely on class and have nothing to do with race or color. During my encounter with the crew from a major international network, I insisted that they interview João, the black movement militant who had set the media machine in motion.

As the camera rolled several days later, João spoke for nearly an hour. To my surprise, the clip that was finally broadcast included his telling comment that foreign researchers received the public's attention while Brazilian militants' steadfast attempts to focus awareness on racism were routinely dismissed and ignored. Later, when I spoke with João privately, he was reassuring. Despite the brevity of the clips, they included some of my comments about my informants' encounters with racism and police brutality. The racist sensationalism, on one level at least, had defeated itself.

Days and weeks later, people whom I had never met formally on the morro told me that they were pleased that I had "spoken well of the community." Dona Janete's son Efraim, however, warned me about the death squads, particularly those that were made up of out-of-uniform police officers. These "types," along with the "X-Nines," a species of masked police informers, were known to occasionally prowl about the hill in the dead of night. "The police are not going to like what you said," Efraim cautioned, "You must be very careful what you say in Brazil."

It was precisely the fact that the existence of racism is routinely denied, heavily qualified, and/or noticeably unmentioned in everyday talk in Brazil that motivated my research in Rio de Janeiro. Although middle-class Brazilians, including academics, characterized me either as extremely brave or, more often, as *maluco,* or crazy, to live in a favela, my concern had never been with the shantytown as such. My decision to live on a morro was based on the fact that it was an urban, bounded, close-knit community in which poor Brazilians of African descent—the principle victims of racism—predominated.

A year after I left Morro do Sangue Bom, the época de paz collapsed entirely and the peaceful community that I describe here no longer exists. To my mind, the significance of the fact that my research was conducted in a favela lies not in the reputed exoticism and marginality of such communities—they house 18 percent of Rio's population, after all— but in the fact that Morro do Sangue Bom, like many other hillside shantytowns in the city, is situated within what has became a maelstrom of all-too-real violence. That people such as those on the morro—a very clear majority of whom are law-abiding and critical of criminal activity—should have become the principal victims of this violence is rarely noted. That their vulnerability is, however indirectly, itself one of the consequences not only of poverty but of the racism that keeps them impoverished is conventionally ignored. The histories of small places like Morro do Sangue Bom have, I believe, a bearing on our attempts to understand the larger issues that animate contemporary scholarship. I return to the story of Morro do Sangue Bom and its residents in a brief epilogue.

Chapter 2   Talk

Discourses on Color and Race

"It is an incontestable fact," Charles Wagley emphasized nearly forty years ago in his account of race relations in Brazil, that "there was early and extensive miscegenation between the Portuguese and both the Indian and the Negro" (1963, 7). This "incontestable fact" is also a kind of myth of origin in Brazil. Although miscegenation has certainly been widespread in other countries of the New World, Brazil is renowned for the extent to which its national discourse portrays *mistura*, or mixture, as a defining and celebrated feature of the nation. The existence of a plethora of terms that describe or name a person's color or racial characteristics is also an incontestable fact, one that remains much remarked upon both in everyday discourse and in the scholarly literature on race and racial classification in Brazil.[1] Brazilians, it is said, do not conceptualize race as a simple dichotomy between black and white, but rather, they recognize and name many intermediate categories: *moreno, mulato, sarará, marrom bom-bom,* to cite but a few.

The claims made in everyday discourse and in much of Brazilianist scholarship suggest that these incontestable facts—widespread miscegenation and what are assumed to be multiple categories of race—have virtually erased the boundaries of racial identity in Brazil. "As far as actual behavior is concerned," Marvin Harris has asserted, "races do not exist for the Brazilians" (1964, 64). Moreover, because it is assumed that Brazilians tend to attribute racial or color characteristics to themselves and others on the basis of appearance rather than descent, racial identity—understood in bipolar terms at least—is said to be difficult or impossible to define for the those who are *nem preto, nem branco* (neither black nor white).

The interpretation of the larger sociological and political significance of these facts—and assumptions—lies at the heart of the debate on how best to characterize race relations in Brazil. Many Brazilians and Brazilianist scholars argue that the existence of what appear to be multiple racial categories can be taken as evidence that Brazil has avoided the ideological essentialism that plagues countries such as the United States and South Africa. Lacking such rigid essentialism and leaning always towards fluidity, ambiguity, and the blurring of racial boundaries, Brazilians, it is asserted, have neither the ideological conviction nor the stable target necessary to create and maintain consistently racialized patterns of oppression.

Other scholars and most of those involved in Brazil's black movement argue, on the other hand, that color (or blackness) is always sharply distinguished from whiteness and the qualities and privileges associated with it. The close correlation between color and class structure—another incontestable fact—is taken as sufficient evidence that the apparent multiplicity of racial categories serves as a mystifying ideology that not only conceals the racialized nature of oppression but also prevents the development of social movements that attempt to expose such oppression.

This chapter examines racial meanings and concepts of racial identity by focusing explicitly on language and its use. People in Morro do Sangue Bom, I discovered, use race-color terminology in a variety of ways, and they insist that the meaning of these terms depends, to a very significant degree, on context. Any given race or color term can, in a given conversation, be used to describe, to tease, to insult, or to flatter. To assume, as so many anthropologists do, that these terms function simply as static categories in a "system of racial classification" (see especially Harris 1970; Sanjek 1971) is to miss not only the many other linguistic functions that these terms serve but also the ways in which people such as those in Morro do Sangue Bom construct their own sense of identity.

After spending more than a year and a half listening to everyday speech in Morro do Sangue Bom and discussing the meanings of race-color terms with my informants, I concluded that words related to race and/or color tend to be used in three fairly distinct discourses or registers. Each of these discourses emphasizes different ways of conceptualizing the cultural semantics and politics of race and color.

I begin with a rather radical observation: contrary to conventional wisdom, people in Morro do Sangue Bom do, in fact, conceptualize racial being as essentially bipolar. Just as is the case in countries such as the United States, my informants saw the racial world as one divided between *branco* (white) and *negro* (black). Although the colloquial expression *passou por branco, negro é* (If you're not white, you're black) is fairly common in Brazil, its significance has been overlooked. I refer to the contexts and forms through which this bipolar vision of race is articulated as the *discourse on race*.

If people like those in Morro do Sangue Bom see the racial world in simple terms of black and white, what then is the meaning or function of their notoriously complex color vocabulary? In many everyday contexts, I argue, these terms are used to describe rather than to classify oneself and others. Moreover, what is being described is not a reified notion of race but rather a necessarily imprecise perception of *cor,* or color. I hope to demonstrate that both distinctions—that between description and classification and that between race and color—are critical to an understanding of the cultural construction of race in Brazil. When color terms are used as provisional descriptions of one's own or another's appearance, I call this usage the *descriptive discourse*.

In what I believe is the most frequently employed register, race-color terms are used in what my informants were apt to call "a way of treating someone." Words like *moreno* (brown) are, in such contexts, used pragmatically rather than referentially. Their function, in other words, is not to describe or refer to another person in an objective or taxonomic sense but rather to treat them in a particular way, much as one does when choosing between the formal *o senhor* or the informal *você* when addressing someone in Brazilian Portuguese. When they are used in this pragmatic sense, race-color terms typically serve as polite euphemisms for blackness. They do not, in such cases, either describe or classify. I call this euphemistic, etiquette-driven manner of speaking the *pragmatic discourse*.

Taken together, these three registers both reflect and construct what I believe is a profound ambivalence about concepts of race, color, and racialized identity. On one level, people in Morro do Sangue Bom embrace a sense of shared race to a much greater degree than the extant literature on racial identity in Brazil would suggest is the case. On the other hand, their employment of race-color terms, particularly within the pragmatic discourse, bespeaks a culturally articulated yearning to escape from all that is negatively associated with blackness.

As a foreigner attempting, as a first step, to learn the semantics of race-color terms, I quickly discovered that what I had initially believed to be simple questions often required, in the view of many informants, elaborate responses that might include qualifications, illustrations, asides, and what often appeared to be "double-voiced" quotations (Bakhtin 1981). People in

Morro do Sangue Bom, it was clear, were quite conscious of the complexity of registers in which they used race-color terms, and they constantly reminded me that "it depends on how it is said." My reliance on metadiscourse—the way in which my informants talked about their talk—is thus especially evident in the following pages.

Color, Context, and Description in Morro do Sangue Bom

Soon after I arrived in Morro do Sangue Bom, I began an informal survey, in order to introduce myself to the community as well as to get a sense of household composition, employment, religious affiliation, origin, and race or color identification. Before beginning the census interview, I asked several friends, including Joia, to make sure that I was wording my questions properly. The word *raça*, or race, Joia said, would shock people and would not do. "Raça is a word used for dogs and so on," she said, referring to the word's double meaning of "race" and "breed." Her brother-in-law Guilherme disagreed. "No, it's a normal word, we say *raça branca* [white race] and *raça negra* [black race]," he said, "Everyone understands it." There was a great deal of meaning embedded in their apparently simple disagreement, and it defined, in some ways, the shape of the puzzle that I was to confront throughout my research on the morro. I decided to take Joia's advice, however, and asked people, "What is your color?" or "How do you name your color?"

Asking people to name their color may be an unusual request in Morro do Sangue Bom, but, as I discovered, it is not an entirely unfamiliar one. Several informants told me that census takers had asked them to identify their color, although none could recall the names of the organizations conducting the census. In the past, birth certificates included information about race, and the identity cards issued to young men who performed mandatory military service carried this information as well. Almost inevitably, it seemed, people of African descent were designated in these official government documents as *pardo*, an intermediate term that connotes a light brown or even yellowish complexion as well as racial mixture.

Although I interviewed people in all areas of the hillside, truly random sampling was precluded by a number of factors. Moreover, because I asked interviewees to provide a term both for themselves and for the other members of their households, there was a discrepancy between those who engaged in self-identification and those who were described or classified by others. I found it impossible to conduct all of the interviews in private, and the discussions that my questions sometimes provoked were, in fact, particularly revealing. The survey thus proved to be a valuable tool in my attempts to understand the local race-color vocabulary and the nature of the ambiguities surrounding its use.

Beginning my survey interviews, the first people I approached were two women sitting outside their dilapidated home, enjoying a cigarette in the sunshine. The older woman had fairly dark skin and tightly kinked hair, which people usually call *cabelo ruim,* or bad hair. The younger woman's skin was a medium-light shade of brown, and her hair was curly, what people often call *cabelo razoável,* or reasonable hair. When I asked how they identified their colors, both said "*morena.*"

On the same day, I interviewed a young woman who was sitting on the steps outside her home. Her thick black hair was pulled into a tight knot, her skin was a very light shade of brown, and her nose and lips were narrow. In her arms, she cradled an infant, lighter than herself, with soft downy black curls. I predicted that she would refer to herself as *morena* or *parda,* both of which are conventionally viewed as intermediate terms. However, she entirely bypassed all of the intermediate terms. "*Negra,*" she said, "and my son is *negro* also." I counted her, her son, and her father as *negros,* or blacks, although many who were considerably darker than she I counted as *moreno* or *pardo.*

A teenage boy, who was a very eager interviewee, paused when we came to the color question. In a gesture I had come to recognize as common, he held his arms out before him, looking from one to the other. His skin was a bronze color and his hair was dark and very curly. He chuckled and finally said, "*Moreno.*" "And the others who live with you?" I asked. Having established himself as a point of reference, he quickly answered, "One is dark (*escuro*), one is *morena,* my mother is darker than I am, my stepfather is white and his son is *mulato.*"

It was only after I had been in the community for several months that I began to fully understand that each of the cases I describe above exemplified a larger pattern. Much of the literature on racial classification echoes Kottak's claim: "Through their classification system Brazilians recognize and attempt to describe the phenotypical variation that exists in their population" (1992, 2). If this were an accurate and complete representation of the function of race-color terms, the first two women I interviewed should have chosen different terms to describe or classify themselves, for they were markedly different in appearance. Harris's claim that "Brazilians will call almost any combination of facial features" (1970, 12) *moreno* is more accurate—it was certainly the most common, most neutral, and most polite term in Morro do Sangue Bom—but this fact should, logically, call into the question the notion that this and other race-color terms actually constitute what we might appropriately refer to as a "system of racial classification" (Harris 1970).

In the second case I describe, the light-skinned young woman provided the term *negro* for herself and her family. Once again, if Kottak's claim were accurate she should have chosen from among the large number of intermediate terms. She did, in fact, classify herself, and she relied on a simplified bipolar system in doing so.

In the third scenario I describe, the teenage interviewee revealed uncertainty about his own color. His description of his family is notable although, as I discovered, hardly unusual: "One is dark (*escuro*), one is *morena*, my mother is darker than I am, my stepfather is white and his son is *mulato*." This informant used a combination of words that are conventionally understood in the literature as classificatory terms with comparative descriptions. He did not *classify* his own mother at all but said simply that she was darker than he was. His response (and so many others that I heard) indicates that part of the semantic ambiguity surrounding the vocabulary of race and color is based on the fact that the words' meanings (as well as their discursive functions) shift according to both implicit and explicit points of reference. Moreover, this informant and many others apparently understood my question not as a request to classify themselves and their families but as a request to describe them in terms of appearance.

Returning to the survey data itself, it is clear that different informants interpreted my question about color in different ways. Was I asking them to classify themselves in racial terms, to describe their color in relative terms, or to tell me how they would typically be referred to in polite everyday conversation? I could not, obviously, assume that the responses I collected in my survey were conceptually or linguistically equivalent. Generally speaking, what most of my informants were manipulating was language itself rather a reified notion of identity or membership in a taxonomical category.

What the results of my survey do reveal, however, is the total number of terms that my informants used and the relative proportion of those referring to themselves or others in their households as white (or, in one case, *claro*) versus those using other (nonwhite) terms. I sampled seventy-two households. In providing terms for themselves and the other members of their households, 419 responses were obtained. In total, only twelve terms were used in the entire sample, and of these, three were used on only one occasion (or to refer to only one individual). Of all those for whom terms were provided, 76 percent were given nonwhite terms. Sixty-three percent of this nonwhite group were referred to with terms usually thought to denote intermediate colors, while 37 percent were called either *preto* (the color black), *negro* (of the black race) or *escuro* (dark). Despite my awareness of the fact that my question about color could be and was interpreted in different ways, the survey confirmed my impression that 75 to 80 percent of the people living in Morro do Sangue Bom were nonwhite or of color.[2]

Although the qualifications, uncertainty, and imprecision that I encountered while conducting my survey were tremendously instructive, such surveys tell us little about how race and/or color terms are used in ordinary conversations. Within everyday discourse, in fact, references to a person's color or race tend to occur only within a few limited contexts. Typically, these references tend to be made when two or more interlocutors are conversationally establishing the identity of a common acquaintance. "Have you seen Rosa?" one person might ask another. "Who?" the other might ask. "That *pretinha*, Rosa," the first might respond, "that little black one." Similarly, color references may be made when a speaker does not know a person's name. "How is your girlfriend, that *moreninha?*" one might ask, referring to the person as a little *morena*. In addition, when one is describing a person who is unknown to one's interlocutor, references to color may be made. "He has my color but his hair is good," one might say, or alternatively, "He's a real *negão!*" (big black one). Notably, such references tend not to occur in the presence of the person being identified or described, although on occasion, one might call out to another, "Hey there, *morena!*" In some cases, people with extremely common names may be given nicknames that refer to their color, so that a woman can be called "Maria Pretinha," or "Little Black Maria," to distinguish her from other women named Maria who have lighter skin. The color of babies is referred to more often than that of adults, particularly when neighbors and relatives gather around a newborn. Babies and toddlers may also be directly addressed with color terms, such that one may say to a little girl, "Hey, *moreninha*, come and give me a kiss!"

References to race and color that occur in everyday conversations can be, and often are, more complicated than I am describing here, of course. Nevertheless, these more or less neutral usages are among the most common ones in Morro do Sangue Bom, and they represent a particular mode or register of discourse. In such cases, the person being referred to, clearly, is not being classified or categorized but is simply being described, or alternatively, referred to with a polite term.

Another context in which references to race or color tend to be made is in *brincadeira*, or joking. One man might say to another in greeting, "Hey there, *negão!*" Brincadeira tends to engage words that connote not merely color but blackness; they explicitly refer to the darkness or imputed darkness of a person. The brincadeira that engages these words is intended, typically, to mark intimacy, and as such, it is less neutral and more freighted with complex and ironic associations than the descriptive and polite usages I describe above.

As with all highly ironized forms of joking, racialized brincadeira can and does backfire on occasion, and even when it is successful, it often gives rise to a kind of laughter that is laced with awkwardness. The verbal repartee such brincadeira can provoke, moreover, is often edged with antagonism. "*Negão? Who are you calling negão!*" one might respond.

Generally speaking, with the exception of the limited contexts I describe above, references to an interlocutor's color or race tend to be avoided in Morro do Sangue Bom. Speaking explicitly about color or race is thought to be, in most contexts, gauche and impolite. I came to understand this fact not only by listening to those around me but by observing how my own color was referred to—or, far more commonly, not referred to.

Jokes were occasionally made about my color, and while they never offended me, there was an awareness on both sides of what might be called a mild social trespass. On one occasion, I was sitting on Joia's couch with one leg propped up on a chair. Joia's brother-in-law Guilherme, with whom I had a warm relationship, came into the house and said, "I saw your white leg sticking out as I was coming in and I asked myself, 'Who is that with a cast on her leg?' " I thought his brincadeira was genuinely funny and began to giggle, but Joia said in mock indignation, "Tell him to go take it in the ass, Beth!" It was precisely the trespass, the impoliteness of the exchange, that constituted the punch of Guilherme's brincadeira.

As will be seen, it is darkness far more than lightness that is hedged about with negative associations, awkwardness, and, in linguistic terms, euphemism. When race-color terms are used, softening diminutives are nearly always preferred. Although race and color are, in a sense, not supposed to be noticed or granted significance, racialized attributes are a focus of cultural awareness and preoccupation. Predictably, heated altercations are often peppered with (and sometimes caused by) deliberate violations of this etiquette. A host of racial slurs exist and are universally known in Morro do Sangue Bom and elsewhere in Brazil. *Macaco* (monkey), *preto palhaço* (black buffoon), and *nego safado* (impudent nigger) are among the more common epithets, and they are often heard from the mouths of bullying police officers and angry children.

In sum, race-color terms are only occasionally used to actually classify individuals in truly racial terms. In what I call the discourse of description, color terms are used in a primarily adjectival rather than a nominal sense. They attempt to describe a person's unique configuration of phenotypical traits, not their membership in a discreet category. If a speaker refers to a man as *mulato*, in most ordinary everyday contexts, his meaning will be much closer to "he is a man with medium brownish skin" than "he belongs to a distinct racial group called *mulato*." Because these words, when used in this way, are attempts to describe color, they are necessarily provisional. The fact that Brazilians show a striking lack of consensus in their judgment of which terms best describe which set of features (Harris 1970) is, when considered in this light, both logical and predictable. Color perception, as we know, is a notoriously subjective phenomenon; what is medium brown for one is reddish tan for another and cinnamon for yet another.

The distinction I am drawing between classification and description as well as between race and color will become clearer in my discussion of the discourse on race. As will become evident, *raça* is conceptualized as a more fundamental, immutable, and deep quality than *cor*, which is, of necessity, always imprecise. If one is not white, one is, according to my informants in Morro do Sangue Bom, of the *raça negra*, or black race.

The Discourse on Race

Basing their argument largely on the fact that Brazilians do, in certain contexts, distinguish between light- and dark-skinned people of color, previous researchers have overwhelmingly asserted that light-skinned people of color occupy different racial categories and sociocultural positions that are significantly more favorable than those categories and positions available to those who are unambiguously black.[3]

The reputed significance of the *mulato* (mulatto) as a distinct racial and class category was articulated most forcefully by Carl Degler in *Neither Black nor White: Slavery and Race Relations in Brazil and the United States* (1971), a classic discussion of comparative race relations. Basing his analysis on the extant literature (including historical sources) rather than on ethnographic research, Degler argued that light-skinned Brazilians of color, unlike those in the United States, are able to strategically pursue what he called a "mulatto escape hatch," whereby they are permitted to climb the socioeconomic ladder and thus achieve a position intermediate between those of whites and blacks. The argument of Degler and others (see, for example, Harris 1964), while offering an elegant explanation for some of the differences between North American and Brazilian cultural patterns, is unsupported by conclusive evidence that light-skinned people of color do, in fact, fare better than dark-skinned people in contemporary Brazil.[4]

More recently, researchers have challenged the notion that light-skinned people of color occupy positions of greater socioeconomic advantage than those filled by people with dark skin. Basing his argument on a detailed analysis of 1976 census data, Nelson do Valle Silva has concluded that *mulatos* and *negros* constitute, in socioeconomic terms, a "homogeneous group" (1985,

49); both are very disadvantaged vis-à-vis whites, even when the variable of educational achievement is controlled. Other researchers, such as Carlos Hasenbalg (1985), have joined with Silva in reworking the language through which racialized discrimination is discussed, in referring not to distinctions between three or more groups but to those between whites and nonwhites.

In a similar vein, two historians of Brazilian race relations, Thomas Skidmore (1993b) and George Reid Andrews (1991), have also urged a rethinking of Brazilian racial categories—at least as they are conceived in structural terms. Citing both Silva's work and the discourse of Brazil's black movement, Skidmore argues that the conclusions drawn from research on racial classification may have been under-informed and premature. He suggests that Brazil may be much closer to a biracial model than has previously been assumed. Andrews also argues against the assumption of significant social differences between blacks and those of "mixed race." He concludes in his historical study of black-white relations in São Paulo: "I have chosen to emphasize the commonalties between the two groups as well as the black-white racial dichotomy, which, I believe, accurately describes twentieth century Brazilian society" (1991, 254).[5]

If Silva's conclusions are correct, I wondered, how is the statistically undifferentiated positioning of light- and dark-skinned people of color either contradicted or confirmed by the ways in which Brazilians of African descent talk about themselves, their notions of identity, and their experiences? How does their use of race-color terms relate to these issues? In even more fundamental terms, do people such as those in Morro do Sangue Bom view light-skinned and dark-skinned people of color as members of separate racial categories?

After I felt I had achieved a degree of competence in my understanding of the admittedly slippery rules that govern what I call the discourse of color description, I approached Elena with my household survey. A woman in her mid-forties, Elena was married to José, Joia's stepfather. Elena's skin was very dark and her hair fell in shiny waves; it was what people on the hill often called *cabelo bom*, or good hair. Her facial features were what she herself called "fine features." Her particular combination of phenotypical traits was somewhat unusual; it was such mixed appearance, I thought, following previous researchers, that provided the raison d'etre for the plethora of race-color terms. Following the statistically prominent (but hardly consensual) "dark skin, good hair" definition of the common term *morena*, I would have described her with that term; or, perhaps, because she had told me that her mother was white and her father *preto*, I might have called her a *mulata*. José's features also presented something of a descriptive challenge, but one with which I believed the race-color lexicon was rather precisely equipped to deal. His skin was ruddy and freckled and his hair was kinky and reddish-colored. I took his appearance to be classically *sarará*.

When I asked Elena to describe her own color, she said, "*Preta*," or black. "And José?" I asked. "*Preto* also," she responded without hesitation. "Only white and black exist," she told me, "The rest of those things don't exist." Later in our conversation, when I asked her to explain, she said, "That's right, only *preto* and *branco* exist. The other things don't exist— *mulato, moreno* [all that]. We say *mulato*, but that doesn't exist, no. We've mixed it all up right? *Branco, moreno, mulato*, I don't know what all, but they don't exist, no."

Elena was suggesting that intermediate terms such as *mulato* and *moreno* were best understood as figures of speech rather than as racial categories. Others echoed her view. My friend and landlady Dona Janete, for example, referred to such words with a certain disparagement. "That's all an invention of the people," she explained.

My friend Neusa, a dark-skinned woman in her twenties, also cautioned me against the impulse toward literalism. As I had with many others, I asked Neusa to list the race-color terms she could think of and to tell me which terms were considered offensive. Our conversation was as follows:

ROBIN: Is *negro* offensive?

NEUSA: *Negro*. Look, it's like this—it depends on the sense in which the person is speaking, you see? Sometimes the word negro is used to discriminate. It is not valorizing, you see? It is discriminating. But it depends on how you put it.

ROBIN: And *mulato*—can it be offensive?

NEUSA: No! Look, so many [words] exist exactly so that one is not totally of a *negro* color. So they use the *mulata* color, the *parda* color, the *morena* color, to treat the person as if they were a little lighter, a little like, less discriminated against.

What Neusa implied, of course, was that words like *parda, mulata*, and *morena* functioned as polite, even euphemistic terms that avoided, or at least softened, the negative associations carried in the term *negro*. As had others, she explained that such terms were not racial categories in anything remotely like a literal sense, for, as everyone knew, there were but two races: "So, these things do not exist. One is white, or one is black. But people feel so humiliated to be *negro*. The *negro* was a slave. The *negro* suffered. The *negro* was treated like an animal. All that. But here, it is truly correct to say that one is white or one is black (*preto*). No one can be anything else."

Yvonne, a woman in her late twenties, also emphasized the notion that "one is white or one is black." Because Yvonne was one of Joia's closet friends, I had known her since I first arrived in Morro do Sangue Bom. Yvonne was never one to beat around the bush about anything, and her conversation often had a directness that I found refreshing. As I had with so many others, I explained to her that I was trying to understand the words that described color and race. After she had provided a number of terms, I asked Yvonne to describe the appearance of a *preto*, the first of the terms she had listed:

ROBIN: What does a *preto* look like?
YVONNE: A *preto*? Oh, for me, preto is the one who doesn't pass for white (*Preto é aquele que não passou de branco*).
ROBIN: What? I don't understand.
YVONNE: If one is not white, one is black (*preto*).

Yvonne had used a fairly common colloquial expression, and I was to hear it, and its variations, repeated a number of times in Morro do Sangue Bom. One day, for example, I was interviewing Nestor, a very clever man in his thirties, who was one of Daniel's younger brothers:

ROBIN: So, a question. You said in the other interview that we did that you are a *negro*. Didn't you say that? [He nods.] So, I'm confused because you could be *moreno*, or *pardo* or *negro*, or whatever—
NESTOR: It is because the color, it passes—for example, the definition is the following: passed by white is preto (*passou de branco, preto é*). I define it this way . . .
ROBIN: But this expression, passed by white is *preto*—
NESTOR: It defines—passed by white is *preto*—it defines everything. One who doesn't have light skin is a *negro*, in general. Everyone! In Brazil, this is so. It's hard in Brazil to find a person with really light skin.
ROBIN: So, there really is, in your mind at least, a separation between white and black (*negro*)?
NESTOR: That's right.
ROBIN: So, you can say, in this other sense, in this sense that we are talking now, that most of these people [*morenos, pardos,* etc.] are *negros* also? Is that right? Because they aren't white?
NESTOR: In Brazil, yeah. The majority. I will tell you the following: 98 percent is all *negro*. It's a mixture. Passed by white is *preto*. There are very few pure whites here in Brazil, right? Because there is a great deal of racial mixture.

ROBIN: But a mixed person also has this idea that he is a *negro*?
NESTOR: That's right.

A notable feature of Nestor's explanation is his suggestion that a mixed person or racial mixture is not an identity that is in any significant way distinct from *preto* or *negro*. On the contrary, he asserts, all those who are not white, whatever the degree of darkness or lightness their skin possesses, are black.

I interviewed Joia's half sister Susana on several occasions. When we talked about race and racism, she might, depending on the conversational context, refer to herself as a *negra*, a *preta*, or a *parda*. She clarified the issue for me when I asked her to list all the race-color terms she could think of and then define them. "*Preto, negro*, right?" she began and paused to think. She continued, "*Moreno*. They say that. There's a guy here, he's a *mulato* from Paraiba. He calls me *morena*, you know? He doesn't call me *preta* or *pretinha*. He says it like, 'Hey, *morena*! Hey, *morena*!'"

Before she had even completed her list, Susana gave a typical example of the way in which the term *morena* was used as a euphemism—perhaps an affectionate one—for blackness. Susana, for her part, referred to her acquaintance as a *mulato*. Our conversation continued:

ROBIN: So, you said *mulato* also.
SUSANA: That's right.
ROBIN: What else? It can be slang too.
SUSANA: *Neguinho*. I think that's all.
ROBIN: But before, you said *pardo* also.
SUSANA: Yeah, that's right, there's *pardo* also.
ROBIN: So, what does *preto* mean?
SUSANA: *Negro*.
ROBIN: What does *negro* mean?
SUSANA: *Preto*. [We laugh.]
ROBIN: Is there a difference or not?
SUSANA: No. I think it's the same thing.
ROBIN: What does *moreno* mean?
SUSANA: *Preto*.
ROBIN: What does *mulato* mean?
SUSANA: Put *negro* down.
ROBIN: *Mulato* is *negro* also?
SUSANA: Yeah.
ROBIN: What does *neguinho* mean?
SUSANA: *Preto*.

ROBIN: What does *pardo* mean?
SUSANA: *Preto*.
ROBIN: OK. Are you remembering any other words?
SUSANA: No.

My interview with Rosa, a woman in her forties, echoed my conversation with Susana and helped to untangle its possible meanings. As had many other informants, Rosa interpreted my request for color terms as one that referred only to those words that described nonwhites:

ROSA: *Preto, moreno, mulato, pardo, russo*. If the hair isn't straight,
    they're *negro*, right?
ROBIN: And what else?
ROSA: There are Japanese, for example, but they're white.
ROBIN: OK, what does *preto* mean?
ROSA: *Preto* is *preto*, right? [We laugh.]
ROBIN: What does *moreno* mean?
ROSA: It's *preto* also, right? It's the same thing.
ROBIN: What does *mulato* mean?
ROSA: For me, that's *preto* also.
ROBIN: What does *pardo* mean?
ROSA: Light-colored people with hard hair. I think it's *preto*.

As Rosa and I were talking, her friend Carla dropped in and began reheating coffee on the stove. A woman in her twenties, Carla had very light skin, what I would have described, using the language of color description, as *puxada por branca*, or leaning toward white. Her color was closer to mine than to Rosa's. Her hair was covered by a scarf.

"Like her, like her color," Rosa said, gesturing toward Carla. "But the hair—show her your hair, Carla. It's hard. The hair is hard." I was embarrassed by this exchange, but Carla obligingly removed the scarf from her head for a moment and then re-tied it. I began, "So, a light person with hard hair is—." "Is *negra*," Rosa said, finishing my sentence. Turning to Carla, she said, "Aren't you? Are you white?" Rosa's direct, unsoftened question startled me.

"No," Carla said simply. She had not balked at the two radically simplified choices Rosa had presented. Having been invited into the conversation, Carla asked us what it was about. I explained that I was doing research on race and racism. Carla immediately told me that a man for whom she had once worked as a domestic servant was unabashedly racist. Despite her light skin color, her employer had "found her color horrible"—had said so directly, in fact—and had made her suffer for it in other ways. Using a colloquial expression that I would hear many times over, Carla said, "I simply told him that we are all going to the same little hole." Her reference, of course, was to the shared mortality of all people, the fundamental equality among all who would go, eventually, to their graves.[6]

The tendency, at least in some contexts, to see oneself as a *negro* or *preto*, regardless of the distinctions that are made in the discourse of color description, is undoubtedly informed by the hard understandings of shared experience. Analucia, a woman in her thirties, defined her blackness in these terms but to an even greater degree; she did so on the basis of a racialized solidarity that, according to so much of the literature, should not exist in Brazil. Analucia often dropped in to chat with Joia, and the two of them would engage in a mock brusqueness. "Hey, woman!" they would greet each other. As happened between so many households on the morro, Joia and Analucia constantly borrowed one another's kitchen utensils, clothing, and food.

Analucia was a very light-skinned woman whose hair was what most people would describe as *meio duro*, or somewhat hard—different, in other words, from the "really bad hair" that is stereotypically associated with people who are *pretos*. I thought of her simply as *branca*, or white, and I fully expected her to describe herself as such. Analucia's husband, Jorge, was very dark-skinned and their attractive daughters were also dark.

I used my survey questions to open my interview with Analucia. When I asked her about her color, she said, "I am *parda*, but I am of the black race (*da raça negra*)." Later in our conversation, I told Analucia that I was confused about how she had identified herself. She explained that her family was "a mixture," and our conversation continued:

ROBIN: But you identify more with the black race?
ANALUCIA: Yes, with the black race. Because we—well, I—consider myself of the black race because my family has black (*negro*), right? My father was *mulato*, but my mother was white. But I consider myself to be of the black race. All my children are black (*negros*), my husband is black (*negro*), so I consider myself of the black race also.

As other informants had, Analucia described herself not on the basis of her own unique appearance but according to notions of racial ancestry. She directly contradicted the assertion made by many (e.g., Harris and Kottak 1963; Harris 1964) that Brazilians classify themselves by appearance rather than by "hypodescent"—the tendency, that is, to identify one's racial membership through the minority parent. Analucia's reference to herself as "of the black race" is clearly conditioned, moreover, by her conscious stance of solidarity with her husband and her children.

Analucia told me a particularly interesting story that suggested that her self-identification as a member of the *raça negra* was more than merely rhetorical, or a response to the conversational context of our interview. One day, when she was visiting a friend in the hospital, she rode on the elevator with a black man and several white women. After the man got off the elevator, the women made racist comments about him. "They thought that I was white too," Analucia said with a sneer. She corrected them, however, and said, "Look, I am a *negra* too and you should not talk like that!"

Dona Janete also suggested, in one of our interviews, that people who were of intermediate colors were, by definition, *negros*. In the same conversation, she referred to her son, Jacinto, as a *negro* and as a *mestiço*. "So, *mulato, moreno, jambo*, all these people can be of the black race?" I asked her. "Of the black race, yes," Dona Janete replied, as though I had asked a foolish question. Neither of Dona Janete's two sons were very dark—their father, Seu Arnoldo, was white. Yet, she insisted that both were *negros*: "Because isn't the mother *negra*? Am I not *negra*? I am *negra*. That's what I think."[7]

When I interviewed Alberto, Joia and Daniel's sixteen-year-old son, I decided to test, as I had with Dona Janete, some of the understandings I was beginning to form about the distinctions made between notions of color and race and the various ways in which the term *negro* could be used. When I asked Alberto his color, he said, "*Moreno*. Or *mulato*. But on my identity card it says I am *pardo*." "Can *moreno* also mean *negro*?" "Yes, it can," he replied without hesitation, "because *moreno* is not white. It is dark." Once again, a color term was oppositionally contrasted to white. "But the word *negro* offends many people, right?" I asked Alberto. "Yes," he explained, "but it depends on the way a person says it." I thought for a moment, and continued:

> ROBIN: OK, here's an example. Let's say two men are talking about you
> over at Joãozinho's bar and you can hear them but they can't see
> you standing there. One says to the other, "I saw Alberto yesterday."
> The other says, "Which Alberto?" and the first one says, "Alberto,
> that *negro*." What would you think?
>
> ALBERTO: It's just a description.
>
> ROBIN: Would you be thinking that you're not really *negro*?
>
> ALBERTO: I am a *negro*!

The meaning the term *negro* had in Alberto's final explanation is made more clear by contrasting it to the word *preto*. When I asked people the difference between the two terms, a few people told me that "*negro* is darker than *preto*." Others told me that there was no difference. Most people, however, told me that "*preto* is color, *negro* is race."[8]

This distinction between color—of which there are many, obviously—and race—of which there are, according to most of my informants, only two—was clarified by Joia's stepfather, José. He used his stepdaughter as an example of someone whose color was an intermediate shade but who was, nevertheless, a *negra,* or a member of the black race: "Now, Joia is black (*preta*). But people call her *morena.* Why? Because of her color. She isn't black (*preta*) like the color of your clothes. So, she's *morena.* . . . On her identity card, it says *parda.* . . . [But] deep down, everyone is *preto.* Look there [gestures towards the people going about their business on the hillside]. Some are lighter, some are darker, but they're all *negros.*"

In all of these metadiscursive comments, it is clear that for many people in Morro do Sangue Bom, intermediate terms such as *moreno, pardo, mulato,* and *sarará* are not true racial categories. They are color terms that describe an individual's appearance—and provisionally, at that. If one is *de cor,* or of color, my informants believed, one was, ipso facto, a *negro,* a member of the *raça negra.*

A bipolar conception of racial identity was also articulated in other, non-metadiscursive contexts. In the most obvious instance, when informants spoke to me about their encounters with racism, they would, regardless of their color, often refer, in simple and straightforward terms, to *brancos e negros* (whites and blacks). In this and similar cases, the white race and the black race were figured as oppositional and mutually exclusive categories.

In yet other instances, the notion that one is a member of the black race regardless of color was articulated with a measure of pride. During my conversations with Susana, for example, she repeatedly used locutions such as *raça negra* (black race), *nossa raça* (our race), and *sangue negro,* or black blood, which, she asserted, was stronger than *sangue branca,* or white blood. Dona Janete, who sometimes described herself as a *parda,* said, in the context of Nelson Mandela's brief visit to Rio in 1992, "I like him because he struggles for my race." "I adore my color," Nestor said one day. As if to clarify his meaning, he added, "I adore my race!" While such comments were very occasional in Morro do Sangue Bom (in the sense of both infrequent and contextually determined), they articulated a sense of racial identity and belonging—which was not merely local but stretched, however tentatively (as in Dona Janete's statement), toward transnational conceptions of identity.

In arguing that the notion of multiple racial categories has been exaggerated in the anthropological literature, I do not intend to assert that differences in color are insignificant to Brazilians such as those who live in Morro do Sangue Bom. Color differences can play a role in the decisions and behaviors associated with courtship and marriage, as shall be seen. What I call the discourse on race, in addition, is not particularly salient in everyday discourse but becomes most evident in the kind of metadiscursive statements I have quoted. The bipolar conception of racial identity is, I would argue, a universally held notion that remains largely, although not entirely, unvoiced. Democracia racial is as much a system of etiquette as it is an ideology, and as such it stipulates that Brazilians of all colors and classes eschew discourses that figure their nation as divided along a rigid color line.

It is clear, however, that if informants such as those in Morro do Sangue Bom are asked not merely to produce race-color terms but to reflect on their meanings and usage—if they are asked to scratch beneath the polite surface of their own speech—they readily articulate a vision that belies the platitudes of mixture and miscegenation that characterize the discourses of democracia racial. As I argue next, it is not only these discourses that tend to muffle the discourse on race but also their opposite: the denigration of blackness.

Negro *and Other* "Hard Words"

Although so many of my informants insisted that they and others on the hill were *negros* regardless of the degree of darkness of their skin, the term *negro* is polysemic; it can, in many contexts, be deeply wounding. In addition to its usage as a fairly neutral word that refers to racial identity, the term *negro* can be used in a pragmatic sense, to insult, demean, and humiliate. An examination of this word's power clarifies many of the apparent contradictions and distortions in race and/or color discourses and explains the predominance of those registers in which references to blackness are avoided, softened, and/or euphemized.

Joia's nine-year-old son, Tiago, as I have noted, had a special knack for linguistic explication, and I often relied on him to help me understand the meaning of words. As I suspected would be the case, my interview with him proved to be especially useful. He told me that both *preto* and *negro* referred to someone who was *escuro,* or dark, and I asked him if there was any difference in their meaning. Without missing a beat, he responded: "There is no difference except that *negro* is a name (*apelido*) that the whites gave to the blacks (*pretos*). Like once I saw a film and there was a white man beating a black man (*preto*) and he kept saying, 'What is your name, *negro?!* What is your name, *negro?!*' He kept calling him *negro.*"

Tiago's comments confused me at first. I had difficulty seeing beyond the referential use of the word *negro* as a generic term for dark-skinned people of color, and in the scenario Tiago described, I thought the white man was simply using the word *negro* in this generic sense, as a provisional substitution really, for the man's name. Its power to connote, to invoke, to point to a host of painful associations was evident enough, but in conceptualizing its power as that of reference and connotation, I failed to grasp its performative function, or to understand the slippage between oblique references to power and the literal enactment of power. As I continued to learn the language of race and color, I came to understand that Tiago was telling me that calling a man a *negro* not only invoked an entire history of domination but was the linguistic equivalent of beating him with a whip.

The point was also forcefully clarified for me during one of my first visits to an organization associated with the black movement. I asked a woman activist whom I met there, "Why is it that people don't like being called *negro?*" With unmistakable ire, she stood over me and spat, "How would you like it if someone called you a worthless, ugly thing, shit, dirt, less than a dog!"[9] I had my answer: in some contexts in Brazil, calling someone a *negro* is culturally and politically equivalent to the North American use of the term *nigger.* Insert this word as the most appropriate English gloss for the scenario Tiago described and its performative force becomes immediately apparent.

As I later learned, Tiago's etymological understanding of the term was hardly idiosyncratic. "The word *negro* is offensive because it is what the masters called the slaves," Rosa explained.[10] Rosa was suggesting that masters used the term *negro* not as a racial classification for people of color but as an epithet. "That is a word used to criticize," others told me. "It means you want to humiliate someone."

Dona Janete summarized the comments of many when she said, "I think that people should avoid calling others *negro.* I feel offended when I am called 'that *negra* over there.' I don't want to be called that. I have a name! I never baptized myself as *negra.* In my consciousness, well, you know that I am a *negra,* but no one talks like that." When Dona Janete said, "You know that I am a *negra,*" she was distinguishing between the referential usage of the term (as one referring to racial identity) and the pragmatic usage.

The negative usage of the term *negro* is not limited to its use as an epithet. Within another discursive register, the *negro* is an abstract, even imaginary figure in Brazil. Often shortened to *nego,* the term is frequently used to refer to a perpetual other who exists, untamed, at the margins of society. The expression "If the *negro* doesn't shit coming in, he shits going out" is well known in Brazil, as in other parts of Latin America. In 1969, Florestan Fernandes noted, in the urban context of São Paulo, "The word *Negro* becomes interchangeable with words such as drunkard or boozer, bum, carouser, and thief; and *Negro* woman becomes interchangeable with streetwalker" (1969, 176). What Fernandes failed to note, of course, is that a white boozer would not be called a *negro*. Despite the abstraction with which the word is used in certain discursive registers, and the argument among Brazilians that it is "just a way of speaking," it remains anchored within notions that are unmistakably racial.

Everyday discourse on Morro do Sangue Bom, as elsewhere in Brazil, articulates a profound association between devalued or even despised physical traits and blackness. While this association may be articulated in expressions such as "The *negro* has an ugly face. . . . he hasn't got lips, they're rubber tires" (qtd. by Harris 1956, 122), it can also be articulated in personalized discourses which refer to the real people in one's social universe (cf. Maggie 1992; Pacheco 1986). A typical comment was made by a woman in her thirties about a man whom she detested: "My god, he was so ugly, black as coal, so dark, really *negro!*"

Within everyday discourses, the most common discursive construction of devalued blackness occurs precisely in those locutions which begin "He is *negro* but" or, alternatively, "He is very *preto* but." In one of many cases I overheard, a woman in her twenties was telling two of her friends about an acquaintance of hers (unknown to her interlocutors) who had recently died of leptospirosis. Concluding her sad story, she said, "He was very, very *preto*, but he was a really cool guy, you know?" Such locutions are ubiquitous, and they spell out the assumptions and associations underlying notions of blackness. One is said to be *preto* or *negro* "but very cool," "but very intelligent," "but really nice," "but very responsible," "but hardworking," "but he/she has a car." During the entire period of my fieldwork, I never heard anyone challenge the implicit assumptions within such locutions, and I was never able to perceive a correlation between the frequency with which people engaged in such locutions and the color of either speakers or hearers.

These assumptions are evident in other types of coded speech as well—even when the speaker is ostensibly rejecting the assumptions. I met, for example, an upper-middle-class white woman who had scandalized her friends and family by dating a much younger and very handsome middle-class black man. "I have learned," she told me, as though soberly defending her choice, "that appearance does not matter." "But he's so handsome!" I blurted. We were both embarrassed by the exchange, although for different reasons. She had spoken of his blackness and her willingness to excuse or overlook it and not of his attractiveness.

While *negro* represents, in both a historical and a cultural sense, the central signifier around which the panoply of negative notions of blackness coalesce, it is but one of many words that, depending on context, can signify the same or similar notions. Joia, for example, told me, "*Preto* (black) hurts less than *negro*," but she added, "It depends on how it is said." The devaluation of blackness is also articulated through a wide variety of slang terms. *Crioulo*, for example, has evolved from a word signifying a Brazilian-born slave to one that is used as an epithet. As a nineteen-year-old boy told me, "You say *crioulo* when you want to curse someone." Another very common word is *macaco*, which, literally translated, means monkey. "It is very racial," Alberto said of the word. "It is a word that the police often use." All of these terms, of course, are understood as epithets, and they can be spoken either within a confrontation or behind a person's back.

Negro and similar words that simultaneously connote darkness, ugliness, marginality, and immorality are not, of course, the only terms that are burdened with such pervasive and largely unexamined meanings. All terms are located, both symbolically and discursively, within a hierarchy that posits both aesthetic and moral values. *Negro* is at the bottom of this hierarchy, and white is at the top. Positive valuations of whiteness are articulated in everyday discourses, and once again the color of speakers and hearers appears to be of no significance. Value-laden references to race and color, it often seemed to me, tended to be employed especially in those conversational contexts in which a person's death or impending death was remarked upon. Speaking to her husband, one friend said, "Do you remember Susana, that very pretty light-skinned woman? She is dying of AIDS!" For several minutes she continued to refer to the woman's physical appearance. "And she is so beautiful; she is *clarinha* (light-skinned); she has *olhos claros* (light eyes) and *cabelo bom* (good hair)! It's just so sad!" This was all spoken as though these traits made the woman's illness and likely death all the more tragic.

The valuation of racialized traits is, in a fairly direct linguistic sense, inscribed within the very words used to describe those traits. The expression "bad hair" is an obvious case in point. I often had the sense that as a foreigner I was sharply struck by such expressions, whereas my informants used them in an extremely facile and apparently unconscious manner. *Nariz chato*, which means flat nose, carries additional linguistic associations. The word *chato* is among the most common of slang terms and is used to refer to whatever is thought to be lousy, bad, unpleasant, obnoxious, or troublesome. Thus, when one young woman mentioned that she did not like her own nose because, as she said, "It is ugly, really *chato*," I believe she intended the word to be understood in both of its senses. Notably, when I contradicted her and said that her nose was very pretty, she replied, "No, Beth, *your* nose is very pretty!" The lips of *negros* are called *labios grossos*, literally, thick lips, but as with the double meaning of the word *gross* in English, it can also mean crude, coarse, or disgusting.

Predictably, words used to define what are thought of as white features have double meanings that connote positive qualities. The word *fino*, which translates as narrow, is used to describe the lips and noses of white people. It also means fine or refined, as in the expression *gente fina*, or refined people. White people's faces are also described as *bem feita*, or well-made, and, as many in Morro do Sangue Bom told me, white people always have so-called *cabelo bom*, or good hair.

All of these associations, whether they involve moral qualities or physical features (or both simultaneously), are not restricted to *negros* and *brancos*. They represent, rather, the extremes within a color hierarchy. Thus, one who is not quite *preto* or *negro* is said to have *cabelo razoável*, or reasonable hair. *Pardo* was defined by one woman as "darker than white but better than *sarará*." Another woman, believing as some do that *preto* is not always synonymous with *negro*, defined the former as "more or less the same but less dark than the *negro*, more pretty."

Given the fact that blackness is overwhelmingly associated with negative qualities, it is little wonder that references to race and color are highly circumscribed—hemmed in, in fact, by a universally understood and conscientiously practiced etiquette. In Morro do Sangue Bom, everyday conversations, as well as the way people talk about their conversations, reveal that politeness tends to be preferred over clarity of reference, description, or classification. What my informants called "hard words" are typically covered over with euphemism, softening diminutives, and other pragmatic, rather than referential, terms and forms of address.

The Pragmatic Discourse of Color

As I have indicated, the question I put to informants about their color during my brief survey interviews was, in fact, a very complicated one, and it was often met with laughter, uncertainty, and, when others were present, discussion. In response to my question, a woman with curly hair and a tannish complexion said, "I am *branca*." She then extended her arm, looked at it, chuckled, and added, "A little bit *morena*, right?" In another case, I introduced myself to a man who was repairing the cement steps outside his home after a heavy rainstorm. He gave his own color as *negro*, and I asked him about his wife's color. "*Branca*," he said. Smiling, he then looked down at the ground, chuckled sardonically, and added, "She isn't you know, but that's what we say."

One day I asked Maria, Joia's next-door neighbor, if she would do the survey interview with me. Her eight-year-old daughter, Ana, with whom I was particularly friendly, was present, and she attended the interview closely. Maria's skin was tan and her hair was curly. Her husband, João, who was driving his delivery truck that day, was, as I knew, occasionally referred to in brincadeira as a *negão*, or big black man. His skin was very dark, he kept his crisp hair cut very close, and he was very tall and broad shouldered. João and Maria's three children were darker than their mother and lighter than their father.

When I came to the color question, Maria laughed shyly and said of herself, "I'm called white, but I'm not really. I'm—I don't know—*morena?*" When I asked about João, she said without hesitation, "*Moreno.*" Ana said, a split second later, "*Negro,*" covered her mouth, and giggled. Maria turned to her daughter and said sharply, "No, he is not!" Ana's giggling became uncontrollable and once again, she said, "*Negro.*" Maria was clearly embarrassed. In an attempt to cover the awkwardness of the moment, I pretended to ignore Ana and asked, "And the children?" "*Morenos,*" Maria replied. "Except for me," Ana said, thrusting her chest forward, "I am a *negão!*" Maria shook her head, rolled her eyes, and said, "Stop!" The three of us burst into laughter.

Like the young man I had interviewed who distinguished between his wife's real color and "what we say," Maria told me that what she was called was different from how she really appeared. Moreover, Maria, Ana, and I all knew that João was not, according to the discourse of color description, *moreno.* She intended the word as a polite euphemism for her husband's darkness. It was partly Ana's awareness that I enjoyed brincadeira and partly the mischievous impulse that children often have to expose and play with the squeamishness underlying the delicacy and politeness of adult discourse that motivated her to contradict her mother.

Other informants qualified the terms that they used. Often, they intended not only to answer my question as best they could (using the discourse of color description) but to teach me about, or to signal their own awareness of, the ways in which the race-color lexicon was systematically manipulated. A dark-skinned woman in her forties whom I had just met said, for example, "I am *preta* (black). People say *morena,* but I think I am really *preta.*"

It was clear in these and similar cases that when distinctions were made between what people said and some notion of real color, the real color was always, by the standards of the discourse of color description, darker. What people said, then, served to lighten the person to whom they referred. As Neusa told me, "Look, so many [words] exist exactly so that one is not totally of a *negro* color." Cutting straight to the point, another informant told me, "*Moreno* is used so as not to call someone *negro.*"[11]

This polite register shares many features with other linguistic registers or markers that emphasize the pragmatic rather than the referential function of language (Crapanzano 1992; Lutz and Abu-Lughod 1990; Lucy 1993; Silverstein 1976, 1979.) A comment of Alberto, Joia's oldest son, provides a working definition of the pragmatic dimension that I have emphasized in all of the above examples. When I asked Alberto the meaning of the term *neguinho*—the diminutive of *negro*—he responded, "It is a manner of treating someone." When they are employed in the pragmatic register, such diminutives, as well as words like *moreno*, refer less to a person's real color than to the relationship between speakers. When used pragmatically, these words *do* something rather than *say* something, or in Alberto's astute terms they are a "manner of treating" rather than of describing or classifying someone. In social terms, the pragmatic use of intermediate race-color terms functions to demonstrate respect and/or affection. "*Moreno* and *pardo* are words that people like," an eleven-year-old girl told me. "They are good words." By using such terms, of course, one avoids "hard words" and the feelings of hurt and offense that they cause.

What is consciously regarded as euphemistic substitution even occurs when the person being described is not present. When I asked Dona Janete to provide terms for a number of people with whom we were both acquainted, she gave terms such as *moreno* and *jambo* and softening diminutives such as *pretinho*. When we had finished with the list, she leaned back in her chair, sighed with relief, and said, "Good. I have not called anyone a *negro*."

Diminutives, as is clear in Dona Janete's responses, function in much the same way as do terms such as *moreno*. The most common diminutives are *pretinho*, *escurinho*, and *neguinho*. The term *pretinho* is usually glossed as "little black," and indeed it is sometimes used to describe a child or an adult of diminutive stature. Far more often, however, its meaning is closer to "a little bit black." It modifies the term *preto* by softening it. *Pretinho* even suggests a kind of cuteness. Roberta, a young woman in her twenties, echoed others when she told me that the term is *carinhosa*, or affectionate, at the same time that it is *bem delicada*, or quite delicate. "Instead of saying *preto*," Joia's stepfather informed me, "it is better to call a person *escurinho*" (a little bit dark).

Words such as *pretinho*, *escurinho*, and *neguinho* can be contrasted to hard words with considerable dramatic effect, as Tomas noted when he talked about the tendency of policemen to hurl racial epithets at young men such as himself: "[The word] *crioulo* is very offensive. *Negro! Crioulo!* [Police officers] never call us *escurinho*. They never call us *pretinho*."

When race-color terms are used in what I call the pragmatic discourse, they have, like all euphemisms, a double edge. This is especially obvious in the case of diminutives. The same young woman who explained that diminutives are both affectionate and delicate pointed out that they can be, at the same time, condescending. Talking generally about what she called the "racism in Brazilian society," she said, "Even within a given conversation, you are going to talk about someone, and how is it? If it was a white person, you wouldn't call him *branquinho,* no. But if the person was a *preto,* you say it like this—you say, 'That *pretinho.*' You already have that [condescending] idea in your head."

Roberta's comments are ethnographically accurate, for white adults are rarely referred to as *branquinho,* while adult people of color routinely receive the diminutive. This is true regardless of the color of the speaker, and it was the fact that people of color automatically, as it were, use diminutives that Roberta wanted to emphasize. *Pretinho* seeks to soften and soothe, but its echo gently, or sometimes aggressively, infantalizes. It is intended to index affection but in a wayward fashion; it simultaneously invokes the relentless presence of a cultural hierarchy within which the *preto* occupies a pitiable position.

The term *neguinho* is also, as I was told by many people, an affectionate word, yet it too has a condescending edge. White middle-class men as well as poor men of color may sometimes call their wives *minha neguinha* (my little black one), and the wives, ostensibly, like it when they do so. In this sense it is proprietary, and, while affectionate, the speaker asserts a personal claim and a superiority over the hearer. Although it can be used for a white person, the colonial etymology of *neguinho* is evident, and several people in Morro do Sangue Bom told me that they objected to it. "*Neguinho,*" Tomas said frowning. "I don't like anyone to call me that."

Sometimes Tiago called his mother *minha neguinha.* Joia, of course, would grab a broom or other handy object and in feigned fury chase Tiago around and around the dining-room table until both collapsed in exhaustion on the couch. The punch of Tiago's *brincadeira* was three-fold: it communicated incestuous innuendo, it asserted that Tiago's status was higher than that of his mother, and it flirted, as the term always does, with a derogatory racial reference.

When they are used pragmatically, intermediate terms such as *moreno* and *pardo* also have this condescending dimension. Although calling a dark-skinned woman *morena* is a form of flattery, some, such as Susana, objected to its implications: "It offends because people who are quite black (*bem pretinha*) are called *morena.* They say I am *morena* because I am black (*preta*). You see?"

For Susana, the pragmatic use of the term *morena* engages the same rather paradoxical dilemma as do all euphemisms. The intent of the speaker who uses a euphemism is, typically, to soften, conceal, or discursively dismiss the unpleasantness of the original referent—the word or concept for which the euphemism is a substitution. Yet in using the euphemism, which is an unmistakably pragmatic act, the speaker summons that original referent. When someone calls Susana *morena,* she inevitably hears the echo of *preta* ringing silently but somehow palpably in the air. As Susana and others in Morro do Sangue Bom are aware, terms like *morena*, as well as softening diminutives, are euphemistic precisely because it is thought that one *ought* to be ashamed of being a *preta*. Once, when I asked Joia's close friend Yvonne to describe Joia's color, she responded with the term *pretinha*. Joia, who had been chopping vegetables in the kitchen, stepped into the room and shook her knife in a mock threat. "I heard that!" she warned. "Poor thing!" Yvonne teased.

Questioning Brazil's System of Racial Classification

Much of the contemporary anthropological discourse about Brazil's multiple racial categories is based on research conducted in the late 1960s and early 1970s by Marvin Harris (1970) and Roger Sanjek (1971). Although the point is typically overlooked in the numerous references to the research, Harris intended his influential article "Referential Ambiguity in the Calculus of Brazilian Racial Identity" (1970) as a critique of the so-called New Ethnography of the era, and his methodology was therefore modeled on componential analysis. Harris asked one hundred Brazilian informants to provide race terms for a set of black and white cartoonlike drawings that represented people with different skin shades, facial features, and hair types. This technique elicited 492 terms. Working with the same methodology but limiting his research to a single village, Sanjek (1971) elicited 116 terms.

Both researchers emphasized the ambiguity of Brazilian race-color vocabulary, but they nevertheless maintained that the terms that they elicited in this fashion constituted "racial categories," "raciological taxonomies," the "Brazilian system of racial classification," and/or the "Brazilian calculation of racial identity." What I would call the literalist assumptions embedded in their labeling of their data—which was collected not through traditional, grounded ethnographic means but by highly artificial, experimental methods—have been uncritically adopted by a generation of Brazilianist scholars.

My primary theoretical argument in this chapter has been that it is not a true concept of racial identity, nor racial categories, nor a system of racial classification that most Brazilians are engaging and manipulating when they use these race-color terms but rather language itself.[12] That people in Morro do Sangue Bom manipulate the language of race and color at a largely conscious level is evident. "Why do you have so many words for a person's color?" I asked a young man named Celso during my survey interview. He reflected for a moment and replied, "Well, you know that the Brazilian, he adores slang, right? Here in Rio, there are people from all over the country, so it's an exchange of slang." For Celso, the explanation lay not in a homologous or literal relationship between racial identity and the lexicon but in the peculiar and often self-consciously artful forms of engagement—and avoidance—that he and his countrymen have with their language.

My conversation with José, Joia's sardonic father-in-law, also helped me to understand that Brazilians such as those in Morro do Sangue Bom are apt, in many moments, to view race-color terms as existing within a space of linguistic play. In a comment I quoted earlier in this chapter, José described the majority of people living on the morro: "Some are darker, some are lighter, but they're all *negros*." He paused after this comment and then continued, "They're all *preto. Preto*, no! Everyone is *crioulo!*"

Crioulo, of course, is an epithet, and in using it José smiled, much in the way that one might wink, to signal a shift in register. His pedagogical intentions were twofold. He wanted me to understand that all people of color were *negros*, regardless of how they might be described or politely addressed. In addition, he was teaching me that all of the confusing terms were best understood as words from which one might choose in order to communicate one's social intentions—to flatter, perhaps, or to tease, or, in his own use of the term *crioulo*, to insult.

Several days after this conversation with José, I was sitting on the couch in Joia's house chatting with her and her older son, Alberto. José came through the open door and asked me, in the tone of an instructor testing a pupil, "Now Beth, what would you call the color of Alberto?" (Alberto, recall, had told me that his own appearance could be described as *moreno, mulato,* or *pardo*, but that in racial terms he was a *negro*.) I looked apologetically at Alberto and then said with mock authority, "Alberto? He is a *pedo engarrafado*." "Exactly!" José exclaimed amidst much laughter. This term, I had previously learned, literally means bottled fart, and it describes a person whose color (as opposed to race) is indefinite or difficult to describe. It is insulting to call someone a fart, of course, but I had chosen the term because it allowed me to show that I understood José's lecture about the linguistic play that underlies so much race-color talk—and it allowed me, at the same time, to compliment Alberto by suggesting that he was not particularly dark. The etymology of the term *pedo engarrafado*, from all that I could gather, was unknown.

I could well imagine the sly amusement with which Celso, José, Alberto, and others on the morro might approach a task such as that which Harris (1970) and Sanjek (1971) put to their informants. Confronted with a stack of drawings on which differently shaded human faces were depicted, they might well have interpreted the task as a test of wit and linguistic creativity. Seen in this light, it would appear that in eliciting more than four hundred color terms, some of which appear to be entirely nonsensical, Harris was not tapping the "Brazilian system of racial classification," as he insisted, but the creative (and often humorous) poetics of color description—or in Celso's terms, the Brazilian adoration of slang.

My review of the pragmatic discourse reveals that the ambiguity of race-color terms is not limited to their semantic elasticity but is just as fully based on the distinction between the separate linguistic functions that Brazilians speakers engage in their use of the terms. I would argue that much of the misrepresentation of what Brazilians are so often doing when they employ a race-color term is based on the fact that speech acts that are essentially pragmatic in function are so often interpreted as literal references. Michael Silverstein (1976, 1979), an anthropological linguist who has done a great deal to call our attention to the critical cultural and communicative function of pragmatic language, has noted the degree to which our attempts to understand situated talk is distorted by an overemphasis on the referential function of language. It was precisely this type of distortion that my informants in Morro do Sangue Bom warned me against when they repeatedly insisted that race-color terms were often "a way of treating someone" rather than taxonomical categories.

One day when I went to visit Dona Janete, I found her chatting with another friend, Dona Nilda. They were swapping stories about their work as domestic servants, and Dona Nilda said that her least favorite employer had been an African diplomat. He was cold and authoritarian, she said. "And he was *preto* (black), like us," she explained, coming to the point. "Speak for yourself, I am *parda!*" Dona Janete put in and guffawed. I did not yet know Dona Janete well, and I was unfamiliar with her irreverent wit. Because she was, in fact, quite a bit lighter than Dona Nilda, I assumed that she thought herself to be in a different (and implicitly superior) racial category.

I was wrong, of course. As I came to know Dona Janete, I learned that she wholeheartedly considered herself a *negra*. Dona Janete's *brincadeira*, or joke, certainly skirted the borders of good taste, but it was a particularly revealing one. As she explained to me later, words such as *parda* were "an invention of the people." What she was mocking was not Dona Nilda's presumption of racial solidarity but the opposite: she was poking fun at the delicacy of the term *parda* and all that was implied in the existence of an etiquette that shied away from, softened, and euphemized blackness.

There is, as Dona Janete's joke made clear, something akin to an implicit ideology that is embedded within each of the registers in which race-color terms are used. Terms such as *moreno, pardo,* and others that connote intermediate skin colors are by far the most commonly employed in everyday speech. In the most immediate sense, such terms function, I would argue, as a kind of leveling mechanism. A degree of ideological resistance can and should be read not only into the pragmatic discourse but into the descriptive discourse of color as well. The descriptive discourse, in focusing one's attention on the uniqueness of an individual's appearance (rather than membership in one of a set of mutually exclusive categories), stretches toward a de-essentializing and dismantling of race and its insidious significance. The pragmatic discourse, an "invention of the people," insists that everyone be addressed with a neutral intermediate term, and it thus stretches toward a democratic leveling of color distinctions. Ideologically speaking, these registers resist the cultural hierarchy of race and color and all that it suggests about invidious distinctions, esthetic beauty, and moral worth. Although people in Morro do Sangue Bom soundly denounce democracia racial as an accurate description of the world in which they live, their use of the polite register is, in a sense, an attempt to support its prescriptive beliefs: neither race nor color *should* matter because all are members of the (miscegenated) Brazilian family.

Dona Janete's joke, however, also calls attention to the paradox underlying these ideological implications. Even if the intention of speakers is often to level differences, all of the words in the lexicon are anchored, semantically speaking, within a vision of value and hierarchy. Because there is a constant interplay of referencing, indexing, connoting, and evasion that occurs both in the minds of interlocutors and in the rapid shifting from one register to another in everyday speech, true escape from that hierarchy is impossible. As Susana told me, she dislikes it when people call her *morena* because she is aware of the term's deeper implications: she is being condescended to precisely because her darkness is both noted and considered unfortunate. Susana and my other informants in Morro do Sangue Bom understood that while the language of race and color is articulated from within a space of linguistic play, it is also circumscribed within a space of cultural and ideological entrapment.

In teaching me about the language of race and color, people in Morro do Sangue Bom engaged in metadiscursive narratives through which the descriptive and pragmatic discourses were figured as a superficial scrim beneath which a different and implacable reality was concealed. Dona Janete's reference to most of the race-color terms as an "invention of the people" held a double implication: the descriptive and pragmatic discourses were best understood as manipulations of language itself rather than identity. "Deep down" underneath such invention was the bedrock reality of racialized polarization and opposition. This, I would argue, is a theoretically appropriate way to describe the manner in which the significations of race and color are culturally and discursively ordered in Brazil. The discourse on race—the only one, I would assert, that truly articulates a system of racial classification in Brazil—simultaneously engages an essentialist, naturalized notion of racial being and what I would suggest is a more conscious and objective awareness of the fact that blackness is constructed through the shared experience of discrimination and prejudice and is thus a product of oppression. It is in this latter sense, especially, that the discourse on race disavows the platitudes of democracia racial.

These metadiscursive narratives are theoretically appropriate for the additional reason that the discourse on race is neither a totalizing nor even a dominant one but is, in places like Morro do Sangue Bom, subterranean. Its reality as both a kind of hidden discourse and a cultural vision, I believe, is fully illustrated by the consistent way in which my informants deconstructed their own language. The employment of euphemisms in the service of a universally understood etiquette, the often conscious manipulation of semantic ambiguity, and the desire to eschew references to blackness were all framed as forms of linguistic agency that in one sense or anther comment on the implicit understanding that "there are only two races."

As will be seen in the following chapter, all of the discourses I have described are embedded within a larger arena in which silence, rather than talk, is most evident. Democracia racial—whether we call it a myth, an ideology, a discourse, or a dream—is a fragile dam that requires careful tending. As this chapter suggests, people in Morro do Sangue Bom participate in its upkeep through their everyday talk, even as they sometimes undermine, in quiet and subterranean ways, its foundation.

Chapter 3   Silence

Racism and Cultural Censorship

AFTER SPENDING FIVE and a half months in Brazil in 1940 and 1941, the African American sociologist E. Franklin Frazier wrote, "There is in Brazil, little discussion of the racial or color situation. It appears that there is an unexpressed understanding among all elements in the population not to discuss the racial situation, at least as a contemporary phenomenon" (qtd. in Hellwig 1992, 131). More than half a century later, Frazier's observation remains essentially accurate. While some scholars and black movement militants have been developing sociological analyses of racism and espousing antiracist discourses since at least the 1930s, their numbers remain small and the contexts in which these discourses are articulated continue to be extremely limited. The discussion of issues related to racial prejudice and discrimination in everyday discourse is, relatively speaking, a rarity, and this appears to be true, as Frazier noted, of all colors and social classes in Brazil.

In the discourses of democracia racial, the lack of talk about racism in Brazil is taken as prima facie evidence that racial prejudice and discrimination, as a set of social and/or political problems, are not significant enough to provoke discussion. Observations such as Frazier's are regarded, moreover, as ethnocentric judgments, made because North Americans obsess over their own dilemma to such a degree that they fail to understand that no such dilemma exists for Brazilians.

Although Frazier himself appears to have been partly swayed by this argument (see Hellwig 1992), his comment does more than simply underline the political and sociological differences between Brazil and the United States. In referring to unexpressed understandings, he suggests if not censorship (which did, in fact, occur during the military dictatorship of the 1970s) then a kind of tacit, unexamined, and yet deeply pervasive etiquette of silence. This silence, I want to argue, is meaningful; it is not merely a lack of talk or an unmarked absence, as has been suggested, but a perceptible lacuna within discourse.

"The law for the negro is to keep his mouth shut," Dona Janete told me one day when we were talking about the fact that she and others in her community were acutely aware of racism but rarely, if ever, spoke of it. What required explanation, and the question at the center of this chapter, is why did Dona Janete, by her own admission, decide not to talk about the realities of racism with her sons, her husband, and the many friends she had in the community? This silence, as I will argue, is best conceptualized as a form of *cultural censorship* that has deep roots not only in the specious claims of democracia racial but also in the psychology of oppression.

Theoretical Treatments of Silence

Silence represents a particularly difficult puzzle, both in the realm of ethnography and in theory building.[1] In the social sciences, it tends to be discussed in relation to one of two issues: the macro level of discourse (or the lack of discourse) in public domains and the micro level of sociolinguistics and the analysis of speech acts. In the former case, discussions of silence usually center on censorship. While censorship is sometimes used in a metaphorical sense (see, for example, Bourdieu 1991), it typically refers to the enforcement of silence by identifiable agents, usually the state and/or its representatives. Censorship is defined as a primary means by which states control opposition and resistance. As one writer has remarked, "A kind of macro silence of oppression is a desirable state for all power groups that are afraid that the mere expression and exchange of opinions or the free flow of information will threaten the existing status quo" (Jaworski 1993, 115). Theories of enforced censorship, however, cannot account for the maintenance of silence in the apparent absence of censors, identifiable agents who police discourse and punish infractions against an official code.

A number of writers have used the concept of linguistic domination to account for the silence of subordinate groups. In Bourdieu's vision, for example, dominance and power are exercised through the unequal distribution of "linguistic legitimacy" and "competence," which are defined as the forms and styles of speech practiced by the dominant group (1991, 71–72). Bourdieu emphasizes the notion that direct control of the speech of subordinate groups is rarely necessary, for the members of such groups share the beliefs, assumptions, and values of the linguistic markets in which their speech is (negatively) judged.

The most fully developed work on muted or silent groups remains that of feminist sociolinguists. At the macro level of analysis, a number of writers have focused on women's limited access to the arenas of public discourse, their internalization of beliefs about the inadequacy of girls' and women's speech, and the historically entrenched unofficial censorship of women's political criticism (see, for example, Harding 1975; Houston and Kramarae 1991; Lakoff 1975; McConnell-Ginet et al. 1980; Thorne and Henley 1975). Houston and Kramarae note that "silencing is used to isolate people disempowered by their gender, race, and class, even in the speaking contexts of their daily lives" (1991, 338).

Silence that is embedded within conversation has been examined by sociolinguists, who assert that it is, in some contexts at least, a communicative act. As one writer has noted for such occasions, "similar inferencing processes are employed to interpret the meaning of what is not spoken as in interpreting what is said" (Saville-Troike 1985, 7). In a perceptive analysis of silence among the Italian families he studied, George Saunders argues that silence is one of two expressive styles. Drawing on the anthropology of emotions, he writes that "silence may be an indication of conflicting or problematic emotions, emotions which must be monitored, controlled, or inhibited in expression because of their potential consequences" (1985, 175; see also, Basso 1970, 1979). In ethnographic studies such as these, silence is seen as a code choice similar to that assumed to operate in linguistic production.

An additional, more recently elaborated area of scholarship that may bear a relationship to silence is that which focuses on history and the production of social memory. As a number of scholars have noted, the production of social memory is anything but a neutral process. Discussions of history and memory suggest an overlap with the issue of silence in that social memory, as a politically motivated representation of the past, presupposes the coexistence of forms of collective forgetting or, in the terms I am outlining here, of lacunae within discourse. As one writer has observed, "As remembering is a social act, so too is forgetting. The contemporary landscape of memory is created through the modern ars memoria, which involve not so much feats of hypermnesia as of strategic forgetting" (Kirmayer 1996, 191). In a similar vein, another writer has remarked, "The absence of memory is just as socially constructed as memory itself, and with an equally strong intervention of morally and ideologically grounded claims to truth" (Irwin-Zareka 1994, 116). In *Between History and Histories: The Making of Silences and Commemorations*

(Sider and Smith 1997), Sider has provocatively argued that the "creation of culture is also, simultaneously and necessarily, the creation of silence . . . we can have no significant understanding of any culture unless we know the silences that are were *institutionally* created and guaranteed along with it" (1997, 74–75, emphasis in original).

All of these works articulate a general recognition of the fact that various sorts of patterned silences play roles in constructing the shape of social and political life; and, to differing degrees, they suggest a set of theoretical questions that partly overlap with those that motivate my discussion of silence in Morro do Sangue Bom. The silences they describe, however, differ in fundamental ways from the silence my informants practice. This chapter is primarily concerned with the fact that people in Morro do Sangue Bom tend to refrain from discussions of racism even in the contexts of community and family—in those places, in other words, where state-sponsored surveillance and coercion are absent. Poor Brazilians of African descent do not represent a silent or muted group in the sense described by feminist sociolinguistics because as working-class people they often speak volubly about the injustice of poverty. Their silence is highly specific rather than totalizing.

The silence that surrounds the issue of racism in Morro do Sangue Bom (and in Brazil generally) is properly conceptualized, I would argue, as cultural censorship. Although there are meaningful, even profound psychological motivations underlying my informants' silence, the censorship is socially shared; the rules for its observance are culturally codified. As will be seen in chapter 6, in which I discuss middle-class whites, the cultural censorship surrounding racism in Brazil crosses social boundaries. It is not, however, seamless. Different groups in Brazil—particularly those as divided as poor Brazilians of African descent are from middle-class whites—have markedly different interests at stake in the suppression of talk about racism.

This chapter focuses on how people in Morro do Sangue Bom account for the silence they practice in their own community. Although, according to the familiar literary tropes, "silence is palpable" or "pregnant with meaning," it is, in and of itself, difficult to describe in ethnographic terms. As was the case in the previous chapter then, my discussion of cultural censorship relies, to a great degree, on metadiscourse: the ways in which informant's acknowledge, frame their explanations for, and describe the experience of silence.

Accounts of Silence in Morro do Sangue Bom

As I have noted in the first chapter, I rarely heard impromptu discussions of racism in everyday conversations in Morro do Sangue Bom, particularly during the early months of my fieldwork. Later, when I conducted in-depth interviews with people, the issue of the lack of talk about racism, as well as the denial of racism, was often broached not by myself but by informants. When it was not, I asked direct questions about the issue. For example, after informants described personal experiences that involved racism, I often asked them if they had recounted these same experiences to others, such as friends and family. Much of what follows is based not on silence itself but on informants' comments about and descriptions of silence and their accounts of why people "don't want to talk about it" and choose to *ficar calado*, or stay silent.[2]

Very few of my informants in Morro do Sangue Bom told me that they tended to discuss racism, even with their intimate associates. Yvonne, for example, was typical in her assertion that the issue was not discussed within her family; yet, atypically, she told me that she and her friends sometimes conversed about it. The manner in which she framed her comments is instructive: "No. You know why, Beth? Because I don't dwell on it. (*Eu não ligo.*) But also because [in my family] we almost never talked about it. Oh, but with friends I have. . . . I have [other] friends also, who live nearby, who talk a lot about this, right? And they always think that it really exists, this horrible prejudice, here in Brazil, and that it's never going to end."

When Yvonne says that she and her friends discuss racism, she points out that "they always think that it really exists." Yvonne's allusion to a cultural argument that centers directly on the question of whether or not racism truly exists in Brazil was immediately familiar to me, for it framed so many of the comments that people provided in response to my questions. While this may have been partly due to the way I often posed my questions, this initial framing of the issue would continue to dominate people's narratives—particularly their comments about silence—long after it was conversationally established that I was entirely persuaded by the authority of their claims and had responded to their narration of painful experiences.

After Jonas, a man in his late twenties, spoke with considerable frustration about his experiences with racism, I asked him if his friends tended to recount similar experiences to him. He responded rather curtly, "Some tell what happens; some don't tell. It's like I already told you, the subject is rarely touched on, but I believe [racism] exists." The comments of Analucia show a similar concern to carefully assert the reality of racism while acknowledging the silence surrounding it. She had finished telling me the story that I describe in the previous chapter, in which several white women, believing that Analucia was white also, made racist comments about a black man. Analucia scolded them. I asked her if any of the other people present who had witnessed the exchange had said anything to her after the confrontation, either in support or refutation of her angry comments: "No, they stayed silent. I mean, it's like that Beth. It's concealed, but there is racism. Here in Brazil, it will never end, never end; it's never going to end. Many can say, 'Oh no, there's none of that, there isn't prejudice against the negro.' They won't say anything because, I think, here, no one accepts [the reality of] this business of discrimination against negros."

Silence and/or the discourses that deny the existence of racism in Brazil are highlighted in these comments. As other informants had, Analucia, in fact, imitates and mocks the discourse of denial. I believe that my interviewees did not, for the most part, feel that I was in need of suasion or had failed to understand the import of their words. Rather, particularly when they referred to silence, they framed their comments as a kind of defensive counterargument against an invisible interlocutor. If at times I had the impression that they had never before discussed their experiences, interpretations, and opinions in such detail, I also had the sense that both their narratives of racism and their comments on silence were spoken from a private history of tortured inner dialogue, a kind of *esprit d'escalier*, or staircase wit. Although their comments were generously intended to enlighten a foreign researcher, they were also, at identifiable moments, directed toward all of the people who had denied their experience and misread their silence.

My awareness of the dearth of explicit discussions about racism was repeatedly confirmed by people's responses to my direct questions about the extent to which racism was a subject of conversations within families and between friends. When I asked Paulinho, a man in his forties, if his parents had ever discussed racism in his presence, his response was typical. Although he described a childhood spent in the Bahian countryside, his comments were echoed by others with more urban origins. The all-consuming demands of day-to-day survival left no time or energy for the discussion of issues such as racism: "No, there was that whole thing at home, that business of being in the country, all that, planting manioc, making manioc flour, that whole thing. So everything was more or less just consumed with this, and fishing, you know? . . . When I was nine years old, I felt that [awareness of racism]. I came home and I said to my mother, 'Mom, someone called me a monkey!' You understand? And she just said, 'Answer back, insult them back.'. . . So, like that, after that business of throwing insults, it starts up, that whole thing, right, and it's too much."

His mother's response, Paulinho suggested, was hardly adequate.[3] Other informants told me that during the time they were children, cross-generational conversation was, in general, very restricted. Elena, who grew up in the countryside of Espirito Santo, said, "It's not like today. There was a lack of information, and parents didn't converse with children as they do now." Like Elena, a number of informants suggested that their parents lacked the sophistication to engage in discussions of racism.

I also asked many of my informants if they had heard stories about slavery when they were growing up. When I asked Dona Janete, she recounted several but then added, "The adults at that time didn't converse with children, right? It's hard for you to understand this, but we didn't have the right to listen to the conversations of our elders. When the parents were conversing like that, we had to leave, to work, to take care of our younger siblings. So I didn't hear things like that."

The few stories about slavery that Dona Janete did recount were painful ones, involving routine privation and gratuitous torture. When she said that children "didn't have the right to listen to conversations," I believe she was suggesting not only that relations between parents and children were more formal than they are currently but also that children were deliberately shielded from certain conversations.[4] Very few informants, in fact, were able to recall hearing stories about the slavery era, although the grandparents and great-grandparents of a number of the older people I knew had been slaves. Paulinho, whom I have quoted above, was an exception in that he told me that his great-grandfather would "get the children together and tell stories, so many incredible stories." Although Paulinho referred to the content of these stories in a pained and somewhat vague way, he was able to recall their effect on him: "My great-grandfather told about all that, stories so bad that he would wind up crying, the poor guy, and then he would change the subject, because he was crying so much. This made me so upset and angry. . . . This for me—I was a child and he passed this on to me. I said, 'My God, what was done to my great-grandmothers, my great-grandfathers?' That whole thing. And they died. I didn't get to know them well. And I kept thinking about this: Was it the same for them?"

In Paulinho's last line ("Was it the same for them?") he was referring to stories about rape and beating, the stories that his great-grandfather had reported as happening not to him but to others, his friends of the slave quarters. Paulinho told me that as a result of these stories, which he had heard at the age of seven or eight, he had become a "very rebellious child."

Dona Janete's son, Jacinto, also told me several very truncated stories from the slavery era, stories that his mother had told him. He then said, "My mother told us a lot. . . . She told us so many things. I don't dwell on it (*Eu não ligo muito*). Because it's so sad. I don't like [these stories] from the past. What humans do to each other! I think we should leave those times behind. Oh, but there is slavery still today, right? . . . Slavery is like racism. It hasn't ended; it's just gotten more sophisticated. And this isn't going to end. It exists today, a concealed kind of slavery (*escravidão embaixo do pano*).

Both men obviously suffered distress on hearing these stories and in retelling them to me, in however abbreviated a fashion. When Jacinto said, "I don't dwell on it," his face became contorted and he waved his arm about as though dispelling a cloud of smoke.

Most people told me, however, that their parents had talked about neither slavery nor racism when they were growing up. When I asked younger informants in their teens and twenties if their parents had ever discussed racism with them, they rarely elaborated on their responses, saying simply, "No, they never talked about it" or "They don't dwell on it."

Some informants, such as Paulinho, suggested that the lack of open discussion (which could hypothetically involve warnings, advice, or reassurance) within the family caused them pain and frustration during their childhood or adolescence. In this regard, the comments of Rosa are worth quoting at length; they recount the searing experience of a sudden confrontation with prejudice and the failure to find sufficient familial support and reassurance. When I asked Rosa if she was able to recall the first time she became aware of racism, she paused for nearly a minute and then began to recount an experience she had had at the age of sixteen or seventeen:

> I remember. It was in Belo Horizonte [a major city in the state of
> Minas Gerais]. I came to Belo Horizonte and worked for a family
> there [as a domestic servant]. And on the same street, I knew a girl, a
> very light-skinned girl. So my friend said to me, "Let's go out on
> Saturday night." I said, "Let's go." She had a white friend. So at 9:30
> at night, she came over and we went over to this friend's house to
> call her to come out with us. . . . But when her friend saw me, she
> didn't want to go out anymore. She spoke directly to me. "But why
> don't you want to go out anymore?" I asked. "Oh, because you're
> black (preta)." She didn't like dark people. . . . And from that day
> forward, I thought, "What is this difference?" Of whites not liking
> blacks, blacks not liking whites? You know? There has to be some
> root to it, from the mother or father. I knew there had to be a reason,
> but I thought, "How absurd!"

At this point in her narrative, Rosa paused, and I asked her if she had also told her mother or another relative what had happened. She continued:

> I talked about it with my mother. My mother just said, "What
> nonsense, that had nothing to do with it!" [And I said,] "Then why
> didn't she go out with my friend just because I was with her?" [My
> mother said,] "Because you were poorly dressed." That's what my

mother said. [I said,] "No, Mom, I was all neat and pretty, just like her." . . . You know? All she said was that perhaps I was poorly dressed. I said, "No, mom, it wasn't because of that, no!" My mother didn't believe me.

Rosa paused again, and I asked, "You were very angry then?" Almost shouting, she responded, "I knew it was because I was a preta! Because I was a negra! This bullshit shouldn't exist, but it does!"

Rosa's narrative culminates in her insistence that despite her mother's denial, she knew beyond a doubt that she had encountered racial prejudice. When she described—in fact, replayed—the conversation with her mother, the speed and pitch of her voice increased and she repeatedly left out the pronouns that indicate who was speaking in the original conversation. In her last statement ("This bullshit shouldn't exist"), I believe Rosa was not merely making a prescriptive moral statement. I had heard such pronouncements many times, and while they were often spoken with some feeling, they had the conversational ring of oft-repeated truisms. Rosa's statement, on the other hand, sounded like "talking back." Speaking, as it were, to her mother and, by extension, to the discourse of denial and to silence, she was saying in effect, "I know it shouldn't exist, but denying that it exists doesn't erase the reality of what really happens." In calling herself first a preta, then a negra, Rosa rejects politeness and euphemism and at the same time speaks in the voice of the other, what she herself, in a different moment of our conversation, had called "what the masters called the slaves." Despite this experience, Rosa told me that she had never discussed racism with her own children.

The silence surrounding racism in Morro do Sangue Bom is not absolute. Although people told me stories about racism, ones they had not told their friends and families, a number of people were able to recount secondhand stories—encounters with racism that were suffered by parents, spouses, children, and friends. Rosa had, in fact, mentioned that her twelve-year-old son had told her that a white neighbor had called him racist names and that the neighbor "didn't like pretos." Clearly, she and her son had had at least one conversation about the issue. For Rosa, somehow, this conversation and others she might have had with her children were not deemed significant or were not recalled.

Although it was not absolute, I often had the sense that the silence observed within families and between families was somehow at cross-purposes. This was especially clear when I interviewed Dona Janete and her son Jacinto on separate occasions. Both had spoken at length about racism. While Dona Janete said, "Thank God, nothing ever happened to me," she felt that both of her sons, in being dismissed from or ill-treated in their jobs, had been discriminated against. Generally, she felt that racism was very pervasive. Yet when I asked her if she had ever discussed racism with her sons, she said, "Have I conversed with my sons about this? I never said anything because they don't feel this. They think that everyone accepts them. The only thing was [my sons' difficulties on the job]. . . . So they never complained about being discriminated against. And it doesn't enter their heads that they could be discriminated against in some place."

When I interviewed Jacinto, he spoke at length about a variety of situations in which he had felt victimized by prejudice and discrimination, ranging from his reception in restaurants, to his rejection by his future (white) parents-in-law, to being dismissed from a job. When I asked him if his mother had ever discussed racism with him, he told me she had not. I clarified my question by asking, "Did she ever say anything, you know, like, 'You have to struggle because there is racism'?" He responded, "Oh well, [she said] you have to study to be someone in life . . . because of that business—these days you have to study because those of us who don't study won't be anything; it would be worse." I asked him, "Did she ever advise you in a more direct way about racism?" "No, no, she didn't advise me. . . . She doesn't have much of a notion of—she never had—my parents never struggled ideologically, in this movement business, racism, those things. They never did because each one is caught up in day-to-day thing, right? So, she just told us to study, to study because at least you could [get] a job that's more or less . . . but these days it doesn't help!"

Both Jacinto and Dona Janete believe that the other is naive about the realities of racism; and there is a suggestion, though not explicit, in the comments of both of a desire not to undercut this naiveté with open discussions of what both clearly know and feel. Neither, it seems, wants to disabuse the other of a false sense of safety and optimism. In this sense, the silence they observe with each other is protective. Though it is almost certain that Dona Janete and her son Jacinto have, on occasion, at least mentioned issues and personal experiences related to racism, neither recalls, or wants to recall, these conversations.

"Trying Not to Remember": Accounting for Silence

My interview with Guilherme, Daniel's youngest brother, was particularly revealing. Guilherme was somewhat shy, and like many such people, he occasionally made parsimonious but astute comments that got right to the point of topics that others approached with more circumspection. I asked him if, during his childhood or adolescence, his parents or others in his family ever talked about the issue of racism. "No, never," he replied. I asked him, "Why do you think it is that people don't talk about it very much?" He responded, "Oh, well, people want to forget and let it pass. That's why people don't talk about it. It's a form of forgetting, of trying not to remember."

Guilherme then abruptly brought up the issue of slavery: "These days, people will even say to you, 'Give thanks to God and Princesa Isabel that you are free. Because you are a negro. A slave.' That happens; there are people who say that to you. I mean, it's racism. It doesn't do to keep talking about it. It doesn't resolve anything. It doesn't change things. If racism comes from the big person, right, on top, well, it's hard for the person on the bottom to say anything."

For Guilherme then, the relative silence surrounding racism is not a mere absence of talk. Within this silence there is a kind of purposefulness, the involvement of agency, for it is a "form of forgetting" or, more precisely, of "trying not to remember." Several overlapping meanings are suggested in Guilherme's mimicking of the racist jibe, "Give thanks to God and Princesa Isabel that you are free. Because you are a negro and a slave." (Princesa Isabel is credited with abolishing slavery in Brazil in 1888.) Given the context of our conversation, Guilherme was suggesting that if one does speak openly about or against racist mistreatment, one is likely to met with such a comment—the force of which people in Morro do Sangue Bom refer to as "putting one in one's place." There is, of course, a sense of threat carried in the insult—it is a command really, to *ficar calada,* or keep one's mouth shut. This sense of threat is carried further in Guilherme's reference to the "big person," the "one on top" whose power compels silence.

What was especially notable in Guilherme's response to my question was his abrupt shift between his reference to *talking about* racism (among intimates, for example) and references to *talking back* to a racist interlocutor. This shift occurred in the responses of a number of other informants. I felt certain that Guilherme understood that my question concerned conversations *about* racism, such as those that might occur with one's family and friends. Yet for him and others, the acts of talking about and talking back, while certainly separate, were closely related. His comments on the ineffectiveness of talk, its failure to accomplish change, were also echoed by many.

During my conversation with Jonas (whom I have quoted earlier), I asked him, "Why is it that people don't talk much about racism?" He replied, "There isn't a way for it to be resolved. If someone mistreats me because of my color, am I going to punch him? I can't do that. You just have to let it go. Let it go, right, let it go (*deixa pra la*). You can't even—you can't lose your temper (*esquenta a cabeça*) over it. You forget what's happening. It passes. I let it go. I think this is the best way of resolving it."

Jonas had arrived at this apparently complacent position through a painful route. He had told me about an experience in which he had gone, literally in tears, to the police station to make a formal complaint of racial discrimination. The police had told him to "calm down" and to "not lose his temper" or get "hotheaded" (*não esquenta a cabeça*). In the end, precisely as Jonas asserted, nothing was resolved. Like Guilherme, Jonas understood my question, yet he responded not with an explanation for the lack of talk among friends and family but by commenting on the impotence one feels in face-to-face encounters with racism. Neither talking about nor talking back mends the injustice, and physical violence is, if not impossible, certainly untenable. In the absence of redress, Jonas thought it best to "forget" and "let it go."

Tomas, a young man of nineteen, made similar comments. After he had described a number of occasions in which he felt he had been harassed or discriminated against because of his color, I asked him if he had told anyone else about what had happened. "No, no, I didn't tell anyone, no. I got really sad (*fiquei triste*) about what happened," he said.

Because of my own cultural assumptions about painful emotions and the consequent desire to unload one's feelings by talking about them and the events that provoked them, I asked him, "But didn't you want to tell someone?" "I didn't want to tell anyone, no," he responded in a soft voice. "I got very sad." Pressing further, I asked, "But why didn't you want to tell anyone?" "Because it doesn't do any good. It doesn't do any good (*não adianta*), no. It does nothing, nothing, nothing. And to whom will I complain? There is no one to whom I can complain. I know that we have human rights, right? But to complain—there's no way, so you have to let it go. It doesn't do any good."

Evidently, Tomas did not share my psychoanalytic, essentially hydraulic model of emotions and talk; he implied that telling the story would not relieve his feelings but would lead to a painful reliving of them. The word he used, *triste*, like the word *nervoso*, is often used as a gloss for a host of emotions in Morro do Sangue Bom. While nervoso may suggest a kind of fearful anxiety, as the word *nervous* does in English, it frequently implies an emotion closer to an incapacitating anger or perturbation, the kind that can provoke tears of pent-up frustration. It may also suggest a fear of losing control, of unleashing one's anger. Thus, when Jonas described his feelings on arriving at the police station to lodge a complaint, he used the word *nervoso* and implied that his attempt to seek legal redress might have been more successful had he not been crying and in a state of pent-up rage. *Triste*, on the other hand, may describe anything from an abstract and vague melancholy to despondency and grief. It implies, at any rate, a passive withdrawal into the self, a private and quiet nursing of wounds.

Although I had asked Tomas why he did not tell his friends or family what had happened, he turned for elaboration and explanation finally to the impossibly of accomplishing legal or moral redress. There was, in fact, no one to whom he could complain, especially given the fact that most of his stories involved police harassment. Who could he trust to champion and defend what he appropriately called his "human rights?" Once again, the futility of discussing experiences with one's intimates is tied to the futility and even danger of direct confrontation and protest.

The danger of talking back was also described by Dona Janete, although her comments were more equivocal. After she had reported to me that her sons had been discriminated against, I asked her if they had protested their treatment. She said, "No, no one talks, no. Because I think that here in Brazil there is a problem of everyone keeping silent. Many people feel it, but they stay silent. They never shout (*nunca grita*). They never shout, 'Oh, I want a better job, I want I don't know what all.' They never protest (*gritar*), right? I think that here in Brazil there is this craziness of feeling something and not protesting. A thing of people staying silent, of not talking."

I asked Dona Janete why people stay silent. She replied, "I think they have fear, right, my daughter? Of repression. Because if you want something in a job and any white wants to do something to you there, they aren't going to defend the dark one, even though the little dark one (*escurinho*) is right. They're not going to question the white one, they're going to question the dark one. So if anyone is going to have to go, the white doesn't go, the dark one goes. There is a fear of speaking."

It is clear from these comments that what Guilherme calls the "big person," "the one on top," is not a mere figure of speech for people in Morro do Sangue Bom. These words may refer variously to state-sanctioned force, usually in the form of the police, or to the patrons and business managers who control one's access to informal clientage and formal employment and thus to the material sustenance of oneself and one's family. The threat of force, the possibility of being subjected not only to demoralization but to violence and economic privation as a punishment for talking back, is very real. This fact would seem to offer a powerful explanation for the silence of people such as Tomas. Indeed, political repression, which is primarily constituted by the constant, arbitrary police harassment that occurs in the war-torn city of Rio, exists as a constant backdrop to silence and the kind of self-conscious complacency and passivity described by Jonas. Yet, as I have suggested, talking back and talking about are very different acts that occur in very different contexts, and while my informants seemed to discursively draw the two together into one explanatory web, they certainly recognized the distinction between them. The question remained: Why did people in Morro do Sangue Bom refrain from talking about racism even in the intimate and safe contexts of community and family?

I often had the sense that the telling of these stories involved not only an emotional reliving of the actual experience but also a kind of confrontation with one's powerlessness in the face of the big person, the one on top. In narrating such experiences, one almost inevitably casts oneself as defenseless and dependent. If my informants' narratives of racism sometimes seemed to be articulated in a confessional register, what was being confessed was not only vulnerability but the demoralizing and humiliating failure to defend oneself. Thus, to recount such experiences, even to one's intimates, seems to entail a kind of *vergonha,* or shame.

When I asked Robertson, a young man of twenty, why people tended not to talk about their personal experiences with racism, he said, "Perhaps they feel ashamed over their suffering. They withdraw themselves with shame. Or perhaps when you suffer over something, you don't want to tell people, you don't want to explain, because you're afraid that, afterwards, people will treat you the same way. They might think it's your fault."

The implications of Robertson's comments were echoed by others. A woman in her fifties who spoke articulately about various forms of racism in the public sphere nevertheless responded to my question about her own experience by saying, "I, at least, have always gotten along with white people. I was never discriminated against because I have always tried to get along and people like me. So, that's how I am. I have always tried also to learn and to give. There really are dark people who are very discriminated against when they're badly behaved, when they have no manners. So they become discriminated against."

The notion that people of color may provoke racialized discrimination by behaving badly or presenting an unkempt appearance was articulated by a number of informants. When I asked Tomas if his mother ever talked to him about racism, he said, "My mother conversed with us. Because I like to wear certain clothes, to dress as I please, in shorts and a cap, and to wear my hair [in a fashionable style]. So that's why. People who always go in shorts, without a shirt on, who wear necklaces and wear their hair [like this]—people who have this hair are stopped by the police, you know? [My mother] says, 'It's because you have this hair that the police stop you. You have go out with your hair combed down, always very neat.'"[5]

When I asked Tomas if his mother had explicitly said anything else about racism, he responded, "She never involved herself with it, no." It should be recalled also that Rosa's mother insisted that her experience of being rejected by a white woman was because she must have been "badly dressed."

There is thus an ambivalence that is articulated about the social and political nature of racism. At times, racism is figured as an overwhelming, inevitable force, one that variously resides rather abstractly in the society, or in the persons of powerful people who abuse their authority. It may even be seen as residing, as I demonstrate in chapter 5, within one's own family or within oneself. In any case, "it will never end" and one is defenseless and powerless against it. On the other hand, in comments such as those above, it is implied that one may be able to avoid racist mistreatment by controlling one's self-presentation—by behaving well, by serving others, and by wearing neatly pressed, conservative clothing and modest hairstyles.

This issue has implications for the understanding of silence in that it helps to elucidate the notion that vergonha, or shame, may play a role in the construction of silence. This shame may be related of the narration of oneself as defenseless, even cowardly, or to the fear that others may turn the blame in the wrong direction, as Robertson suggested. In both cases, to talk of one's one experience with racism involves a negative and uncomplimentary figuring of oneself and, perhaps by extension, of one's community or *raça* (race).

Yvonne, whom I quoted at the beginning of this chapter, acknowledged that, in general, the subject of racism is rarely discussed. I asked her why she thought this was the case: "No, [people] don't converse [about racism]. I think they don't feel unsettled (*não sente incomodado*) by it. I don't know. I don't know how to explain, well, why not, you know? I think it's a little like that—there's no way to change things. Accommodation, right? There's no way to change things; it doesn't help, you know. 'I'm not going to get ahead,' right? . . . It's fear also, you know, fear of competing with the white. I think it's accommodation, fear, a lack of hope, of faith, of not believing in oneself, right? 'I can, I am able, I'm going to go out there, but I'm not going to succeed.' It's a lot of that."

Yvonne's comments, like those of many others on the morro, account for silence in primarily psychological terms. There is in these comments a kind of politics, what Yvonne calls "accommodation." While a collective acquiescence is implied both by silence itself and by informants' accounts of and accounting for silence, I believe that what Yvonne and others refer to is a more private kind of psychological accommodation. The overriding concern that these comments ultimately express is not with the politics of either discourse or silence but with protecting oneself and one's intimates from the eruption of anger and the festering of emotional pain.

Yvonne also echoed many others in her statement that talking "doesn't help." By now these expressions are familiar to the reader and they deserve comment. In Portuguese, the expressions *não adianta* (it doesn't help, advance, or improve things), *deixa pra lá* (let it go, leave it be, or perhaps more colloquially, don't let it get to you), *não liga* (don't dwell on it, don't concern or involve yourself with it), and *não esquenta a cabeça* (literally, don't get hotheaded, or don't lose your temper) are continually intoned in the context of stories about racism. As can be observed in the above quotes, they are particularly ubiquitous in the comments informants make when accounting for silence on the subject of racism.

These expressions appear, at least partly, to be descriptions of strategies that are consciously adopted at the moment in which encounters with racism occur. As Jonas said, "If someone mistreats me because of my color, am I going to punch him? I can't do that. You just have to let it go." In such moments, it seems, these expressions constitute a kind of inner dialogue spoken to oneself with the intention of quelling the painful emotions, including anger and humiliation, that racism provokes. They muzzle angry outbursts and smother the dangerous impulse to defend oneself with violence. We might call them, in this sense, words of accommodation, but it is a forced accommodation that comes from the knowledge of personal and collective vulnerability in the face of "the one on top."

In accounts of silence, these expressions both refer to and index silence, the impulse or decision to not speak, to not tell of one's own experience or introduce the specter of collective humiliation into ordinary conversations. As Tomas said, "It made me sad. . . . It doesn't help, it doesn't help. . . . you have to let it go, it doesn't help." In psychological terms, it appears that these expressions are an attempt to bring closure to wounding experiences. They also represent a kind of dismissive gesture, a ritualized locution that is meant to dispel the cloud of anger and frustration that inevitably descends on both the storyteller and the listener. In social terms, these expressions signal or command a return to silence. They suggest not only psychological suppression but the closure of social discourse about the realities of racism and injustice.

Ultimately, I feel, for many in Morro do Sangue Bom, silence is directed toward the containment of anger and psychological pain. My own assumptions (shared, in fact, by most middle-class Brazilians and more than a few social scientists) that speaking of one's pain helps to ease that pain and that the articulation of anger may profitably lead to personal action and/or political mobilization seemed to hold no sway on the morro. Talk cannot overcome but, in fact, evokes what Yvonne called "fear, a lack of hope, of faith, of not believing in oneself."

If it can be said that people on the morro have what Frazier called an "unexpressed understanding" not to discuss the innumerable slights, insults, humiliations, and rejections that are suffered in the day-to-day world (qtd. in Hellwig 1992, 131), they do so not because they lack the words, the analytical sophistication, or the discursive strategies to do so (cf. Twine 1998), and not because they believe racism is insignificant, but because to do so would involve a kind of personal and collective surrender. The paradox of silence resides precisely in the fact that it implies and objectively constitutes a kind of political accommodation to oppression at the same time that it allows people such as those in Morro do Sangue Bom to let it go, to forget, to at least partially contain the wounds of victimization and carve out a world in which to live with dignity and laughter.

Silence and Sainthood: The Legend of Escrava Anastácia

Although silence seems to be constructed and maintained through unexpressed understandings and is indexed in discourse—particularly in expressions such as "let it go," "it doesn't help," and "don't concern yourself with it"—it appears to be, relatively speaking, unmarked and unremarked. It is as though silence, the act of trying not to remember, is itself buried in a kind of forgetting. While the metaphor of psychological repression seems to offer itself at this juncture, it is not a truly apt one, for people in Morro do Sangue Bom know very well that racism is pervasive and wounding—their forgetting, in this sense, is unsuccessful. Still, if silence is meaningful, we might expect it, much in the manner of repressed material, to surface or to be marked, in however displaced a fashion, in genres other than everyday discourse. I believe that the story of silence is, in fact, represented in the figure of Escrava Anastácia, a popular saint whose image and mythical biography are well known in Rio de Janeiro.

I first became aware of Escrava Anastácia (or Slave Anastácia) very early in my fieldwork. Her image is reproduced on placards, religious pamphlets, wall hangings, and religious medals and in the plaster busts that are sold in Rio's religious shops. While Anastácia is believed to bestow mercy on her devotees, there is nothing gentle in her image. She is always portrayed from the neck up. She has the short, tight hair, dark skin, and broad nose of a negra. When she is represented in color, as in the plaster busts, her eyes are blue and they are said to be very penetrating. Her neck is encased by a thick iron collar and her mouth is choked by an iron muzzle, a device that is called a *mordaça*. As her name implies, Anastácia was a slave woman, and as her image unambiguously reveals, she was a victim of what were once conventional methods of punishment and torture.

The origin of the Anastácia legend is clouded in controversy. The image of Anastácia seems to have originated in an illustration of an anonymous slave drawn by the French artist M. J. Arago, who traveled to Brazil in 1817. Beginning in 1971, Arago's illustration was exhibited in the Museu do Negro (housed in the Igreja do Rosario, a traditionally black church) in Rio de Janeiro. The director of the museum, a man by the name of Yolando Guerra, evidently had a vision about the illustration and began to elaborate what later became the biography of Escrava Anastácia. This, at any rate, is the account given by church authorities who investigated the Anastácia legend. In 1987 they concluded that Anastácia, also called Santa Anastácia, or Saint Anastácia, never existed. Her image was removed from the Igreja do Rosario, much to the consternation of a number of my informants. Aware of but unmindful of the church's pronouncement, devotees of Anastácia now congregate at a temple dedicated to her in Madureira, in Rio's North Zone.

I am not concerned here with the controversy surrounding the popular saint, nor with the religious beliefs and practices that are associated with Escrava Anastácia.[6] While living in Morro do Sangue Bom, my concern was with the ways in which informants narrated the story of Anastácia and how they explained the presence of the mordaça, or muzzle, in which she is depicted.

Like all popular saints, Anastácia is believed to intercede for those in dire need and to perform miracles for her devotees. More than a few of my informants told me that they believed in Anastácia; they had addressed many prayers to her and they were answered. At the same time, however, people in Morro do Sangue Bom were aware of the fact that Anastácia's sainthood was rejected by church authorities. I asked Dona Janete why this was the case. She responded with a hoot of laughter, "Oh, it must be because she is a black woman, right, my daughter? If she were white, she could be a saint but she is a preta!"

Other informants, while not professing belief in Anastácia, called her the *protetora dos negros,* or the protector of the blacks, and in one case she was called a great *orixá,* or god of the Candomblé pantheon. Even *crentes,* or Protestants, who did not believe in Anastácia's sainthood were nevertheless able to narrate at least parts of the Anastácia story. This familiarity is due, in large part, to the fact that a telenovela, or miniseries, about Anastácia was aired on a major Brazilian network in 1990. There are, of course, many versions of the Anastácia story, and the novela's screenwriter no doubt mixed some of the common elements from popular, oral versions of her biography and those found in religious pamphlets with elements from his own imagination.

Elena, who was a *crente*, declared herself immune to the claims of Anastácia's sainthood, but she recapped the novela with considerable enthusiasm. Her narration contains most of the elements I heard in other informants' narrations and thus serves as a template:

> Escrava Anastácia was a slave who they say was sacrificed. She was a really beautiful slave woman, really black with blue eyes. She was enslaved by a plantation owner. He put her to doing really brutalizing work, you know? But she did it without complaining. But he wanted her, wanted her as a woman. She didn't want that, no way. So he put her in the stocks and flogged her.
>
> The people in the slave quarters were her friends. She was the leader of the slaves. Anything that had to be done, she was always in front. If, for example, there was a sick person, she went to them to lay on hands and cure them. So out in the slave quarters, she helped the negros.
>
> When the [plantation owner] saw that she didn't want to be his woman, he said, "Fine, you're going to take care of my children. I'll give my children a black doll with blue eyes." So, she took care of the children but he kept bothering her. So, he said, "Since you don't accept me, I'm going to do something so that you will never again speak in your life." So he put an iron collar on her neck and an iron mordaça, squeezing her mouth and nose. I mean, because she was always helping her people, he would really enslave her, so she would never speak again. So, she stayed that way and continued to take care of the children, without ever speaking.
>
> She was getting sick and the plantation owner called a doctor. The doctor told him to take the collar and mordaça off her. She said, "Put it back on. My hour has come." The doctor put it back on because there was nothing more he could do for her.
>
> So, the plantation owner's son was tubercular. He was complaining, crying in pain. So the man came, the plantation owner, who put the collar on her. He kissed her hands and said, "For the love of God, save my son's life. I don't want to lose my son." She put her hand on [the boy's] head and passed her hands over him very slowly. Once she got down to his feet, she took her hands away and closed her eyes. The boy got up and called his parents. Then they

said, "Thank God, thanks to Anastácia, my son is cured!" So everyone was happy. But they could do nothing more for her because when she finished curing him, she closed her eyes and died.

In Elena's narrative, Anastácia was sacrificed both because she rejected her master's advances and because she was a leader to her people, the slaves who shared her burdens on the plantation. As Elena had, most people who talked to me about Anastácia touched on both of these elements, although some emphasized one over the other. Perhaps predictably and logically, a few of my informants provided versions in which it was suggested that Anastácia did not succeed in repelling her master's abuse; she was raped, yet remained proud to the end (see also Guillermoprieto 1990, 179). In such accounts, stoicism in the face of violation is emphasized. Other informants, however, emphasized not Anastácia's victimization but her heroism. Although Jorge expressed doubt about popular saints in general, his attempt to narrate the story of Anastácia was emotional:

"I don't understand it well; I don't understand her story well. I saw a little on television. Anastácia. She was a protector, right? She was a saint. She was a woman who died muzzled (*amordaçada*) for her people, for her race. God! I mean, she was a person who died for her race! You understand, she died for her race. That guy took the mordaça off and it was pure gangrene in her mouth. She died from that. Why? To defend her people, to help her people. She gave her hand to her people."

When informants did not spontaneously bring up the issue of Anastácia's mordaça, or muzzle, I asked them about its significance. The word *mordaça*, as well as its verb form, *amordaçar*, and its adjective form, *amordaçada*, were known by everyone who discussed Anastácia with me. Also called a *folha de Flandres*, the mordaça was a commonly used disciplinary device during the era of slavery. According to most historical sources, its purpose was to prevent slaves from drinking cane liquor and/or from eating dirt.[7] Both my informants' comments and standard dictionary definitions pose a rather different purpose for the mordaça, however. The *Novo Dicionario Aurelio* defines the word *mordaça* as "an object with which someone's mouth is plugged with the end that they can neither speak nor protest (*grite*)." Figuratively, the word is defined as "repression of the liberty to write or to speak." The verb form, *amordaçar*, is defined as "to impede speech."

When I asked Yvonne about Anastácia, she did not mention the issue of her master's sexual advances or abuses. She said that Anastácia "struggled for the race, right, for the slaves, and after she died, I think that people continued believing in her." When I asked her, "What is the significance of that thing she has?" Yvonne replied, "The mordaça on her mouth, right? . . . Now, it is said that there are people who talk too much, and it is said that she talked a lot; she really talked so . . . It's because she talked so much that he put that mordaça on her."

Other responses were similar but lacked Yvonne's hesitation. A number of people told me that Anastácia's master locked her into the mordaça to prevent her from telling others about his abuse. A man in his thirties told me, "I think she suffered because she was used as an object; her master used her like an object. . . . That mordaça, they say that it was so that she could not protest." A woman in her forties told me that Anastácia had "already done many miracles" for her, and she said, "It was so she couldn't tell [others] what the master did with her, you know? He muzzled her mouth. . . . Because of what she had gone through, she couldn't say anything to anyone with that iron mordaça on her mouth. I believe in her."

Susana, Joia's half-sister, made similar comments. She told me that Anastácia's master tried to rape her. She resisted and he put the mordaça on her: "Because then she didn't shout. It was so she couldn't call for help. Because she was muzzled, she didn't yell, you understand? So he muzzled her so she couldn't protest, and from that she died bit by bit, without food, without speaking, and without drinking, right?"

In all of these comments, the purpose of the mordaça was related to a literal muzzling of Anastácia. Specifically, it prevented her from telling others, her friends and supporters in the slave quarters, what was being done to her. In these narratives, Anastácia was muzzled not only as punishment for her (possible) resistance or outspoken leadership in the slave quarters but also so that she could not *gritar*, or reveal, the abuse she had suffered. Although we might expect that the master would be, in a sense, omnipotent—not required at any rate to justify or defend his actions, however brutal—his exploitation and abuse of Anastácia must be kept a secret.

Other informants also explained, although in more general terms, the logic of the mordaça in terms of the prohibition that was imposed on Anastácia against speaking. A woman in her sixties said, "He didn't give her the right to express what she was feeling. He muzzled her so she had no way of speaking. She became mute." A woman in her twenties told me, "She was a person who had a facility in speaking, for communicating messages. People believed in her prayers. And the mordaça signified a form of impeding her speech." A teenage boy simply said, "She had power in the word. She was muzzled so she would not speak anymore." When I asked Analucia about the significance of the mordaça, she said, "Because the mordaça prevents the person from speaking, right? . . . You can't say anything of what you know and what you have heard. . . . I think this is what happened to Escrava Anastácia. She didn't get to tell her story."

As she had on other occasions, Dona Janete pulled the threads of these ideas together into a masterful interpretation. She had not seen the *telenovela*. Much to her consternation, her husband and sons were given to compulsive channel surfing on the family television. She told me that Anastácia was sacrificed because of her beauty. "She was killed, little by little, right? . . . He put that mordaça on her face, right on her mouth." "And why did she have the mordaça?" I asked Dona Janete. She replied,

> It must have been for her to suffer from not speaking. Like here, everyone shuts their mouths, right? So, they shut Anastácia's mouth. The first thing they did was to put that mordaça on her and she didn't speak anymore. . . . She had it here, around her head and everything. Meaning, the law for the negro is to really keep silent (*de calar mesmo*). It has been thus since slavery, right? The law for the negro is to keep silent. It began through Anastácia, right? They put it right on her mouth. Why didn't they put it some other place, around her middle, on her legs, in some other place? They put it right on her mouth. . . . She was sacrificed little by little and she could say nothing. . . . So I think it was clearly this. They put it on her so she couldn't speak of what was happening to her, and it was like that until the end of her life.

As my quotations suggest, informants' explanations of the significance of Anastácia's mordaça were remarkably consistent. It is clear, however, that there are many ways of reading the Anastácia story. For Alma Guillermoprieto, a Mexican journalist, the story is, in a fundamental sense, about the cultural erotics of race in Brazil. As she writes, "I was interested in Anastácia because her legend was explicitly concerned with the relationship between black women and white men, and while that relationship is at the center of the Brazilian universe, it is rarely addressed from the black point of view" (1990, 179).

The extent to which Guillermoprieto's brief analysis represents or comments on "the black point of view" is questionable, but her suggestion that Anastácia's blue eyes imply miscegenation has recently been elaborated by Burdick (1998). It may well be that some of Anastácia's devotees view her as a stereotypical model of the beautiful mulata and that the legend logically incorporates an overvaluation of white characteristics. Yet close attention to the precise ways in which my informants in Morro do Sangue Bom talked about Anastácia suggests that, regardless of the implication of her blue eyes, she is viewed as a negra. Generally speaking, people in Morro do Sangue Bom claim her as one of their own, and they refer to her not as a mulata, but as a preta and a negra, and it is said that she "died for her race."

In a very different interpretation, the story of Anastácia can be read as a parable about servitude, particularly the domestic servitude of women. Nearly all of the women I knew in Morro do Sangue Bom had worked as *empregadas*, or maids, at some point in their lives; most, in fact, worked in the homes of white middle-class families from the time they were teenagers. As I indicate in the following chapter, women often describe situations in which they feel slighted, exploited, and insulted while performing domestic service for others. Usually, they have to hold their tongues. Talking back, of course, can lead to abrupt dismissal. Although Anastácia was a slave and a saint, her life was not so different from theirs.

Within such a reading, Anastácia represents the picture of the (nearly) perfect servant. As Elena said, she was put to "really brutalizing work . . . But she did it without complaining." Although abused and shackled, she "continued to take care of the children." While condemned to a slow, painful, and unjust death, she roused herself to save the master's son just before expiring. For these generous, saintly, feminine, and submissive qualities, it seems, Anastácia is revered. For the dominant, she is the model of one who provides good service; and for people such as those in Morro do Sangue Bom, she suggests that long-suffering patience and subordination are rewarded in the spiritual realm. To bear one's burdens without complaint, moreover, is thought to demonstrate dignity of character.

This is, perhaps, the most ambiguous angle of the Anastácia story. On the one hand, she is revered for her resistance, and on the other, she is lauded for her ability to turn the other cheek and to suffer in a silence that, while forced, is maintained in dignity. Read crudely as a political parable, it could be said that the message of the Anastácia story is that this is what happens to you when you try to resist your exploitation. What such an equation leaves out is the other message: that the dignity and humanity of the slave remain inviolable. The master, while a monster, is a pitiable one, alienated from his own humanity.

While Anastácia's blue eyes may touch the cultural nexus of meanings associated with miscegenation and the superiority of the mulata, and while Anastácia does model the dominant vision of servitude and black womanhood, these readings do not address what seems to be the dramatic motif at the heart of narratives about Anastácia: her forced silence. Anastácia's story is far more explicitly concerned with the brutality of slavery and, by extension, with the reality of racism—and the silence surrounding it. For Dona Janete, it seems, the Anastácia story is somewhat like a myth of origin: Anastácia "suffers from not speaking," and this is compared to "Like here, everyone shuts their mouths." The significance of Anastácia's torture is that it dramatizes "the law for the negros," which is "to keep silent." As Dona Janete further remarks, it has "been thus since slavery."

The parallels between the Anastácia legend and the silence surrounding racism in contemporary Brazil are fairly obvious. Her silence is directly linked to the overwhelming force of domination, just as my informants' explanations for their own silence are repeatedly linked to the very real danger of talking back in encounters with racism. Anastácia's story is thus analogous to the concealment of contemporary forms of racism, forms said to be *incubado* (literally incubated, or covert), *embaixo do pano* (under the cloth), and *mascarado* (masked). All of these expressions refer to the more or less covert practices that support and constitute racism as well as to the unexpressed understandings that undergird silence and the discourse of denial. Anastácia's story thus also enacts and depicts, in symbolic form, the social, cultural, and psychological injunctions against talking about racism even in nonconfrontational, intimate contexts. She symbolizes the wounds of racism and exploitation as well as the muzzling that is manifest in the self-censorship of people such as those in Morro do Sangue Bom.

Like Escrava Anastácia herself, poor Brazilians of African descent are entangled in a cultural, ideological, and psychological web in which neither resistance nor resignation are ever absolute. We cannot sum up their position with facile references to false consciousness because they know the truth. Nor can we romanticize their attachment to Anastácia and claim that it unambiguously expresses solidarity and active resistance, for like Anastácia, they remain, for the most part, silent about what is happening to them. I believe that the popularity of Escrava Anastácia is due in large measure to her ability to symbolically represent both the oppression of African Brazilians and the muzzling or silencing of their voices—their inability to talk back and talk about what is really happening under the concealment and obfuscation entailed in the discourses of democracia racial. From what people call her *força,* or strength, and from her "penetrating gaze," she tells their story without words. Escrava Anastácia is, in the direct spiritual sense that frames her sainthood among poor people of color, one who listens to their *grita:* their shout, their protest, their call for help.

As will be seen in the following chapter on narratives of racism, my informants in Morro do Sangue Bom were acutely conscious of racism, and while middle-class whites (and some scholars) might interpret their silence as an acceptance of the platitudes of democracia racial, my quotation of their reflections on the issue demonstrates the existence of a far more complicated cultural, political, and psychological scenario. Although it is something of a misnomer to refer to the silence they hold even among intimate associates as a choice—for cultural censorship carries a great deal of force, even if it is not based on explicit coercion—they nevertheless describe it as a strategy of protection and defense. While the practice of cultural censorship appears to mask the existence of anti-hegemonic consciousness, I argue that it does not, at the same time, preclude it.

Rather than conceptualizing dominant ideologies such as democracia racial as monolithic, internally coherent models which subordinate groups can either entirely accept or entirely reject, I would argue, finally, that successful systems of power—composed of contradictions, platitudes, blind alleys, and ambiguity—entangle people such as those in Morro do Sangue in precisely these kinds of deadlocks. The silence my informants practice is simultaneously a public form of accommodation and a private (if at the same time communal) form of resistance.

Chapter 4

Narratives

Racism on the Asphalt

AFTER SPENDING MONTHS listening intently for conversations about racism on the morro, I began to elicit such conversations myself by conducting focused interviews with informants. I had come to understand that racism was a delicate and difficult topic, and I relied on my friends' patience and understanding as I tentatively began to explore ways to ask probing questions sensitively, while at the same time offering reassurance that, despite my whiteness and my foreignness, I recognized the fact that racism was a serious problem.

One of the first people I interviewed was Tiago, who was nine years old at the time. When I asked him what racism was he said, "Those who don't like themselves." In this comment, Tiago implied that racism was not merely about relationships between people of color and whites but could also be about one's relationship with oneself and with other people of color. When I asked him if his parents had ever discussed the issue with him, he said they had not. He had, however, overheard at least one conversation between his parents: "They even say that slavery in Brazil has not yet ended. They say it hasn't ended because the rich make the poor into workers. And this always continues. Slavery in Brazil has not ended."

Tiago also understood, it seemed, that racism was part of a historical trajectory extending from the institution of slavery to the current exploitation of black workers. Toward the end of the interview I asked Tiago about race-color terminology. As I have noted, Tiago had a knack for linguistic explication that was superior to that of any of the adults I knew. While most informants understood my question about terminology as a request for words referring to the color or race of individuals, Tiago added a unique twist. He began his list with three words: *estragou*, *negro*, and *branquelo*. I asked him what estragou meant. He responded, "For example, I, who am preto, make something, and a rich person comes along who has more power than I do and he orders that which I made to be knocked down, and he builds something bigger. He destroyed (estragou) that which I made."

Despite Tiago's assertion that his parents never discussed racism with him in a direct way, he not only understood the destructive power of racism in the lives of people of color but could also communicate his understanding through the use of an evocative and succinct metaphor. As I was to learn, his tendency to mix the vocabulary of race and color ("I, who am *preto*") with that of class ("a rich person who has more power") was typical of informants of all ages.

Tiago's second word, negro, is often used, as I have emphasized in chapter 2, to denigrate people of color, while *branquelo* is a slang term—often used as an epithet—that describes a white person with an arrogant and hostile disposition. His choice of words not only bifurcated the racial world but suggested opposition as well.

At the end of our interview, I asked Tiago if he wanted to add anything that he thought I ought to know concerning racism. He pondered for a moment and told me that that very day he had spent the afternoon outside of the morro, in a park close to his school. He had been playing in the hot sun and had become very thirsty. He went to three houses asking for a glass of water and was refused. At the fourth house, he told me, a pleasant woman gave him a glass of water. "She was *preta*, dark also," he said, as though he were offering an explanation.

Although he was one of my youngest informants, Tiago's interview shared several elements—in addition to the marked tendency to refer to color and class in the same breath—with those of many adult informants. Among the most notable of these common elements that merit emphasis was Tiago's reference to what is usually called "internalized racism." Many of my informants in Morro do Sangue Bom referred to "the racism of the negro himself." Frequently, these references were made during the early moments of interviews and they required no specific prompting from me.

A second element that Tiago's comments shared with those of many adults in Morro do Sangue Bom was represented by his seemingly abrupt and belated recall of an incident that he felt might be related to racism. Just as Tiago had, many informants recalled and described events in the very recent past as the interview was winding to a close. Because I have chosen not to quote interviews in their entirety, this kind of sequencing within the narratives can only be partially conveyed in the pages that follow. When I was interviewing Susana, one of Tiago's aunts, for example, she interrupted the flow of her own narrative by interjecting several times, "Oh! I remember something else now." Undoubtedly, this pattern of abrupt recall is, to some extent, common to all narratives of experience. However, the belated quality of these eruptions was, I believe, unusual, and it is, I would suggest, a result of several overlapping factors.

Narratives of racism represent, in the climate of silence, a kind of suppressed discourse (Etter-Lewis 1991). Expressions such as "let it go" not only index a desire not to discuss racism in actual dialogues, but are, no doubt, also repetitive, internalized commands not to dwell on incidents of racism. Many of the narratives that my informants provided on racism not only represented a break with the cultural etiquette that commands silence on issues related to racism, but also articulated a kind of psychological excavation or unpacking. While my interviews with informants most often produced exchanges of a distinctly pedagogic rather than psychoanalytic character, I often had the sense that, in conversing with me, informants were, by degrees, bringing to light a kind of suppressed inner dialogue. Significantly, and perhaps paradoxically, when incidents involving racism were abruptly recalled, they were typically described not as unusual occurrences but as so routine and ordinary that their specificity was forgotten—if only temporarily. This fact is a testament, I believe, to both the pervasive and quotidian nature of many racist practices and the constant psychocultural injunction to let it go.

In narrating their encounters with racism, people in Morro do Sangue Bom articulated both the extreme and commonplace experiences, and interpretations of experiences, that informed them of others' visions of their place in the world. That they did not truly accept those visions is evidenced by their ability and willingness to provide such narratives, as well as by the moral suasion underpinning their stories. Silence, as I discovered during the course of my interviews, was neither as absolute nor as durable as it at first appeared.

Both this and the following chapter are devoted to narratives of racism. The present chapter concerns those narratives in which informants highlight relationships and experiences with people from outside the morro. Generally, but not always, these people are white, and they are frequently identified as being of a higher class than those who reside on the hill. Wage labor is central in the lives of people on the morro, and work on the asphalt arguably represents the most significant context in which racism is encountered. As I hope to show, differences in men's and women's wage labor contribute to differences in the ways they experience, perceive, and interpret racism on the asphalt.

The chapter following this one concerns narratives that emphasize experiences with racism in the more intimate contexts of family and community and with what many of my informants called "the racism of the negro himself." Undoubtedly, many racist practices and discourses are shared by whites and people of color, just as they are shared across class boundaries. It can be argued that separating white-on-black prejudice and discrimination from black-on-black forms of racism introduces an artificial distinction that runs the risk of obfuscating the systemic processes—cultural, ideological, political, psychological, and discursive—through which racism is constructed and maintained. An emphasis on the racism of the negro himself, moreover, might appear to lend credence to the view, expressed by a number of white Brazilians I met, that racism is more a "problem of the negros" than of whites and that the "lack of self-esteem" among people of color is a cause rather than a consequence of racism.

I argue, however, that in failing to draw distinctions between the contexts of racism, one fails also to explore and expose many of the deeper, boundary-penetrating patterns of racist ideology and racialized oppression. An emphasis on the ways in which people of color participate in racist discourses does not blame the victim, but rather highlights the profoundly pervasive and deeply damaging power of hegemonic discourses of value and hierarchy. Furthermore, my informants themselves drew such distinctions; many in Morro do Sangue Bom reserved their greatest invective for people of color whom they saw as racist in their talk and actions. The significance of these issues will be elaborated in the following chapter.

Representing Racism

I define narratives of racism as accounts of specific encounters with racism and as more generalizing theoretical and/or speculative comments on the nature, functions, origins, causes, and consequences of racism. Particularly in countries such as Brazil where racism often operates through highly covert forms, or takes place in private contexts, members of dominant groups may (sometimes legitimately) profess a lack of awareness of racist practices—including verbal practices. White Brazilians, furthermore, are more apt to deny the existence and/or significance of racist discourses and practices. I am thus particularly concerned with the ways in which poor Brazilians of African descent, the principal targets of racism, narrate their experiences. Teun A. van Dijk, himself one of the most prolific analysts of dominant racist discourses, has noted that "we need more research about the actual experiences, interpretations, and evaluations of minority members themselves. They are the real experts on our prejudices" (1984, 77). Members of dominant groups within any country or polity, it should be noted, remain, by the very nature of their position, distant from a knowledge of how they are represented by subordinate groups.

An ever-growing interdisciplinary and international literature focuses on dominant discourses that articulate, produce, reproduce, and disseminate racist ideologies (see, for example, Billig 1988; Crapanzano 1986; van Dijk 1984, 1992, 1993; Wetherell and Potter 1993; Reeves 1983; Smitherman-Donaldson and van Dijk 1988). While such works analyze the cultural and ideological logic of racist discourses, as well as, in some cases, the macro- and micro-structural operations and functions of such discourses, they do not address the ways in which those targeted by racism articulate their experience with, and interpretations of, prejudicial discourses and the discriminatory practices associated with them.

Outside of the richly illustrative genres of fiction and autobiography, published narratives of racism are remarkably rare, given the voluminous, international literature on racism (see, for example, Costa 1982; Gwaltney 1975; Terkel 1992.) Works that take narratives of racism as a unit of analysis within scholarly research are rarer yet (see, for example, Basso 1979; Essed 1988, 1990, 1991; Etter-Lewis 1991; Louw-Potgeiter 1988, 1989; Sousa 1983.) Philomena Essed, one of the few researchers explicitly concerned with narratives of racism, has constructed an elaborate interdisciplinary, theoretical framework with which to analyze accounts of racism. Focusing on narratives provided by professional African American women in California and professional women of Surinamese descent in the Netherlands, Essed emphasizes the everyday, routine nature of these women's encounters with racism, what she calls "oppression in the fabric of everyday life" (1991, 146). I concur with her assertion that "racial and ethnic prejudice has been studied largely from a White point of view. . . . Generally little attention has been paid to the knowledge, beliefs, opinions and attitudes of Blacks with respect to the meaning of racism" (7). Essed takes considerable pains to demonstrate, through discourse analysis and supporting cognitive, historical, and sociological arguments, that her informants' accounts of racism are not ad hoc stories but represent and articulate careful observation and thorough-going interpretation, which includes the weighing of various hypotheses that might explain unacceptable behavior.

A review of works such as that of Essed suggests an underlying problematic in the effort to effectively edit and present narratives of racism. When such narratives are themselves the focus of analysis, rather than illustrations or embellishments of a theoretical argument, the risk of erasure or overshadowing of those narratives through an overbearing style of theoretical framing is always present. This problematic is germane to all ethnographic writing responding to Clifford's (1983) call for a greater recognition of the dubious assumptions underlying the construction of monological and monophonic ethnographic writing, I have chosen to frame my informants' narratives in a more or less conventional fashion, while recognizing that despite their mediated nature, they speak for themselves. In highlighting certain narrative strategies, enlarging upon the contexts my informant's describe, and emphasizing both the similarities and the differences in the ways in which encounters with racism are narrated, I have chosen the risk of an echoing redundancy over that of erasure. Moreover, because the narratives I quote do speak for themselves, I do not presume to capture their total nor even their essential meaning within a static, monological analysis. The narratives are themselves a series of overlapping interpretations, and other readings of these interpretations are possible.

"Because of Color": Defining Racism

Racism was defined by people in Morro do Sangue Bom in a multiplicity of ways, and these definitions, while sometimes produced in response to my direct questions, were typically embedded within more extended narratives of racism. Partly because many of my informants suggested in their narratives that racism was a set of beliefs, attitudes, practices, and/or ways of speaking that could be shared by people of color as well as by whites, racism was rarely defined, implicitly or explicitly, as an ideology or set of practices limited exclusively to whites.

Most people in Morro do Sangue Bom defined racism as a situation in which a "person doesn't like blacks." While people used the word *racismo* in their interviews with me, the words *discriminação* (discrimination) and *preconceito* (prejudice) were used more often. *Preconceito de cor*, or color prejudice, is the most common way of referring to racism generally, and *por causa da cor*, or because of color, was a ubiquitous phrase in narratives of racism.

When people told me that they believed that a certain individual was racist, I asked them why they felt this way. Almost invariably, people began their responses with the comment, "Because he/she doesn't like pretos" or "He/She doesn't like my color." When I asked a teenager to describe racism generally, he said, "The person who keeps staring at us, who makes us leave [a place] because of color."

Not surprisingly, many of my informants focused on the more quotidian aspects of racism in their interviews with me, and while their comments often pointed to or explicitly articulated an awareness of the systemic nature of racism, prejudice and discrimination were often described within, and defined by, personalized experience. To a certain extent, as will be seen, women tended to emphasize the behavior of individuals and to implicitly or explicitly define racism as a product of individual character, whereas men more frequently made comments about the systemic nature of racism, defining it as a "problem of the society."

When discussing racism, both men and women explicitly referred to the interpenetration of class and color prejudice. One's appearance or identification as preto, or of color and poor, or of the morro, were described as mutually reinforcing in their damaging consequences. For example, when I asked nineteen-year-old Tomas if he remembered becoming aware of racism as a child, he told me, "I heard it said that white people didn't like black people, pretos, negros, right? When I was really a child. So, each one has his position, negros with negros and whites with whites. There aren't opportunities for those of us here on the morro, right? . . . You're discriminated against because of color and because of the morro. Because they think the morro has this, the morro has that."

Although both scholarly arguments and popular discourse offer the claim that what might appear to be racism is, in fact, class prejudice, this informant and others emphasized the entanglement of both forms of domination.

In some cases, color prejudice was explicitly compared to other types of prejudice. A man in his early twenties told me that there were, in his opinion, racist people residing on the morro. He qualified his comments, however, by referring to regional prejudices: "There are certain people, I think, principally, on the part of the Northeasterners, they have certain—they don't involve themselves with negros. I don't know if it's everyone, but certain of them have racism. Or, I think it's not necessarily racism. Prejudice can be more than that, right? [It can be] regional. If the guy, if he's from Paraíba, well, the Rio native will accuse the people from Paraíba of being pigs, in the sense that they're dirty. [They'll say that] the guy from Bahia doesn't want to work, that the guy from Minas is untrustworthy. These are prejudices."

As such comments make clear, many people in Morro do Sangue Bom viewed racism as part of a larger tendency to objectify and dominate, or attempt to dominate, others. Color, race, racism, prejudice, and discrimination were frequently used as glosses for describing and interpreting experiences that were primarily, although not always exclusively, related to color and concepts of race.

Although some social scientists concerned with racism insist that it is best understood in systemic structural and/or historical terms, and others, such as social psychologists, define it in individual terms, most people in Morro do

Sangue Bom recognized the interpenetration of both levels or aspects of racism—even while emphasizing one or the other. And while many social scientists are devoted to efforts to disentangle class from color prejudice in analytical terms, many of my informants suggested that such a project is misguided at best; the stigma of blackness and the disadvantages of poverty reinforce one another in ways that are perceived to be inexorable. To analytically separate the two is, in a sense, to miss the point.

The Evil Eye of Racism

Soon after I arrived in Morro do Sangue Bom, I discussed racism with Joia. At the time of our conversation, she did not feel that any of her employers had treated her in an explicitly racist manner, but she was troubled by the way she often felt when she went about her errands in the city, particularly when she went into certain stores. "People stare at you, give you *mau olhado* (nasty looks)," she said. "It's not even that they always think you'll steal something, although that sometimes happens. It's like they find you ugly or something like that, like you shouldn't be there. It's like this," she said and squinted at me sideways, from the corners of her eyes.

I learned more about the nature of Joia's experience and how it differed from my own and that of other whites when I went into a small clothing store in the city to look at some sale items. A woman of color who was dressed in jeans and a neatly pressed blouse came into the store and began to look at sale items as well. We had just begun exchanging comments about the clothing and the prices when a store attendant approached and asked her, "Would you like me to take your bag?" "No, I prefer to keep it with me," the shopper responded politely. After the attendant had turned away, she said to me in a disparaging tone, "Now, why would I want her to take my bag?" Looking at my knapsack, she said, "Did she ask you about your bag?" "No, she didn't say anything to me," I told her. I could not help but notice that the attendant hovered nearby and observed her closely until she left the store. I then became acutely aware of the extent to which my own passages in and out of the fitting room—with my knapsack—seemed to be entirely unnoticed.

People in Morro do Sangue Bom are aware of the communicative power of what Joia had called mau olhado, as well as surveillance, whether blatant or surreptitious. Mau olhado is often translated as evil eye, but it is sometimes used in the more secular sense of a hostile gaze, glance, or stare. When it takes the form of surveillance, it communicates the fact that one's character is judged to be suspect. Mau olhado and similar forms of ostracism, suspicion, and veiled hostility are part of the finely drawn web of interactions that constitute "racismo em baixo do pano," that is, racism that is concealed under the cloth.

The feeling of being stared at was described as occurring in other contexts as well. When I asked Yvonne about racism, she said, "Oh, there are so many [kinds], so many. The kind like when a dark person arrives at a party. People keep staring. People who are better off in life, you understand? So, people like that, generally they keep looking at us with little cause, these people—staring for a long time, right? A party that you were invited to by another person, full of whites, where there are more whites. The pretinho who arrives always feels that they're being a little mistreated."

As though to confirm Yvonne's point, Jacinto also told me about going to a party and feeling very uncomfortable. As he explained, it was a party celebrating a girl's fifteenth birthday. These are usually elaborate affairs, and huge numbers of family, friends, and even barely known acquaintances often attend. Jacinto said, "It was over in Tijuca (a Rio neighborhood), [at the house of] an acquaintance of my brother's. So he and I went, but I felt awful because there was not one negro there! [I thought] 'What am I doing here?' And the people there didn't give us the minimum. The people just said, 'Hello, how are you,' and then they were silent. I thought, 'I'm going to have a soda,' and I had a soda and left—because I was feeling awful! [I was thinking] 'Shit, there are only whites here, nobody else!'"

The party Jacinto attended was in a middle-class neighborhood. We might assume that he had not only crossed class boundaries but, because he was the only negro present, a color boundary as well. As in Yvonne's more generalized description of such occasions, Jacinto felt mistreated. He was denied the courtesy—the friendly exchanges, easy banter, and invitations to conversation—that is expected during such festive occasions. The lack of such courtesy, the silence, he seems to suggest, is not merely an omission but an expression of hostility.

While perhaps a quarter of those living on the morro are white, the correlation between class and color appears to be much higher on the asphalt, and it is here that a person of color from the morro is likely to become more acutely aware of de facto segregation and to ask him or herself, "What am I doing here?" when he or she crosses ostensibly invisible but subjectively perceived boundaries. Their sense of being out of place and the behavior of others that provokes these feelings reflect and, in fact, enact the interpenetrating role of class and color in constructing and maintaining those boundaries. In referring to the sense of being "the only negro in a mountain of whites," it is apparent that whatever their white middle-class neighbors might say, my informants did not reduce the surreptitious forms of prejudice that they felt to purely class-based expressions of hierarchy and opposition. Because people of color so frequently respond to these boundary-maintaining forms of prejudice by withdrawal, moreover, they become, ipso facto, forms of discriminatory exclusion.

"Hard Words"

Several years before I lived in Morro do Sangue Bom, I was boarding with a white middle-class family in the elite neighborhood of Leblon. Carla, one of the members of this family, told me a joke in which a black person was referred to as a monkey. I made a comment to the effect that I could not abide such racist jokes. Startled, Carla turned to me and said, "But negros laugh at them too!" While she spoke neither sensitively nor ironically, her observation, ethnographically speaking, was an important one.

People of color, I noticed, often feel constrained to go along with racist jokes. To do otherwise involves the risk of a kind of self-exposure that produces extreme awkwardness or even overt antagonism. Objecting to racist jokes, as I did, represents, rather ironically, a breech of etiquette. Such jokes undoubtedly have an underhanded, coercive force. Moreover, people of color may themselves tell racist jokes, and as I have noted, they often use racist words in the intimate context of brincadeira. The pragmatic message of both the jokes and the brincadeira shared between people of color may often (if not always) be different from that carried in the joking of whites. Intimacy as well as a complicated, double-voiced irony can be, and often is, communicated in such instances. What Carla was apparently unaware of in observing that people of color often laugh at racist jokes is both the coercive constraint and the rueful irony—as well as the delicate sense of danger—within the laughter that she hears.

As the following narratives will make clear, jokes and epithets are, in many contexts, anything but funny. Even when racist comments or name-calling are cloaked in the idiom of brincadeira or in the form of a piada, or joke, danger is always present and indignation, even if unexpressed, is often aroused.

Jorge told me about such a confrontation. He occasionally plays the drums in *pagode*, a heavily percussive, more or less traditional genre of music that is often (but not exclusively) associated with poor African Brazilians. A wealthy white acquaintance invited him to play music at a party at his house in Niteroi, a large city across the bay from Rio. Although Jorge described the arrangement in the idiom of friendship, he was probably paid for his services. After a long car ride Jorge and his companions arrived at the man's house:

What happens? The guys, myself, for example, I have, even, a feeling of shame when I see this guy's house. You know how it is? He's bringing the really poor, right, bringing pagode, right? . . . And I said [to myself], "What am I doing here?" . . . God, they opened [the door] . . . It was all planted with grass up there; [there was] a pool, a waiter serving and everything. [I thought,] "What am I here for?" So [the host] said, "I don't want you to serve the people here." The guy wanted me to make myself at home; rather than serve, he wanted us to be served. He got a bottle of vodka and put it on top of the table for us. But there were one or two people inside who were making a bad image of us (*fazendo um mau imagem da gente*), you know, making a bad image of us.

Jorge hesitated, as though to make sure I understood his oblique account of what had happened at the party. I pressed him by asking, "What do you mean by 'making a bad image'?" He continued, "A bad image is speaking ill, speaking ill, [saying] *crioulo* [derogatory term for blacks]. You know how it is: 'a crioulo race.' 'What is that crioulo doing here?' . . . He spoke like this: 'Two crioulos together are faggots or they're thieves.' Do you understand?"

Jorge knew, certainly, that I was keenly aware by then of how he might be inclined to react, in psychological terms at least, to being called a crioulo and a faggot in one breath. He also wanted me to understand the profound sense of constraint he felt in protesting his mistreatment. He was stuck in what felt like enemy territory, far from home. Jorge added in closing that he had been invited back to this man's house. "But," he told me in understatement, "I'm not going back anymore."

A number of people, particularly young men, told me that the police very often use racial slurs during incidents of harassment, and they mentioned, as well, that the color of the officer seemed to make no difference in his inclination to throw racist insults. Jacinto told me a number of stories in which the act of racist name-calling was figured as the coup de grâce of racist attacks on one's dignity. Referring to the police, he said, "The police themselves discriminate like this. . . . And really, the policeman is dark also. 'Negro!' [they call us]. . . . The negro himself has this nickname for the negro. Sometimes the white is the thief, but he is never called negro or preto. I've seen this happen many times, and it's already happened to me also."

While the suggestion that a white person could possibly be called a negro or a preto may sound absurd, Jacinto's anguished comment demonstrates, rather precisely, the ways in which terms that are usually glossed as black can, in certain contexts, be easily twisted into attacks on one's character.

Jacinto also observed an incident on a city bus, one that illustrates the anger and indignation that racist name-calling can provoke. In the incident he described, a middle-class black man accidentally bumped into a white woman. She called him, in Jorge's account, a *nego safado* (no-account nigger). The man's response was irate. "[I expect] to be treated like a man, like any white person," Jacinto said, quoting the man, "because I am not a negro! I am a citizen of color."

Nearly all of the illustrations of racism provided by Jacinto in our interview centered around "hard words," the practice of racist name-calling. In detailing his dismissal from a job, for example, he described the escalating tension between himself and one of his superiors. He told me that his manager, a relative of the owner of the firm, finally said to him, "That's why I don't like crioulos!" For Jacinto, the woman's overt name-calling proved, finally, that her criticism of him was not motivated by legitimate supervisory concerns but represented an underhanded form of racist harassment.

Name-calling is considered an especially violent act, in and of itself, yet its force resides also, I believe, in its revelatory aspect. Racist name-calling exposes and unveils what would otherwise be implicit, suppressed, or, as people in Morro do Sangue Bom are apt to say, incubado, or concealed. It directly violates the tenets of democracia racial and lays bare the racialized character of many everyday forms of social antagonism. Or, alternatively, it provides a framework, an ideological raison d'etre, a gloss for what may be, at root, more complicated forms of antagonism, forms that incorporate class- as well as color-based assertions of hierarchy and value. In either case, to insult someone, as my informants said, "by throwing hard words" articulates racism in its own direct and shocking idiom. Hard words leave no room for doubt, no quarter in which meaning can be softened, euphemized, or negotiated. I believe my informants frequently and emphatically recited stories about racist name-calling not only because it is relatively common or because its violent quality makes it inherently memorable and highly amenable to particularly dramatic forms of narration, but also because such stories serve as a heuristic genre. They give voice to, provide proof for, and guide the interpretation of the negative sentiments and covert strategies for expressing antagonism and hierarchy that motivate racism.

Working on the Asphalt: Women and Men

Between Monday and Friday, the day starts very early in Morro do Sangue Bom. Breakfast usually consists of nothing more than hastily consumed bread and heavily sugared coffee. Mothers take children to the day-care center at the bottom of the hill, to the bus that will take them to school, or to the houses of friends or relatives who will watch out for them during working hours. Both men and women make their way down the hill to catch the bus and begin their work on the asphalt, in various locations outside of the morro.

Between five and seven o'clock in the evening, the workers come home, wending their way slowly up the hill. Exhaustion is evident, and almost no one who lives high up on the hill has the energy to make the climb without stopping several times to catch his or her breath and chat with friends and neighbors. Men often stop in one of a number of small bars, where they ask for a "cold one" and exchange stories about their working day with other men. Children as young as four or five spring down the steps at a dangerous pace when they see their mothers laboring up the hill with groceries. "No, Mom, I'm strong; give me a heavier one," I once heard a four-year-old boy say when he was handed a bag of toilet paper. While countless books about the history and culture of Brazil emphasize the profoundly negative associations attached to physical labor in the country, people in Morro do Sangue Bom, many of whom are the descendants of slaves, cannot afford to indulge, for very long, in a fantasy of life without toil. Strength of mind and body and steadfast endurance are essential and highly respected qualities in both women and men. Pobres, or the poor, are very explicitly defined by my informants as "those who must work in order to survive," whereas the rich are "those who don't have to work."

Wage labor and the search for jobs are the most time-consuming and stress-filled activities for nearly all adults in Morro do Sangue Bom. Even those with no formal employment typically engage in *biscate,* a word that refers to activities such as street vending and odd-jobbing. With few exceptions, the people I knew in Morro do Sangue Bom worked in low-paying jobs and earned anywhere between one minimum salary (usually equivalent to eighty to one hundred [U.S.] dollars) to five minimum salaries per month. Those earning in the upper range of this scale were a minority; I knew people in their sixties who had worked steadily since young adulthood yet still brought home less than one hundred dollars a month.

Although there is some overlap in the work that men and women do, their access to different forms of wage labor is highly divergent. An overwhelming majority of the women I knew worked as *empregadas domésticas,* or domestic servants. A smaller number worked in small firms where they made and served coffee and performed janitorial duties, and an even smaller number worked as cashiers or clerks.

Men's occupations were more varied. Among the men I knew well, there were truck drivers, refrigerator repairmen, garbage collectors, plumbers, brick layers, general construction workers, bellhops, messengers, and what are called office boys. Despite their access to a larger variety of jobs, men were unemployed in higher numbers than women. Although a number of women told me that *patroas*—the patrons or middle-class women who hire empregadas domesticas—prefer that their maids be white or light-skinned, jobs in this sector never dry up entirely, and they are not thought to require special skills or formal training, nor even literacy.[1] Domestic service represents a stable occupational niche for poor women of all colors. Men's employment depends to a greater degree on the shifting fortunes of public and private enterprise and, by extension, on the fluctuations that characterize local and extra-local economies as a whole. Both men and women are likely to go through a period of unemployment at some point during their adult lives. For men, these periods are likely to be more frequent and to last longer than they do for women.

Men's and women's attitudes toward wage labor vary and change with shifts in relationships with employers and coworkers as well as with shifts in family life. Everyone who discussed the issue with me felt that they were paid too little for their work, and many felt that their talents, skills, dedication, and loyalty were unrecognized. People in Morro do Sangue Bom nevertheless took pride in their work. The community's unemployed people were a constant reminder of the necessity of work and the measure of independence it affords. Although the men and women of Morro do Sangue Bom were sometimes accused of being lazy and indolent by their middle-class neighbors, those who had secured employment worked much harder than most of those neighbors and knew it.

One of the central questions that motivates this section is, To what extent do men and women experience racism differently? In what ways are their interpretations of racialized or potentially racialized encounters divergent? France Winddance Twine (1995, 1996, 1998), a North American anthropologist, studied this issue closely during fieldwork conducted in "Vasalia," a rural town in the northwestern interior of the state of Rio de Janeiro between 1992 and 1994. A comparison of her conclusions with my own provides an illuminating contrast and reveals the centrality of work-related experience in the construction of racial meanings.

Focusing primarily on African Brazilian women and men in a nonurban locale, Twine (1995, 1996) discovered that there is a very significant "experiential and perceptual gap" between men and women with regard to white racism. Men, who sometimes work and pursue leisure activities in the city of Rio (or, at any rate, outside of the community), are exposed to a much more public world than are women. Traveling from a rural community to the city, they experience a disjuncture similar to the one my informants experience when they leave the morro and descend to the asphalt. The contexts in which

Twine's male informants tended to encounter racism were the same as those described by my male informants: while on the job and while looking for jobs, while traveling to and from work, and in unprovoked episodes of police harassment, episodes that occur outside of the home community. The women Twine interviewed worked as *donas de casa,* or housewives, or in low-paying jobs within the town, and their leisure activities took place within the local community. Their ability to travel outside of the town was highly controlled and circumscribed, and as Twine notes, women's exposure to the world beyond Vasalia was extremely limited. Twine found that her female inform-ants "reported no encounters with racism" (1995, 9). Her observations are very much in line with my own description of the lack of everyday discourse on racism in Morro do Sangue Bom. She observes, in addition, that racism is rarely discussed among her informants—although they had experienced racism, the male informants she quotes did not discuss these experiences with their wives.

If Twine's argument is correct—that experiences with, and recognition of, racism tend to increase with travel outside of the local community—we would expect most women in Morro do Sangue Bom to articulate experiences and perceptions similar to those of men. They do, in fact. While some women told me that they had never had a personal encounter with racism, very few of my female informants denied the pervasiveness of racism, nor did they attempt to underplay its significance. On the contrary, some of the sternest and most illuminating critiques of white racism were articulated by women, some of whom were, in fact, light-skinned. In comparing the way men and women in Morro do Sangue Bom discuss racism, it is evident, however, that differences in both work and leisure-related activities contribute toward gen-der differences in both experiences with and interpretations of racism.

Performing domestic labor for others often begins early in the life of women in Morro do Sangue Bom. While a few of the women I knew were not engaged in domestic service during the time of my research, I did not know of a single woman who had not worked as a maid in a middle-class home during some period in her life. Girls of thirteen or even younger often accompany their mothers to their jobs in middle-class neighborhoods, where they learn what is expected of a domestic servant. A girl may begin her first full-time job at the age of fourteen or fifteen, or even earlier. Many of the women I knew had spent at least a part of their adolescence as live-in maids; i.e., they lived with their employer families and went home only on weekends or Sundays.[2]

Varena's adopted daughter Rosemary was involved in such an arrange-ment during my stay in Morro do Sangue Bom. She slept in a very small maid's room—an appurtenance in nearly all middle-class homes in Rio and elsewhere in Brazil—and rose early to prepare breakfast for the family. While the children attended a private school, she studied for half a day in a public school. In the afternoons and evenings, she cleaned the house, did laundry, and prepared and served the family's dinner. Afterwards she ate her own dinner alone in the kitchen, washed the dishes, put the children to bed, did her homework, and retired until the next morning. She returned to Varena's house late Saturday and stayed until early Monday morning. For these services, Rosemary received less than fifty dollars per month, or one-half of a minimum monthly salary.

Although positions for empregadas and nursemaids are advertised in the papers, most women found positions through their own personal network of women on the morro. Middle-class people, particularly women, who usually hire, fire, and supervise the work of empregadas in familial households, also had personal networks through which information about available workers (gleaned from their own empregadas) was circulated. Jobs with good patroas were considered to be relatively scarce, however, and I knew some women who remained jobless for long stretches of time.

Some of the women I knew had worked for the same family, or different branches of an extended family, for most of their adult lives. As the word used for the employer of a domestic servant suggests, a patroa (or *patrão*) may, in what is considered the most favorable arrangement, serve as a kind of patron as well as an employer. Empregadas may be invited to take leftover food home to their families, they are sometimes given cast-off clothing, and some ask for advances on their salaries or a little help during especially difficult financial shortfalls, such as those induced by medical crises. While empregadas may sometimes discuss personal, even intimate problems with their patroas, I had the impression that the reverse was more often the case. It would, moreover, be impossible for an empregada not to know the intimate details of the lives of the families that employ them; they wash all the clothing and bedclothes, clean every inch of the house or apartment, shop and cook, overhear the conversations and arguments that make up family life, answer the phone and the door, and serve not only the family but also the family's guests.

Much of what goes on in employers' households becomes grist for the frequent and detailed gossip that women in Morro do Sangue Bom exchange and for scathing critiques of the perceived decadence of the wealthy and aspiring-to-be-wealthy classes. Stories are also told sympathetically, however, and women often ask after one another's employer families. When an empregada's patroa or someone in the patroa's family is undergoing a personal crisis, the empregada may give daily updates to her friends on the hill; and her friends in turn will express concern and sympathy, as though she were speaking of her own close friends or family. Undoubtedly, many women on the morro consider their relationships with their patroas to be genuine and important friendships, or even a kind of fictive kin relation. When describing the patroas they had as teenagers, some women on the morro speak gratefully of them as having been "like a mother," and when they refer to long-standing employment with a family with children, they will often say that they have been "like a second mother" to these children.

It is thus difficult to generalize about empregadas' relationships with and feelings about their employers. Most of the women who discussed the issue with me said they had had both good and horrible experiences, and as one who heard many daily updates myself, it became obvious to me that those relationships that were considered to be good (and were thus long-standing) tended to pass through the same ups and downs as do many, more intimate employer-employee relationships. Anger, frustration, and hurt over unpaid wages could be at least temporarily offset by an unexpected gift; gratitude for cast-off furniture could later be overshadowed by the unpleasant behavior of lazy or disrespectful children.

Women's experiences as empregadas, and their manner of recounting those experiences, contained a kind of personalized and ongoing drama that was not present or not so emphasized in men's descriptions of their professional lives. Because of the intimacy of their work and the emotional ambiguity of their role, empregadas often expressed feelings of hurt and betrayal in connection with their employers and their families, whereas men more often expressed feelings of indignation and anger. At least partly as a consequence of this intimacy and ambiguity, it seemed that women were more willing to overlook, excuse, and forgive the lack of sensitivity and consideration or the rudeness and unfairness that was occasionally or often shown to them. I had the impression that racism for them, when and if it occurred, might often be an explanation of last resort.

In my interviews with women in Morro do Sangue Bom, some, such as Dona Janete, did report (like Twine's female informants) that they had never personally encountered racism. Usually, when they discussed this issue they interjected phrases such as, "Thank God, it hasn't happened to me!" Most of the women I interviewed responded to my first question about the existence of racism in Brazil with comments such as, "My God, yes, there is racism here, Beth! Of course! Too much!" Despite that fact, women's narratives did, on occasion, have a more equivocal character than men's narratives; and on the whole, women reported less incidents of encounters with racism than did men.

Some of the ways in which men and women responded differently to my questions about racism were reflected in my interview with Rosa, who was in her forties. Her husband was present during the early part of the interview, but he was listening to a soccer match on the radio. When I asked Rosa if she thought there was racism in Brazil, however, her husband abruptly and loudly interjected a few comments.

ROSA: I have to say that in the house where I work, no [there is no racism].
HUSBAND: But some places have it! Some places have it!
ROSA: There are many racists here.
HUSBAND: The black (*preto*) is like . . . the black is always avoided—
ROSA: There are many racists here—
HUSBAND: You have to have "good appearance." . . . Here in Rio—
ROSA: Here, here in Brazil, here in Rio, there are many racists, yes, you know. It's hidden. Hidden, hidden. People [say,] "Oh, there's none of that," but deep down they're racist.

Rosa began her response with a favorable comment about her own patroa. Before she had a chance to enlarge upon or qualify her comment, her husband (who is, in fact, much lighter than she is) loudly qualified it for her, and his continuing comments refer not to individual cases or personal experience but to general scenarios. His reference to "good appearance" was one that I had heard many times, particularly in my discussions with male informants. As is well known, help-wanted ads often request job applicants with a good appearance, and Rosa's husband, like many others, interpreted this to mean pretos need not apply. Rosa did not disagree with her husband's characterization of racism in Rio and in Brazil, and she elaborated on his comments by pointing out that racism tends to be hidden and discursively denied. She continued, however,

With me, never, there was never racism, you know. I manage to work with people, you know. It's a good relationship. . . . But I have many friends who have racist patroas. They prefer white [empregadas] over black ones (pretas). My patroa? On the contrary, she has more preference for a black empregada than a white one. . . . I think it's the manner of the [black] person, the way of treating others well— because it's not the empregada who does the employing, it's the patroa. So I think when the person really needs [the job], they always treat them, the patroas, with more—with the most affection that they can, with the maximum attention. So, they know how to attend to their needs. This is what my patroa says. I don't know. I think that dark people sometimes have more consideration. They are sometimes more considerate than white empregadas. . . . So, there are many racist patroas. But this one, my patroa, is not racist.

Rosa returned to the description of her relationship with her patroa and suggested that her own deferential behavior contributed to the lack of racialized conflict in the relationship. Her comments are remarkably similar to those of the empregada I quoted in the previous chapter who suggested that one's own ability or inability to get along with and help people was a determining factor in whether or not one would be to subjected to racism. Rosa's (and her patroa's) reference to the manner of the (supposedly typical) black empregada seems to be a description of her greater deference and hard work vis- à -vis the (supposedly typical) white empregada. This was the patroa's formulation, and while Rosa suggested that the black empregada's greater deference might be related to her greater need to hold onto the job, she did not address the implications of this fact, nor the implications of her patroa's association of blackness with deference. Rosa was thankful for the fact that her patroa, unlike others, preferred black servants to white ones.

The often spontaneous positive comments that some women in Morro do Sangue Bom made about their employers reveal how they judge whether their employers are racist or not, and they suggest, more fundamentally, that empregadas view racism as, above all, a personal trait. Another woman in her forties who had just learned that I was studying issues related to racism told me, "My patroa likes negros very much. She is French, but she likes negros very much. She's not racist, no. We drink out of the same glass and we even wear the same clothes. The other day I was very cold and she said, 'You can borrow my sweater,' and I put her sweater on. She's a very cool person."

The issue of indirect contact through shared objects continued to surprise me when I talked to women about their jobs. Why should the sharing of a glass or a sweater be so noteworthy in a country where interracial sex and marriage is celebrated in public discourse, where white children are often cared for by black nursemaids, and where the grab-fest of carnival almost requires physical contact among people of different colors?

As I continued my interviews, a number of women described the opposite type of scenario: while working for their employer families, they were expected to change and shower only in the maid's quarters, they ate and drank from a special set of plates and glasses that were separated from those used by the family, and they were often forbidden to eat the pricier food items, such as meat and cheese, that they themselves prepared. "It's almost always like that," Joia told me on one occasion. Not surprisingly, those who had to observe the practice of separating everything believed that it was motivated by a fear of racial contamination. Rosa put it succinctly: "There's a friend of mine who said that her patroa separated everything, glasses, plates, forks, everything. So, [the patroa] said it was because [my friend] was a negra. She didn't like negros.

[And my friend said,] 'I am black, but the same blood that runs in your veins runs in mine.' But [the patroa said,] 'Oh no, because who knows, the color, no!' So everything was separated."

Although this incident was reported secondhand, Rosa's description of the patroa's flustered inability to defend her actions and attitudes was familiar. When such confrontations are described in narratives of racism, racist whites are often portrayed as stuttering and stumbling over their words and becoming *sem graça*, literally, without grace. Overt verbal confrontations, when they occurred and were described to me, always involved an attempt to shame the racist offender.

Analucia spoke very directly about the preference for light-skinned maids. As I have noted in the second chapter, she herself was very light-skinned but considered herself a negra, in racial terms. When I asked her if she had ever had an experience with racism, she responded, "I have. I came to notice prejudice more when I came to Rio, you understand? Principally in my work with the patroas. They would look at me and say, 'Oh, I think I'll keep you because you're not totally negra.' I wasn't a pure negra, right, I was a mestiça. [So they said,] 'I'll keep you, you aren't negra. If you were a negra, I wouldn't want you.'" I interrupted Analucia:

ROBIN: They said this to you directly?

ANALUCIA: Many times!

ROBIN: Openly?

ANALUCIA: They said it, Beth! I told them that I am a negra. My family is negra. My father is a negro—so then. So, sometimes they said that to me. You know, sometimes a friend of mine who was a negra would come with me, right, and she—they would say, "No, you can't [work here]. No, my husband doesn't like black people." But sometimes the husband didn't even know that the house had an empregada! [They said to my friend,] "Oh, I don't want you [here], no, because my children don't get along with negras." So, they would say to me, "Oh, I'll keep you." Many times I didn't go because if they didn't want a negra, they're not going to accept a mestiça, right?

As a light-skinned woman who identified as a negra, Analucia was particularly aware of certain forms of overt racism. The openness of her patroas' comments about not wanting empregadas who were negra suggests that they assumed that Analucia would, in fact, share their views. As Rosa had, Analucia portrayed her patroas as sem graça (graceless and awkward) in their attempts to justify their prejudice and discrimination.

Hierarchy is both a defining structural feature and a symbolically marked, socially negotiated understanding in empregada-patroa relationships. Domestic servitude is always, regardless of racial or color issues, a particularly vivid enactment of class differences and the unequal privileges and burdens associated with class differences. Poor women's access to wages depends, minimally, not only on their ability to perform work that is culturally demeaning, but also on their ability to outwardly accept their subordinate position. Although middle-class whites often say that their empregadas are like one of the family, an informal, usually unspoken, contract between the employer and employee stipulates the delineation of boundaries, both visible and invisible, that set employees well apart from the families for whom they work. Many women tend to describe these hierarchical relationships—the rough edges of which are often smoothed by intimacy or the presumption of intimacy—as a natural part of their taken-for-granted world.

Accusations of racism were thus not made in a facile manner by my informants who worked as empregadas. None of the women I spoke with explicitly emphasized the racial structuring of empregada-patroa relationships, i.e., the fact that most patroas are white while a majority of empregadas are of African descent. When talking about their work, the issue of racialized employment structures was rarely invoked at all by empregadas; racism was defined and described through the personalized traits of individual patroas. When accusations of racism were made then, they tended to revolve around the demarcation of boundaries that were felt to be extreme, rigid, unnatural, symbolically freighted, and contrary to the tenets of democracia racial.

A few women recounted other types of work-related experiences that they felt involved racism. Yvonne, for example, wanted to stop working as an empregada, but she was rebuffed in her attempt to secure employment that involved interaction with the public. She told me, "This type of thing with jobs, for example, right? There are jobs in which they won't accept [blacks]. For a long time I have been struggling to get a job as a receptionist. I can't find a job. I think it's because of racism. I've already been to various places. I've already been to agencies, and to the firms themselves. They always said they didn't have an opening. And I knew they had openings because there was no one there in the position. And later, after a time, I returned and there was a person working. And the person wasn't—they were white."

Most women do not actively seek jobs as receptionists but are hired as maids through word-of-mouth exchanges within localized networks. As Twine notes, women are "culturally trained to have lower expectations regarding their job opportunities" (1995, 12). I would add, moreover, that because of their double subordination as women of color working in the homes of middle-class whites, their expectations of respectful treatment may also be somewhat lower (and more qualified) than men's expectations. Fair treatment, as several women implied, must be won through a carefully maintained deference, through giving what Rosa called the "maximum attention." Rosemary, the fifteen-year-old I previously referred to, was actively trained by her adoptive mother to take on domestic service and she was not, to my knowledge, encouraged to entertain other possibilities. As Yvonne's experience demonstrates, this cultural training is constructed within, and supported by, discriminatory practices and associated prejudicial discourses about women of color. As several informants told me, "They [white people] think we can only be empregadas."

As I have noted, there is a great deal more variety in men's employment. Men in Morro do Sangue Bom engage in skilled, semiskilled, and unskilled labor, and their professional experiences and trajectories tend to be more varied than those of women. Some men I knew had very stable jobs, and these were usually in the public sector. I knew several men, for example, who worked as garbage collectors in the employ of the city government. Still, unemployment, as I have noted, was higher among men than among women. During moments of unemployment, it is usually a wife's wages from domestic work that keep a family afloat.

As is the case with girls, some boys begin working part-time at the age of about fourteen, often as office boys and messengers. Joia's eldest son, Alberto, began working as an office boy at the age of thirteen. He attended school in the morning and went to his job in the city five afternoons a week. While on the job, he began to learn about computers and software applications, and by the time he was sixteen, he was able, to the surprise of his supervisors, to serve as a troubleshooter when much higher ranking and better-paid employees had difficulties with software applications. Joia was very proud of Alberto's growing expertise, and she felt that he was not treated with the respect that his abilities warranted. "There's a crisis in his office," she told me, "and no one knows what to do. Alberto says he can fix it but no one believes him. They think, 'What can this poor kid from the favela do?' But he asks for a chance, he fixes it, and everybody is just so surprised." Like Rosemary, Alberto was only paid one half of a minimum salary, less than fifty dollars a month. Brazilian labor laws do not require that minors be paid more, regardless of their position or expertise.

Although women work outside of the morro, their world typically remains more circumscribed than that of men. Men tend to seek jobs in the public arena more often than women. They thus have more experience with the job application process, which typically involves speaking with managers, filling out job applications, and sometimes taking a written test. If their job search is successful, they tend to have a circle of coworkers and supervisors, whereas women who work as domestic servants remain within the more private sphere of the employer's home.

Men not only travel to and from work, but also often go out to visit friends in bars or on other morros during weekend nights, while their wives and sisters care for children, perform household chores, and visit one another on the hill. Whereas women are generally fearful of leaving the community after dark, it is not unusual for men to return to the morro at four or five o'clock in the morning on weekends, and many stop in at bars for a few glasses of draft beer during the work week. Men's experience on the asphalt is thus far more varied than that of women.

When I asked men about racism, they were more likely than were women to immediately introduce the issue of job discrimination. Daniel's brother, Nestor, said, for example: "Even though our society wants to hide it, racism is evident. It is in schools, it is in work. The job market for the negro is very restricted. [Racism] certainly exists, yes. Everyone wants to deny it, but it exists."

Many of my male informants, as I have noted, described the experience of applying for jobs and being rejected by potential employers. Usually, these experiences were summed up with the comment, "They always say they don't have an opening." While my informants felt convinced that they were turned away for racist reasons, they were also aware of the fact that in most situations they could not prove that they had been discriminated against. The experience of Jonas, who engaged in odd-jobbing on the morro, was an exception. When I asked him about racism, he said, "Hell, I'd like to discuss what happened to me!" I urged him to continue:

It was awhile ago already, more than a year. I was talking to a guy from here who encouraged me to go [to the place where he had a job]. His name is José and he is lighter than I am. He was employed [at this firm]. He sent me there to take the position that they had open there. . . . He promised me, he promised me a job as a messenger. It was in a firm in the city. I went there and filled out the application properly and [showed] my documents. Then that whole thing started: "Come back on another day; come back on another day." And the day I went back, the woman said [my application was fine,] they only needed to open the position. . . . Then the guy [my friend] said, to my face, "They don't hire black folks (gente preta) here. They don't employ black people, of color." The guy said that to me! . . . After three days, [I went back] and the woman said they didn't have an opening. . . . So, it was racism. . . . And like that, I got very angry; I got on the elevator and went right to the police. . . . I got [to the police station] and the guy there asked me to explain what had happened and I explained. . . . I arrived there crying, crying, crying—I don't know what all—and they told me to take some medicine, a glass of water with sugar. [I said,] "There is a law that can, you know, punish these people! This is a crime; this can't happen!" . . . I told them everything and [the policeman said,] "Don't get hotheaded, no. Let it go." And he gave me a glass of water because I was so upset (nervoso). . . . And I stayed there for a long time. . . . Nothing was resolved. . . . They didn't do anything. I was a bit upset. Let it go. So, these things exist. At the time I was very upset. Speaking with the firm? A super-millionaire? To complain wouldn't have done anything. It's sad, isn't it? I was just wanting a job. Because of color! If you don't like a person's manner, [that's another thing]. So [racism] exists. I think it exists—no!—I don't think! I *know* it does!

Jonas's framing of certain aspects of this experience as a typical job-application scenario was corroborated by the comments of other informants. While one may be rejected summarily, polite evasion seems to occur more frequently. Although Jonas appears to have been treated with a kind of routine and expectable politeness during his first encounter at the firm, the friend who brought him in is evidently later told by a supervisor that Jonas will not be hired because he is black. Being told so, to his face, without evasion or euphemism, is evidently a shocking experience for Jonas. While Jonas suggested that he had resolved not to dwell on this experience, it was clear that he was profoundly discouraged.

Jonas's story is unusual not only because his friend who had inside information told him that he would never get the job because of his color, but also because Jonas went to the police to register a complaint. Despite the silence that typically surrounds experiences with racism, several informants told me similar, secondhand stories about job discrimination. Analucia told me about a conversation she had with a male friend: "In general, he complains; he says he will stay—he will continue being poor because no one will accept him as a worker because he is of color. There's a lot of prejudice. Many times he said, 'Hell, I'm not a thief. I'm not anything; it's just that I'm a negro.' So, they don't accept [people of color], Beth. Here in Brazil no one accepts the negro. He never went [to the police to lodge a complaint]. He thinks it wouldn't do any good. He simply leaves the place with nothing resolved. So, it will never be resolved. He thinks it's never worth the trouble, and he stays angry."

Jonas's sense of hopelessness and his conviction that racism can disbar him from even the most menial of positions was shared by many men in Morro do Sangue Bom. There is a sharp awareness, of course, that lack of education and identification with the lower class (as *favelados*) constitute very significant disadvantages on the job market, yet many men feel that color represents a particularly severe (and immutable) burden in seeking employment and fair treatment. I presented to many informants a hypothetical scenario in which a man of color and a white man, each bearing the same educational and professional qualifications, apply for the same job. Their agreement that the white man would probably succeed at the expense of the black man was unanimous.

The struggle to support oneself and one's family in the face of racialized prejudice and discrimination does not end once a job is secured. Other men, in addition to Jacinto, told me that they were discriminated against while on the job. Nestor, for example, described such an experience:

> I went to work in a bank and I managed to begin. I was taking a
> course along with the job, and I managed to get a better position. . . .
> They put me into a supervisory position. . . . But they didn't give
> me—they didn't recognize me as a boss, because I was a negro, I was
> of color. . . . The boss, the president of the business, was white. And
> most of the people in the bank were all white. So, they preferred a
> person of the light color. . . . I felt this even more so because my
> other colleagues were making it sometimes to a higher position, and
> after analyzing it, you can perceive this. They have the light color,
> right? Their position was recognized and mine wasn't.

Nestor, like Jonas, was unemployed during the entire period of my research. He spent much of his time composing samba music and writing poetry. Many of his poems concerned the neglect of street children, the poverty of those who live in the favela, and the hypocrisy of politicians. Despite his discouragement, Nestor kept up his work as an unrecognized artist devoted to that which was, in his own words, "always polemical, always critical, always fundamental."

Many men told me that they encountered racism, either directly or indirectly, while traveling to and from work. Although some women narrated experiences that occurred on the typically crowded city buses, men's stories were so common as to constitute a distinct genre within their narratives of racism. In many cases, these stories involved police harassment. It occasionally happens in Rio that bandits—usually two men—will board a city bus and, while it is in transit, hold up all of the occupants at gunpoint. I know of only one individual who had actually witnessed such an incident, yet many people in Rio, particularly members of the middle class, are fearful of riding city buses, especially at night. Such incidents are presented as justification for a far more common practice of the police: entering city buses, scanning the passengers, and ordering some commuters—nearly always young black men—to get off the bus for a *geral* (literally, a general) or a *revista* (a review).

Typically, those who are subjected to a geral or a revista are frisked, ordered to turn their pockets inside out, to reveal the contents of any packages that they may be carrying, and to open their mouths for inspection. (The assumption is that small amounts of cocaine may be concealed in the mouth.) They are also likely to be interrogated about where they live, where they are traveling from, what their destination is, and why they are going there. As I previously noted, many of the men who narrated bus stories told me that the police often engage in gratuitous, racist name calling while conducting revistas. If no drugs or weapons are found, the "suspects" are allowed to continue on their way, after waiting for another bus and paying an additional fare. "It's a thing that isn't cool, right?" Nestor said, describing such an occasion. "You're leaving work tired, and all of a sudden [claps his hands together loudly] you fall into a scene like this, right? It isn't cool."

Often these stories are narrated in a very brief fashion. Guilherme described an incident: "Several years ago this happened to me. I was in back of the bus, out in the suburbs, and four cops got on. Two went in front and two went in back. They ordered me to get out. I asked why and they said it was because they were looking for arms. I was wanting to know why I was the only one they ordered off the bus, and the cop said, 'Because you are the only one under suspicion.' The only difference between me and the others was that I was black."

Men also described conflicts with other passengers while on the bus. When I asked Jorge if he had ever encountered racism directly, he began with the following story:

It has happened to me. In this case, I was on the bus, a bus going to the South Zone. So then, I got on the bus and what happened? I saw a woman (*uma senhora*). She was looking for a place to sit. The guy sitting next to me got up, so there was a place. There was a place, but this white woman didn't want to sit in that place, you know? After three or four minutes, she didn't sit down there and she went up to a guy who was sitting in front and requested of him, "Oh, you go sit back there with that dark one there, I'm going to stay up here in front." She said, "I don't want to sit close to that dark one." I looked at her and I said, "Shit, how ridiculous! What a ridiculous thing! It could be that your flesh is more putrid than mine!" That's what I said

to her. So, she didn't say anything, she felt ashamed, right? She was
sem graça.

Robertson, a man of twenty, told me that when he got on the bus he often
noticed that white women would clutch their bags more tightly and dart anxious glances in his direction. On one occasion, he decided to say something.
"I'm not a thief," he gently told the woman. "Oh, no, I wasn't thinking that,"
the woman responded. "She was embarrassed," Robertson told me. "Later she
will be thinking, 'Why did I do this?'"

Men's leisure activities outside of the community also entailed experiences
with racism. Although women may be eyed warily in shops, men who spend their
leisure time on the asphalt are far more subject to the suspicion that they may be
criminals. A man in his thirties, for example, told me that at a late hour one
night, he and his friend stopped in a bakery on their way home from a soccer
game. When they stepped into the bakery the other customers left abruptly: "No
one stayed inside. They went out so afraid because we were negros. With fear!
Then the police were there, at the side of the door. They kept looking at us. . . .
We paid for the bread and we sat down. The whole bakery was ours! [Laughs.]"

Men may also be harassed by the police when they go to visit friends or go
to dances on other morros in the city—which they do far more often than
women. Jacinto told me the following story, almost as an aside:

> It happens constantly. Because it's a thing—if two or three negros are
> walking together, for sure, if a police car passes, they will stop us. It
> doesn't do any good to say anything. Yesterday! Yesterday! I went to
> Cantagalo (a morro in Copacabana) yesterday, up on the morro of
> Cantagalo with a friend of mine. . . . And when we were going back
> down the hill, a police car stopped. It was about two-thirty in the
> morning. And these people, two couples, two white couples, went up
> there to buy drugs, to buy cocaine. They went to buy and they passed
> right by the police. And we, who weren't doing anything, they
> stopped us. They looked me over, ordered me to open my mouth.

In the midst of making generalizing comments about police harassment
then, Jacinto abruptly recalled an incident that had happened the previous
day. His framing of the story corroborated his opening comment that "it happens constantly" and suggested that such encounters are so routine that their
specificity requires no emphasis.

Tomas told me of a similar but even more difficult experience. He began
by describing the difficulty he had, as a black man, in hailing a cab and proceeded to narrate—again, in the manner of an aside—an experience he had
while visiting a nearby morro:

Those of us here don't have it easy. . . . Here it's very difficult for
people of color. [Cab drivers] think we're going to rob them. I just did
this, this past Thursday. I went out to get a taxi from Rio Comprido
to here. I put my hand out and didn't get one, right? I kept putting
my hand out and not one taxi stopped for me. The car [that finally]
stopped for me charged so much, it was very expensive. You
understand, I stayed there for more or less a whole hour waiting for a
taxi! It was already eleven at night, and I had already been stopped
by the police up above. They thought I was there to buy drugs, right,
but I was there for this dance the people up there were having. . . .
And they gave me a geral, right? "Where are you going?" they asked
me, and I said, "Oh, I'm going to that other morro over there, I live
there." Including even, I had to tell them where I lived and all.
Sometimes at night, sometimes it's very dangerous [with] the police;
there can be violence. So this happened up above [on the morro] and
down below the other thing happened. I don't have much luck when
I go out, no. [Chuckles softly.]

As in previously quoted narratives of racism, Tomas described his activities on the asphalt as though they were part of a dangerous journey within
enemy territory. It is no wonder that men prefer to travel by night in groups of
two or three. Although they know that those who live on the asphalt may see
them as all the more fearsome, they are, for their part, hoping for safety in
numbers.[3]

Both men and women protest, implicitly and explicitly, that their person-
hood, their individuality, their character is neither recognized nor respected
by racist whites. Yet their framing of this protest, in many, if not all moments,
reveals differences in both experience and interpretation. Men articulate, to a
greater degree than do women, the conviction that racism is a part of the
backdrop of everyday life, informed by and structured through the agency of
individual personality perhaps, but nevertheless partaking of a routine,
anonymous, and systemic character. Whereas women tend to emphasize relationships between individuals and to rely heavily on a discourse that emphasizes the moral judgment of character, men tend to emphasize relationships
between groups of people, categories constructed through experience and—
we must assume, despite the relative silence—through discourses that construct the dangerous other of the asphalt. Men are more apt to frame racism as
a problem of the *sociedade*, or society, of *political* economy, whereas their wives
may frame it as problem of *pessoas*, or persons, whose engagement is signified
within, and constitutive of, a fundamentally *moral* economy.

When I asked Nestor if he and his wife, Cintia, ever discussed racism, he
told me that they had had disagreements about it. His comments represented

one of the few cases in which an informant told me that he had discussed the issue of racism with a spouse. His response, which spells out far more than his figuring of the differences of opinion between himself and his wife, is worth quoting at length:

> Occasionally we converse, yes. She understands it in another way. She thinks that [systemic] racism doesn't exist. She thinks that it is inside of each person. . . . Racism doesn't exist for her. I think, on the contrary, that it does exist, it clearly exists in our country, right? It reveals itself in all senses. . . . You never see a private school with negros studying there. . . . It is closed, a lid exists. The only ones with the right of access to the best schools are those with greater financial power, and consequently these people are whites—because generally, the negro is a favelado. We have already suffered for many years, and our education is denied us because we have been manipulated, we have been enslaved—meaning the negro is struggling, struggling, struggling this entire time to find a space. But how is he going to find this space if he doesn't have access to culture, which is basic, right? Discrimination! It is rooted.

It is a distinctly sociological notion of structure that Nestor described. I remained confused about his characterization of Cintia's position, for she had described to me, in a private interview, her own experiences and wounded feelings. I asked Nestor to clarify his comments about her position on the issue. He replied, "I think that Cintia thinks that the negro discriminates against himself. The negro makes his own prejudice. . . . So, Cintia thinks that the negro himself discriminates, that's how she puts it. I see it completely differently. I think that racism comes from—it is inside of the formation of our country, do you understand? When the negro came here, he was already a slave. And up until today, the society—now it wants to hide [racism], but it preserves it."

I knew Cintia recognized the pervasiveness of white racism, just as she recognized the ways in which people of color, particularly those who were upwardly mobile, sometimes failed to show solidarity with others. Yet Nestor was at least partially correct in his comment that Cintia viewed racism as more visibly present "inside of each person" rather than in what Nestor called "the formation of our society."

Such differences were also expressed, in separate interviews, by Jorge and his wife, Angela. Like Nestor, Jorge viewed racism as a systemic form of oppression that operates, at its most basic level, through the mutually reinforcing entanglement of racial and class oppression:

> It begins through the great society right? They don't like, in any way, the black race. They don't like the black race, and those of us who

are of the black race remain people of the poor class. And also the
word *favelado* comes into being. . . . This consists of thieves, muggers.
The majority, 75 percent, right, come from the poor class. Because
the guy doesn't have the minimum [necessary] for survival. Because
he's dark he can't—no one wants to employ him. . . . The firm
doesn't give him an opening. So he goes to the other side, thinks of
something [else]. What? He sells drugs, he steals, he mugs people. But
in reality, the real thief isn't just the little dark one, it's the society!

Jorge's wife, Angela, told me that "in Brazil, the negro isn't given a
chance," yet in a way similar to Nestor's framing of Cintia's position, she
believed that racism "comes from the person": "You don't see many black
people with cars, with luxury, living in apartments, you know, with good jobs.
I don't know, maybe it comes from us, ourselves—you know, the race. One
keeps thinking, 'Oh, I'm not going to study, why should I study? I'm not going
to be anything in life because I am preto.' I think it comes from the person; it
doesn't come, you know, from, from—there are many pretos [who say] it is
because of society, but I think it comes from him. . . . It's not so much discrimination, it is from himself."

Living in the sequestered world of the morro and working for a patroa
whom both she and Jorge felt was without prejudice, Angela had not experienced or could not recall experiences such as those her husband had privately
narrated for the benefit of my research. For her, it seems, it is low self esteem
that prevents Brazilians of African descent from seizing the opportunities
associated with upward mobility.

The differences between the ways in which women and men interpret
racism stem, to be sure, from the gendered nature of men's and women's wage
labor and leisure activities as well as from the gendered nature of racist ideology and practice itself. Women of color are seen as submissive and subordinate, suitable, above all, for domestic labor, as possibly polluted and polluting
(or, contrarily, as sexually alluring and available) but not otherwise dangerous.
"White women for marriage, mulatas for sex, and negras for work" is a well-
known aphoristic expression throughout Brazil, and it captures the historically entrenched and constantly fortified view of black women's place in the
world.

Black men are not only viewed as polluted and polluting, but also, in certain contexts, as dangerous. When they ambitiously seek better jobs on the
asphalt and wander the streets outside the favela, they are demonstrating
what is read by the middle class as an ominous refusal to stay in their place.
"A white man running is in a footrace; a black man running is a thief," as the
well-known saying has it. Black men are also viewed as fit for little more than

strenuous physical labor. Such ideological notions both powerfully reflect and structure the boundaries within which most Brazilians of African descent live and work. While such a formulation is undoubtedly simplified, it captures what is essential in what men and women in Morro do Sangue Bom know to be the racist vision of their place in the world.[4]

I do not wish to overemphasize the distinction between the ways in which women and men experience and understand racism, for their narratives bear similarities as well as differences. The men and women of Morro do Sangue Bom live in a shared world of oppression and share understandings about oppression to a much greater degree than do the more rural women and men interviewed by Twine (1995). The differences I have drawn are a matter of emphasis, and both men and women do, on the whole, articulate a set of (normally suppressed) discourses which describe both the individual and the social and political nature of racism. While social scientists investigating inequality tend to favor a view such as that most forcefully articulated by the men of Morro do Sangue Bom, there is nothing in the vision of a hegemonically ordered, culpable society that contradicts a domestic servant's insight into the interpersonal dimensions of quotidian racism. The moral economy that women invoke and the political economy of racism articulated by men are, I would suggest, equally compelling narratives of racism in Brazil.

Accounting for Racism

Often, with little direct prompting from me, informants not only described their personal experiences but also offered general statements about the causes and consequences of racism. As is evident in some of the narratives I have quoted above, these statements often have an interpretive or theoretical cast. In this way also, my informants' comments diverged significantly from those of Twine's informants, for she writes, "My research in rural Brazil reveals that daily encounters with racism do not necessarily lead to an awareness by Afro-Brazilians that racial inequality is a problem in their lives. In Vasalia, few residents appeared to have access to a paradigm for thinking through racial inequality" (1995, 4).

Although there were contradictions, inconsistencies, and divergences both within and between my informants' narratives, the comments of people in Morro do Sangue Bom suggest that many do use a number of overlapping paradigms for thinking about and critiquing racism. Analucia, for example, told me that racism is "rooted" in slavery and that it could be understood by "looking at how our Brazil began." After I acknowledged the importance of the historical frame she proposed, I asked her to speculate on the psychological and social underpinnings of racism. "But tell me more about what you think is in their heads," I asked her. She responded,

> They think, Beth, that the black color—I think it's like this—that the black color doesn't deserve anything. That's my understanding. Because you see that when [a negro] wants to study, they go like this: "But shit, study?! The negro isn't going to manage anything. Why is he going to study?" So, I think they always discriminate against the negro even on this point. You know, they think the negro doesn't have the conditions to raise himself up, to know things, to arrive at the level of the white. This is a great discrimination. They go like this: "Shit, the guy is negro; he's in the kitchen. Why is he going to study?" So I think they have fear that the negro who studies will succeed, that he will become equal to them. This is what I have thought. . . . So I think this is the fear that they have, that the negro will get on his level, in work and in society.

Analucia, clearly, can engage several overlapping paradigms in accounting for the existence and pervasiveness of racism in her country. She frames her understanding of racialized oppression in terms of history and the relationship between racialized discrimination and the maintenance of class boundaries. Brazilianist scholars are apt to hear an echo of their own discussions of racism in Brazil and elsewhere, yet Analucia herself never had the opportunity to study.

Jonas, who told me about his experience of being turned down for a job and being subjected to condescension in the police station, also elaborated on the patterns he saw within and beyond his own experience. "It is rarely commented upon," he said, to signal his awareness that he was speaking against denial and silence:

> The people who know this thing exists can't do anything, you know, [even when] they understand that there's a law against racism. . . . In a job, color is not important; what is important is personality, that you are a correct person, that you have certain abilities. Nothing more [is needed for] that job. So why not? They don't ask you to take a test; they don't ask you to do anything; they just look at you and say they have no openings. And a white goes in after you and he gets the job. So, it exists, but what are we going to do? We have to put this in front, to put it in front of the person who thinks [racism] doesn't exist.

Jonas insisted—as did so many of my informants—that despite the claims of democracia racial, people like himself had no difficulty in perceiving the systemic nature of racism. Above all, it seemed, he wanted me to understand that his and others' silence should not be read as an acceptance of the claims of democracia racial.

Jacinto also spoke about racism in general terms. He used the fact that black domestic servants (as well as black visitors) are typically forced to ride the service elevators of apartment buildings as a metonym for the larger injustices of racism. "I think it's racial discrimination," he said, "because of the skin that you have. And why is this? Because the worker isn't a human being?" What Jacinto emphasized was not simply the existence of racism and its socially conventionalized nature but its moral thrust. He continued, "So why does he have to take this discrimination of going in the worker's entrance rather than the social entrance? Why can't we go in the same way? Aren't we all [eventually] buried in the same ground? When the employer dies, is he not going to the same place? Is not the blood of everyone red?"

When accounting for racism, most informants framed their comments as an argument against silence and what are figured as the platitudinous, naive, and/or obfuscating claims of democracia racial. As such, they have the character of an externalized inner dialogue, a belatedly vocalized *esprit d'escalier*, which finally gives voice to the insights and understandings that remain, for the most part, unspoken in everyday discourses. Their comments challenge the notion that knowledge must proceed from an exposure to coherent public discourses, that internalized paradigms can only solidify in response to dominant, external paradigms. Voiced or unvoiced, oppression is mediated through the bedrock of experience, and many people in Morro do Sangue Bom (silently) argue against the discursive claims that deny the racialized meanings presented by such experience.

The analytic insight, irony, discursive creativity, eloquence, and the fundamental recognition of the moral absurdity of dominant discourses that are embodied within my informants comments seem to suggest that a heteroglossic and parodic vision lies just beneath the surface of both silence and dominant everyday discourses. It is a biting rather than a humorous parody. That this should be true in Morro do Sangue Bom, while it is evidently not in Vasalia, offers testament to the significance of experience, particularly the experience of wage labor in the highly differentiated world of the urban landscape.

In describing the racialized nature of many everyday encounters, in framing such encounters as examples of boundary-maintaining incidents that occur all the time, and in accounting for racism in the language of a structured and structuring hegemony, my informants revealed what is embaixo do pano, or under the concealing fabric, of dominant narratives of race (and silence about racism) in Brazil. Most of my informants are entirely aware of the pedagogical, demystifying character of their narratives, for they constantly referred to the dominant and contradictory claims of democracia racial in their bitterly parodic quotations of its discourses.

"Shit, the guy is negro; he's in the kitchen. Why is he going to study?" Analucia said, mocking a highly conventionalized type of comment that she had evidently heard with her own ears. "Some don't want to talk about it," she informed me, and she quoted what one is likely to hear on the asphalt: "Oh, there isn't [any racism], there isn't, there isn't." This discourse of denial, people in Morro do Sangue Bom suggested, is insistently and tediously repeated. "Even though our society wants to hide it," Nestor instructed me, "racism is evident. . . . It reveals itself in all senses." Although Jonas felt himself to be a wounded soldier in a battle that had already been lost, he asserted, "We have to put this in front of the person who thinks racism doesn't exist." Democracia racial, as many in Morro do Sangue Bom seemed to suggest, is, above all, a fairly transparent form of national hypocrisy that insists that the racialized bases of their powerlessness and entrapment remain unnamed.

Chapter 5   Narratives

Racism at Home

S<small>OON AFTER I ARRIVED</small> in Morro do Sangue Bom, Joia began to tell me stories about her family, her youth, and the early years of her marriage to Daniel. Joia told me that as a teenager, she had hoped to marry a man lighter than herself so that her children "would not be very dark." Daniel was, in fact, lighter than Joia, and they began courting when she was fifteen. "His mother was against it," Joia told me, remembering the early days of her common-law marriage, "She said to him, 'What do you want with that negra, that dark woman?'"

Joia's comments about Daniel's mother surprised me, not only because Dona Sonia was herself a woman of color, descended from an African Brazilian father and an Amerindian mother, but because, to my eyes, the difference in color between Joia and Daniel was quite subtle. As I continued to discuss the issues of race and color with many people on the morro, my eyes became more attuned to Brazilian perceptions, and the difference between Joia and Daniel, once barely noticeable to me, became—while never dramatic—more apparent. Although a number of people in Joia's personal network of family and friends told me that "if you don't pass for white, you are negro" and derided the significance of color distinctions, there were clearly moments in which such differences were important—so important, in fact, that familial relationships could be strained by them.

Joia's experience calls attention to the larger issue of what is often called interracial marriage, or miscegenation. Although the mixed heritage of Brazilians is celebrated by social scientists, by novelists, and within everyday discourses, many of my informants told me that mixed marriages are often fraught with and surrounded by tension and discord. There is perhaps no other arena in which contradictory notions about the significance of race and color are brought into greater relief. Discourses about the shared identities and experiences of all those within the raça negra, or black race, are contradicted in specific contexts by those that attribute different aesthetic and, to a lesser extent, moral values to people of different colors.

Joia's experience also articulates with two other related issues that were emphasized by my informants: what they called "the racism of the negro himself" and racism within the morro community. In the previous chapter I have described the ways in which informants represent the world of the asfalto as a racially bounded, white-controlled space in which people from the morro must make what are sometimes described as perilous journeys away from home. Yet racism itself is not restricted to the social milieu of the asfalto, nor are prejudicial and discriminatory discourses and practices the exclusive province of privileged whites. Racism may be encountered, as Joia's story suggests, not only within one's own community, but within consanguineal and affinal relationships.

Racism must certainly be viewed as a set of ideologies and practices that penetrate class and color boundaries, and attention must be given to the different contexts in which it is articulated. Although recent scholarship on domination has tended to de-emphasize the extent to which subordinate groups participate in hegemonic discourses and practices while highlighting often symbolic forms of resistance (see, for example, Scott 1990), I would argue that a fuller critique of domination requires an examination of hegemony as seen from the ground of subordinate communities.

As in previous chapters, my examination of these other forms of racism—between people of color, within families, and within the community as a whole—is informed less by explicit theoretical paradigms that attempt to address abstract notions of consciousness than it is by the direct comments of informants. This chapter continues the focus on narratives of racism and takes its direction from informants' emphasis on the significance of forms of racism that are, in one sense or another, closer to home. The narratives I quote are, once again, both ethnographic descriptions and analyses; and while they refer to disparate contexts, they are united above all by a sense of betrayal: betrayal within the race, within the community of shared poverty, and within the family.

"Improving the Race": Historical Considerations

The notion of melhorando a raça, or improving the race, is historically rooted in Brazil, and it was critical to the development of Brazilian ideologies concerning the nation and national identity. A brief discussion of these ideologies

helps to locate the issue of contemporary black racism within the broader trajectory of historically documented discourses about race and race mixture.
The development and articulation of the "whitening thesis" among Brazilian
elites of the late nineteenth and early twentieth centuries has been meticu-
lously documented (Skidmore 1993a, 1990; see also, Silva 1989; Seyferth
1985, 1989). Brazil, in addition, had its own eugenics movement; and to a significant extent, the discourses of this movement overlapped with notions of
race and degeneration (Borges 1993; Stepan 1991).

Confronted with, and ideologically vulnerable to, the pseudoscientific
theories of racial superiority/inferiority emanating from the cultural centers of
Europe, Brazilian elites were undermined in their attempts to assert Brazil's
membership within the elect circle of civilized nations. Miscegenation, widely
and openly practiced in Brazil since its inception as a colony of Portugal, was
believed by European, North American, and Latin American elites to lead to
moral, genetic, and physiological degeneracy. The preponderance of both
negros and people of mixed race in the Brazilian population was conceived as
a threat to both national progress and national ethnic or racial unity.

It was in this context that the ideology of branqueamento (also called
embranquecimento), or whitening, and its contradictory ideological corollary,
democracia racial, effloresced. While the belief that the black race was
improved through dilution with white blood, and the notion of the unpreju-
diced "friendly master" predated abolition and the creation of the republic,
such ideas became explicitly codified during this critical moment of nation-
building. Relying on a different, more modern set of theoreticians, and in
response to Brazil's demographic reality, notions of racial degeneracy became
subject to open debate within elite circles. To a very limited extent, the idea
of black inferiority was questioned by a few elites; but more significantly, and
to a far greater degree, the notion of interracial degeneration was challenged.

On the basis of dubious statistics and what Skidmore (1993a) has called
"wishful thinking," a number of Brazilian elites began to argue that the black
population was withering away while the population on a whole was whitening. White blood, many elites came to believe, would triumph over and erase
the negative characteristics carried through undiluted black blood. European
immigration, while directed toward an expected post-abolition labor shortage,
received elite support and governmental subsidization for the additional reason that such immigrants would provide an increased infusion of white blood
(Seyferth 1989). Within a relatively short period of time, it was proposed,
Brazil would become a homogeneous nation of whites. What had previously
been regarded as a fatal and insurmountable weakness of the Brazilian nation
became its strength; continued miscegenation would not only whiten the

population but also operate against the development of the racial antagonism so evident in the United States.

As Skidmore (1993a) has noted, this reversal within elite ideology did not represent a rejection of racist ideologies but rather a compromise with them. Elite public discourses of the era frequently asserted that racial prejudice was relatively absent from Brazil, even while a fear of blackness and a belief in black inferiority were explicitly articulated. In 1899, for example, the noted literary critic José Veríssimo wrote in a newspaper article, "There is no danger . . . that the negro problem will arise in Brazil. Before it could arise it was already resolved by love. Miscegenation has robbed the Negro element of its numerical importance, thinning it down into the white population. . . . As ethnographers assure us, and as can be confirmed at first glance, race mixture is facilitating the prevalence of the superior element. Sooner or later it will perforce eliminate the negro race here" (qtd. in Skidmore 1993a, 73).

Although some writers have suggested that this discourse and the informal and institutional practices associated with it amounted to a genocidal policy (Nascimento 1979), branqueamento was touted by Brazilian elites as a fortuitous inevitability. The celebration of miscegenation as a morally superior and uniquely Brazilian solution, wedded to the notion of democracia racial, was further codified and popularized by Brazil's most famous sociologist, Gilberto Freyre.

The fundamental contradictions within the ideologies of branqueamento and democracia racial, while rarely remarked upon in everyday discourses, have been frequently noted in Brazilianist scholarship. Denise da Silva (1989), for example, has emphasized the fact that the platitudes of democracia racial are conceived in a highly abstract, even mythic way; and as such, they have little bearing, ultimately, on either behavior or social structure. Roberto DaMatta, one of Brazil's preeminent anthropologists, has described *racismo à brasileira* (Brazilian-style racism) as "an ideology which permits the conciliation of a series of contradictory impulses" (1984, 68). These impulses—the simultaneous embracing of the concept of racial mixing and the devaluation of blackness—pervade everyday discourses and social practices.

Scholarly discussions of both branqueamento and democracia racial tend to concern elite constructions of race as they were codified in the late nineteenth and early twentieth centuries. Skidmore's seminal and influential work, for example, focuses exclusively on the "members of a tiny minority that enjoyed the privilege of higher education within this largely illiterate society" (1993a, 218). While it is undoubtedly true that Brazilian elites formulated the whitening thesis in response to the racial preoccupations of Europeans and Americans, the notion of melhorando a raça could not have been a purely elite construction, nor indeed does it seem likely that such a notion would emerge, more or less fully formed, within such a short period of time. Moreover, while Brazilianist scholars associate the celebration of miscegenation and democracia racial with the work of Gilberto Freyre, his work is surely informed as much by what might be called Brazilian "folk" understandings—the historically entrenched public discourses of ordinary Brazilians—as by the intellectual currents of his time.

Color was associated with status and status mobility from the earliest days of the colony, and the notion of a color hierarchy—and its attendant discriminatory practices—certainly predated the Republic (Forbes 1988). The concept of improving the race and the cultural construction of a color hierarchy are more aptly conceptualized not as exclusively elite ideologies, nor even as white ideologies, but as more universally Brazilian ideologies of remarkable durability. Undoubtedly stemming from white power and the onus of slavery, the notion of improving the race was most likely adopted by people of color themselves, as a strategy toward progressive upward mobility (particularly among freemen, who were numerous) during the colonial era. In contemporary terms, the concepts of improving the race, "lightening the family," and "cleaning the color," however contested at times within Morro do Sangue Bom, are nevertheless native to the community (and others like it), and they reflect the yearning to escape from poverty and racism (see Goldstein 1999; Shapiro 1996). Seen in this light, Joia's desire that her husband and her children be lighter than herself was both expectable and understandable.

"The Negro Himself Discriminates against the Other Negro"

There were only a small number of occasions during which people in Morro do Sangue Bom introduced the issue of racism in conversations that were informal and outside of the interview context. Those occasions that did arise, however, were particularly revealing. Several people initiated conversations about the American pop star Michael Jackson. People in my generation were familiar with the Jackson Five, in which Michael Jackson became famous as a teenage vocalist, as well as with his solo career and his rapid climb to superstardom. One day I met Jonas on the steps, and after we exchanged greetings he said, "Can I ask you something? What do you think of Michael Jackson? I remember when he was a kid, in the Jackson Five. You remember?" Jonas continued, "He was negro then, dark, with hard hair. Now he's white. Is he ashamed of being a negro?"

During my fieldwork, Jackson's music video "Black or White" was released, and it was broadcast on national Brazilian television amidst considerable fanfare. The video portrays an unnaturally pale, longhaired Jackson cavorting with a large, multiethnic cast. Nearly everyone I knew had tuned in to watch it. Later, Nestor asked me, "What is that song about?" I told him that Jackson had apparently intended the song as an antiracist statement, and I translated the refrain of the song: "It doesn't matter if you're black or white." "That's just what I thought," Nestor said and added with considerable sarcasm, "If it doesn't matter, then why did he turn himself white?" Jackson had become, it appeared, a race traitor.[1]

In interviews, many volunteered their opinion that Pelé, the internationally renowned Brazilian soccer star, is racist. Later in my fieldwork, I began to ask directly about Pelé, and the responses I heard were remarkably consistent. It appeared that, with only a few exceptions, Pelé, who is arguably Brazil's most famous man of color (and perhaps, internationally, the most famous Brazilian of any color), is reviled by people in Morro do Sangue Bom. I was told that Pelé "stands only for himself" and that "if he wanted to help negros he could, but he chooses not to." The greatest stain on his reputation was his courtship with Xuxa, Brazil's blonde, blue-eyed megastar, as well as his involvement with other white women. "He only goes with blondes, never women of his own color," I was told. Like Michael Jackson, he was viewed as a traitor who denied his race. When I asked why Pelé was only seen with blonde women, several exclaimed, "Because he can, of course!" While he was not excused, the choices Pelé had made, as a man of wealth and prestige, were viewed as predictable and, to an extent, understandable.[2]

Sometimes informants' discussions of black racism revolved around personal experiences; at other times, the issue was discussed more abstractly. Few of my informants, of course, asserted that they themselves favored light skin over dark skin or preferred whites to people of color; Joia's candor in this regard was unusual.

Not surprisingly, a number of the stories I heard that were intended to illustrate black racism concerned name-calling. Analucia, for example, said,

> The funny thing is the negro against the negro. He has prejudice. They say, "Hell, you're a negro, and you want to lower that which is negro?" To debase the other negro—you know how it is? . . . There exists a funny type of policeman. He may not [truly] be against negros, you understand how it is, but the negro [policeman] generally calls the other "crioulo." Do you understand? He calls the other "monkey," while being himself a negro. . . . I don't know, Beth. I don't know if it's in the head of each one. I don't know. I don't think it should exist, prejudice between us, the negro against the negro. . . . They don't want other people to call them "negro" but they insist on

calling others "negro," calling them "monkey," "negão," I don't know what all. . . . Here on the morro I have heard this; it exists.

As I have noted in the previous chapter, Analucia's criticism of black policemen is far from unique. Commenting on his encounter with a black policeman, a young man said, "Here in Brazil, it's true. The black guy wants to trample the other preto. Any black policeman that you see, the majority want to trample the preto." While Analucia, in commenting that the police "may not [truly] be against negros," suggested that racial epithets were more a manner of speaking than the expression of an avowed racist position, others made no such distinction. The use of racist epithets is viewed as diagnostic of genuine racism, which, as many informants pointed out, is paradoxically turned against the self as well as against the raça, or race, as a whole.

Jacinto told me a story about an encounter with black racism on the asfalto. It concerned a dispute between strangers, and like similar stories about the police and others in positions of authority, the conflict seemed to be as much about power as it was about color or race. Of all the stories Jacinto told me, this one was told with the greatest invective, and his narration required very little prompting on my part. Jacinto told me that he had been a trusted employee in a firm he had been working with for two years. He was sent by this firm to deliver a package containing money to a client staying in a hotel in Copacabana:

> When I got to the gate, the security guard was a negro who was [so dark he was] nearly blue. He told me I couldn't go through the social entrance. Why? Because I was a worker, [he told me]. . . . I thought it was an abuse; he was a negro and he didn't let me go through the social entrance. [So I said,] "I'm a worker but I'm not a domestic servant. I've come here on my job. If I don't have the right to go through the social entrance, then I won't deliver the package." "Well, then, you're not going in," [he said to me]. And I said, "Why am I not going in?" And he said, "Stay in your place neguinho (little black one)." He's going to put me in my place, put me in my place as a black worker. So I looked at him like this [and said], "Hey, my friend, what are you? Are you white? Are you something else here? Are you the owner of the hotel? From my point of view, you are a worker also and you are a negro. Why are you discriminating against me?"

Once again, the scenario involved the humiliating request that one use the service rather than the social entrance. Partly because the guard was black, Jacinto challenged him; from his point of view, as he said, they were equals. The guard's use of the word "neguinho" was primarily pragmatic; it referred less to Jacinto's color than to his menial position as a courier vis-à-vis his own more (symbolically) powerful position as a uniformed guard.

It is precisely in this sense that so many informants told me that racism, particularly black racism, "is the person who thinks they are better"—better, often, not in a strictly racial sense but in the sense of authority or what is often called "acquisitive power." Analucia's comment that black police officers who use racial epithets "may not [truly] be against negros" also illustrates the point that the language of race is, in some contexts, primarily pragmatic; the assertion of relative power is articulated through the idiom of race.

Later in the same conversation, Jacinto told me that he thought one of the men associated with the residents' association on the hill was racist. The man he referred to, Helio, was, in fact, one of the very few people I spoke to on the morro who insisted that racism is not a significant problem in Brazil. Jacinto's comments about Helio, and later his own brother, help to further elucidate the commonly articulated notion that black racism is a trait of those who are *ambicioso* (ambitious) and who think they are better:

> Helio, Helio is racist! He doesn't like the negro. Helio discriminates.
> He's up there and he thinks he owns the world. So, he's very
> arrogant. I don't like him. In a party he wants to be the owner of
> everything. Weren't you ever in his house? You didn't notice!? He
> wants to be superior. . . . He keeps talking in the middle of the
> whites. . . . He thinks he's superior to everyone. So, I think it's
> racism. . . . Many people here even say he became a "white negro"—
> meaning he's only a negro in his color, but in his personality, he's
> white. . . . You've seen Michael Jackson? Because he was a negro with
> hard hair, he was with the Jackson Five, completely black. After he
> began to ascend in his life, he began to take baths in milk, to take
> baths in the moon, I don't know what! . . . So, it's this. I think that
> when a person of color, right, preto, negro, begins to go up, he
> forgets. The very negro who helped him, when he [succeeds], he
> forgets. My own brother is racist. . . . The day he becomes someone,
> if he should get there as a musician, if he succeeds, he is going to
> forget us. He is already racist.

I knew that Jacinto's disapproval of the behavior of these two men was shared by others on the morro. While I had never attributed their behavior to racism, I, too, had noticed an arrogant aloofness in these men, an apparent disdain for others that was perceptibly at odds with local etiquette. My being white did not, in fact, afford me respectful treatment from them. What these comments suggest is that for many in Morro do Sangue Bom, black racism, perhaps to a greater extent than white racism, is not merely a matter of color prejudice but is conceived as a way of behaving that deliberately sets one apart from and "above" others in the community.

Although it has been argued that there is very little or no race consciousness among people of color in Brazil, my informants' comments reveal the existence of an expectation of solidarity among people of color. This expectation extends well beyond the community of the morro. Jacinto evidently expected the black doorman to recognize a kind of shared identity—both in color and in social location—that would lead to a subversion of the assumptions and authoritarian practices associated with the distinction between social and service entrances. When his expectations were disappointed, he insisted on the equality—and racial sameness—between himself and the guard. Racist mistreatment at the hands of black officers, no matter how common, still evokes a special kind of outrage. People expressed disappointment in Pelé in terms that were almost personal. "He doesn't care about us down here," I was told. Michael Jackson's foreign lyrics are understood by very few poor Brazilians of color, yet his color-shifting trajectory, well-known to everyone in my own generation, is described in terms of a clear betrayal of people of color everywhere.

On the surface, it would appear that there is little justification for speaking of a "black community" in Brazil. The distinctly American expression is a political one, and it is predicated, among other things, on historically situated and highly public antiracist movements, and discourses that support and constitute a shared sense of cultural distinctiveness. As I have noted, few people in Morro do Sangue Bom are even aware of either historical or contemporary Brazilian black movements; and as this chapter demonstrates, black racism is, according to my informants, pervasive. Yet it is precisely the way stories of black racism are narrated that suggests a set of underlying assumptions and expectations—about black solidarity—that belie the notion that there is no race consciousness, no sense of a black identity, no sense of a larger community among Brazilians of color. Although the sections that follow focus primarily on tensions surrounding race and color within the morro community and within families, it is important to remember that the preoccupation with, and distress over, black racism attests to the fact that value is, indeed, given to black solidarity—and this value can incorporate not only local, but transnational perspectives.

The Internalization of Racism

Tiago, as I noted in the previous chapter, first defined racismo (racism) as "those who don't like themselves." Tiago was certainly not alone in his awareness of the ideological entanglement and psychological damage that racism enacts against the self. Many adults on the morro suggested that negros *tem vergonha da raça*, or feel shame over their race, or, as Angela, Jorge's wife, tried to explain, they have *raiva*, or rage, over "their own color."

When I asked Jacinto why, in his words, "some negros discriminate against other negros," he articulated a psychological (or even psychoanalytic) explanation. Like Angela, he referred to the concept of raiva:

> The negro can't—he can't be someone. The negro can't rise in life. . . . Or when he begins to rise—even when he is your equal, he begins to trample those below, to become prejudiced. He is preto, but he has everything the white has. So, he thinks he is white. He doesn't like the other negro. He is a racist, and not even his mirror tells him [who he is]—because he has rage against the race (*tem raiva da raça*). Like, he has rage against his own color. Sometimes that climate inside the home—he has rage against his father and his mother for being negro, for putting him in the world of the negro. So he dismisses them.

Jacinto's scenario is reminiscent of Frantz Fanon's anguished descriptions of colonized consciousness, in which "a Negro is forever in combat with his own image" (Fanon 1967, 194). Many of the narratives quoted in this chapter, in fact, invite comparison with Fanon and W.E.B. Du Bois (e.g., 1961) and the psychological literature on what has been called "black self hatred"—literature initiated by Kenneth B. Clark in the late 1930s (e.g., Clark 1939, 1940, 1947, 1950)—and, additionally, with more recent debates on African American identity and self-esteem (see especially, Cross 1991). Although the work of Clark and others has fallen out of favor among scholars because its focus on the psychology of the oppressed appears to "blame the victim" (Cross 1991), my informants in Morro do Sangue Bom emphasized the very real quandaries one faces in negotiating one's way through a cultural world in which blackness is denigrated, even while silence about the existence of racism is pervasive. History, as both a cultural and a structural force, as well as the yearning for progressive upward mobility (rather than a concept of individual psychopathology) were often called to account for these quandaries. As Angela explained,

> There are people who don't like themselves, who have shame—because the negro was a slave. You know, so they are ashamed of this. . . . There are many negros who don't marry negra women, of their own color. They prefer white women, blondes, you know? An aunt of mine, in fact, said that she had to "lighten the family," you know? To marry a white, because some preto would darken the

family, you know? This to me is offensive. I feel offended, you know? Because to me, this is racism. . . . Because she isn't giving value to her color, I mean, because I think that a racist preto is devaluing his color, so I don't think it's cool, you know? If I am born a negro, I have to adjust to and to adore my color, right?

Angela's comment that being "born a negro" requires that one "adjust to" one's color is particularly telling. Racism is a feature of history and of the cultural environment, and its constant reproduction in the everyday discourses of racial hierarchy, Angela suggested, places profound burdens on the self. As Angela was herself aware, children of color confront a peculiar crossroad in which they overhear and reproduce racialized insults—and a host of other negative discursive constructions (e.g., "He is black, but he's a nice guy")—at the same time that they are more explicitly taught the prescriptive tenets of democracia racial. Angela was understandably troubled by the fact that her eldest daughter had begun to reproduce racist discourse:

It's because she listens. A lot of people talk. Because there are many black people here who say, "Oh, I don't like pretos." Sometimes it's joking; they're talking by the [open] window [as children are passing by]. Sometimes it's just playing [like when people yell], "Get out of here! I don't like pretos!" So, you know, [my daughter] remembers it like that and then she says it. I am not going to let her grow up with [that idea of] "I don't like pretos." She would become a racist, and I don't want that because she is preta, I am preta, her father is preto, her grandparents are pretos. She has heard things like, "I've never seen a white doing this, only the negro does this," so she says, "I don't like pretos." So she begins to devalue her own color.

Angela's description, I believe, is an accurate account of the discursive processes whereby children both passively internalize and, at the same time, perhaps, learn to actively negotiate among a variety of contradictory registers about race and its meanings. Angela's awareness of, and parental concern about, children's tendency to overhear and reproduce (or even magnify) racist ideas was shared by some other parents. When I interviewed Varena, she told me that when she was fourteen, she was courting a dark-skinned boy. Her mother, who is very dark, as is Varena, said to her, "What are you doing with that negro, with that monkey!" (Racist comments are sometimes entirely explicit and direct.) Immediately after telling me this, Varena added, "You know, Beth, we have a racist in the family." I thought she was referring to her mother, but she added that her eight-year-old daughter, Lucinda, was racist. "She says that she only likes whites, that she doesn't like black boys, things like that." Varena suggested that I interview Lucinda.

When I asked Lucinda if she preferred that her playmates be of one or another color, she replied that any color was fine with her. She evidently understood that her previous remarks, which her mother had overheard, were, while common enough within her surroundings, somehow not entirely acceptable—or were not acceptable, at any rate, in the context in which she articulated them. At the age of eight, she had learned two different discourses about race, one that denigrated blackness and gave more value to whiteness and one that insisted that all people are equal.

What I have described as a quandary is, of course, a circular process involving public and private, cultural and psychological, and political and ideological components. Brazil's racially bifurcated structure—in which children such as Tiago and Lucinda, as well as adults, struggle with issues of identity, exclusion, solidarity, and self-alienation—is the ultimate source of this quandary. It is the concrete, structural association between blackness and poverty, between color and oppression, between the history of enslavement and the contemporary, quotidian manifestations of political and economic marginalization upon which internalized racism and racist discourse most fully rest, rather than upon individualized consciousness or psychopathology. To describe internalized racism, as my informants did, is not to "blame the victim" but to explicitly identify individual selves, families, and subaltern communities as permeable sites (rather than sources) into which racism, as both a structural and an ideological force, penetrates.

When I interviewed Roberta, a woman in her late twenties, she described racism very generally and told me that people "do not valorize the negro." "Who doesn't?" I asked her. "Are you speaking generally?" She replied, "In general. We ourselves. You grow up in society, with this idea. If you encounter a man on a dark street at night, you feel a certain fear. If you see a white man, who is well dressed, oh, then it's fine, right? But if you see a negro, you think he is a bandit, a mugger, and you become afraid. But why? Because you grow up with this idea in your head. It passes [to you] from society."

I asked Roberta if everyone had these ideas in their heads or if they were more common among whites than among people of color. She continued, "No, everyone! Everyone is racist! The Brazilian people are very racist! We ourselves are. It is unfortunate, but it is so. . . . You have the idea in your head. You grow up with this, without even wanting to. Shit! It's the society!"

In Roberta's account, which I believe is an accurate one, racist ideas are not bounded; they are internalized by all Brazilians, regardless of class or color. As Roberta's anguished comments make clear, Brazilians of color are, of course, confronted with psychological burdens and ideological quandaries to which white Brazilians—by virtue of being, as it were, the privileged racial "norm"—are not subject. At the same time, people like Roberta and her neighbors on the hill are better positioned to experience the insight that the concept of racial inferiority is a false idea, but yet "you grow up with this idea in your head." As is the case with all internalized beliefs that are damaging to self and community, there is, as Roberta suggested, a struggle between those ideas that have been inculcated since early childhood and the insight that those ideas are a product of oppression. Whether we call it low self-esteem, internalized racism, or ideas in your head, Roberta's point that "it's the society" is surely the most critical one to make about that struggle.

Racism in the Community

At times, informants themselves brought up the issue of racism within the morro community, but I sometimes asked directly if this was perceived as an issue. Many people told me that racism did exist on the morro and provided examples, yet these examples often had a vagueness that other types of narratives did not.

As Angela told me, racist comments are certainly heard on the morro. "Sometimes people are joking," she said. "[But] you can't see if the person is serious or not." Such equivocal responses were common, and others besides Angela suggested that it was often difficult to distinguish real racism from brincadeira, or joking. This fact is partly due, I believe, to the neighborly ethos that characterizes everyday life on the morro. While the morro is plagued by the same kinds of interpersonal conflicts and tensions that visit any small, tightly knit, and economically stressed community, people prefer to emphasize união, or union. My question about racism on the morro, while recognized as a legitimate and important one, involved the risk of fomenting unfavorable and potentially wounding gossip. Although a number of people referred to specific neighbors, I did not press for more details than those that were readily provided, and I never revealed such details to others.

When I asked nineteen-year-old Tomas about racism on the morro, his response, while somewhat more favorable than those of most, was revealing: "That which exists is little. It doesn't do to distrust people, because each is the neighbor of the other. And the majority is very much of color, right? . . . So, there is very little [racism]. There are people here who come to be racist when one is darker than the other. Or those with money who live in suffering together with us. There is this. He who can buy something better, a color television, or can buy a secondhand car, which is neither bad nor good, he thinks he's better than the other. But the majority is really of color."

Tomas is correct in his characterization of the hill as composed mostly of people of color; approximately one-quarter identify themselves as white while the remainder identify themselves as of color. Stories that concerned the racism of particular individuals who resided on the morro were about equally divided between those that accused whites and those that accused people of color.

Analucia was one of the informants who brought up the issue of racism on the morro without prompting. She referred to a specific individual: "My neighbor here in back [of my house] doesn't like negros. . . . So my husband even came to the point of discussing it with her, because she said, 'If it were up to me, I would kill everyone who is a negro.' That one who lives here behind me! She said it to another neighbor. Jair [my husband] is a negro and she told [my other neighbor] that she would kill everyone who is negro!"

Rosa and her husband told me, "There are many people here on the morro who don't like pretos." They described a white neighbor who openly announced her prejudice. Rosa's husband told me that he conversed with the woman when he encountered her on the steps and paths that traverse the morro but that he did not trust her. "You have to talk with everyone, right?" Rosa said, referring to the morro's neighborly ethos. Nevertheless, others were aware of the woman's racism, and Rosa told me, "No one likes her."

A sense of betrayal is evident in these comments. When the racism of whites on the morro is described, betrayal is not linked to a sense of shared race but to community and class and, more broadly, to the prescriptive tenets of democracia racial. As one informant said, commenting on the racism of white families on the hill, "Why don't they go live on Avenida Atlantica?" The reference is to Copacabana's main thoroughfare, which continues to be associated with wealth and glamour and, by extension, with whiteness. "Why doesn't she go live down below?" Rosa said of her neighbor. Such comments are sarcastic, of course, and they refer, in an ironic fashion, to the shared poverty and class status of all who live on the hill.

Although Rosa and her husband refrained from naming the person to whom they referred, I later came to suspect that it was Dona Elza, one of the few white people I managed to interview on the morro. While only in her early fifties, she was always addressed as "Dona," a formal term rarely used for those on the morro who have not yet advanced well beyond middle age. Dona Elza had emigrated to Rio from the state of Minas Gerais some twenty years before, and she still nursed a passion to purchase a house in her hometown, where, she told me, there were "almost no pretos." Like others who immigrated to the morro, Dona Elza told me that when she first arrived, she "suffered from hunger." She had spent her entire adult life working as an empregada.

Later in our interview, I asked Dona Elza if she thought there were any differences between people of color and whites. She lowered her voice to a whisper: "I think so; I think so. They are gross. They are gross. They are badly brought up. They don't like themselves. They don't like themselves and they don't like us. If they were—I don't like pretos. Very, very preto, who really have the color, you know? That really preto one, it's impossible to understand him." I asked Dona Elza to explain why, in her opinion, these differences existed. She continued, "I don't know. Because they have—because we—who knows—you can see that in jobs, no one wants people of color. My father was terrified [by people of color]. My father, in that time, way back . . . in that time people would come to the house of [my father's father] and they would say, 'Senhor Branco (Mr. White), may I come in?' So, my grandfather would say, 'You may come in,' if they spoke humbly. Now, these days, these days, they are very rude. They are arrogant. And it's just too much. My father also didn't like them, no."

Dona Elza's presumption of a white superiority is very evident here. That she suffered the same hardship as did most of her neighbors—both in the process of moving to the city of Rio from the countryside and in her continued poverty and grueling profession as an empregada—did not seem to enter her equation of her own status vis-à-vis her darker neighbors. Her expectation that others address her formally as "Dona" and use the formal "a senhora" rather than the more common "você" became much clearer to me after our interview. Her central complaint about people of color appeared to be their failure to accord her the special respect she felt she was due as a white woman.

As I had with many other informants on the morro, I asked Dona Elza if she had ever heard people talking about slavery when she was growing up, and she told me, "Yes. They worked. . . . That business of the whip, they had to have respect, no matter what. Now, no. Now it's the biggest abuse! I don't trust them. Some treat you better, right, but it's hard to find [such people]. It's hard."

I asked Dona Elza if her mother also had a terror of people of color, and she said, "My mother wasn't very—well, she didn't complain [about pretos]. [Her father] was quite moreno; he wasn't preto, but he was moreno, so she had no way of speaking, right?" Dona Elza's laughter was tinged with embarrassment. When I asked her if her father had forbidden her to date men of color, she gave me a surprised look and exclaimed, "No, it wasn't necessary!" I asked her if her husband, from whom she was estranged, shared her feelings, and she told me, "He thinks this. He thinks the same thing."

At the conclusion of our interview, I asked Dona Elza if she had anything else to add to her comments about relations between whites and people of color, and she repeated, in slightly different terms, her complaint about their lack of humility and respect: "As I told you, they don't like whites." I asked her why she felt this way, if a person of color had ever spoken to her aggressively or treated her in an overtly rude fashion. She continued in a whisper, "No, it's just the disrespect they have for us, so we are knowing they are different. It's the way the preto treats us. . . . Inside the bus [for example], there are people of such bad character that I am afraid to look in their faces! I have a terror of even looking in their faces. Some whites are bad too, but they are imitating [the preto]."

I was confused and upset after my departure from Dona Elza's house. I was acquainted with her through several friends, including Joia and Elena, both of whom were Dona Elza's next-door neighbors. While neither considered her a truly close friend, both were very cordial with her and invited her to parties. Several weeks before our interview, Dona Elza had, in fact, gone to the birthday party of Elena's husband, José. She sat quietly by herself and did not samba on the verandah with the other guests. Her husband, who reportedly shared her prejudice, worked as a carpenter for Joia's husband, who had hired him, over a long term, to help him reconstruct his and Joia's home. When he became extremely ill and bedridden, it was Joia who took him covered plates of hot food and urged him to build up his strength and see a doctor.

As Rosa and her husband had explained, "You have to talk to everyone," even, they suggested, people like Dona Elza. Or, as Tomas told me, "It doesn't do to distrust people, because each is the neighbor of the other." Such sentiments and the cordial behavior associated with them appear to override, in most ordinary contexts at least, the kinds of confrontations and social distancing that the expression of attitudes such as Dona Elza's might otherwise be expected to produce. Evidently, both Dona Elza's views and the dislike that some of her neighbors felt for her remained submerged, for the most part, beneath the surface of the routinely polite exchanges that characterize social interaction on the morro. That such would be the case in a community whose members both avoid discussions of racism and eschew overt confrontation generally is not surprising. Yet, as several informants told me, "everyone knows."

Jacinto also reported that on the morro "there are many people who say they don't like negros." He told me about a particular individual who had a reputation for being racist. Married to a white man, she herself was what Jacinto called a negra: "She talks, talks loudly, for everyone to hear, that she doesn't like pretos and she doesn't like the morro. And the person who fed her and brought her up was a negra, a true negra with hard hair—that's who took care of her. Her mother is white and her father was moreno. But no, she doesn't like pretos."

I knew that the woman Jacinto referred to was a close friend of his mother, Dona Janete. They were so close, in fact, that when the woman and her husband succeeded in realizing their long-held ambition of moving into a middle-class apartment, they sold their morro home to Dona Janete and her family for a very low, nominal price.

A number of researchers involved with the UNESCO (United Nations Educational, Scientific, and Cultural Organization) studies of the 1950s suggested that while Brazilians engage in overtly racist discourses, such discourses have little bearing on "social behavior" (Wagley 1963b, 126). Such notions underestimate the multidimensional significance of discourse (itself erroneously defined as somehow distinct from behavior) and ignore the innumerable scenarios in which racially motivated discrimination (as opposed to "mere prejudice") occurs in both formal and informal contexts in Brazil. Nevertheless, the general observation that those (of whatever color) who participate in racist discourses may have cordial and even intimate relationships with people of color remains ethnographically accurate.

To suggest, as the UNESCO researchers did, that discourse, or culturally patterned verbal behavior, is insignificant vis-à-vis supposedly more genuine and meaningful face-to-face cordiality or, alternatively, that racist comments reveal true attitudes that belie more superficial behaviors is, I believe, to miss the point. While my informants were themselves naturally concerned with the notion of what they call the reality—what people really think and who they are deep, deep down—there is, theoretically speaking, little in the way of secure grounds for claiming the static primacy of one tendency over the other within the flow of quotidian interactions such as those that occur in Morro do Sangue Bom. Both participation in racist discourses and cordiality are genuine, meaningful, and context-driven, and both remain open, as the above narratives suggest, to a variety of interpretations and responses. Jacinto was incensed by his neighbor's declarations of racism, and his description of her coldhearted betrayal was vivid. Wary always of fomenting gossip and ill-feeling, I did not discuss the issue with Dona Janete, yet I do not doubt that she would have defended her friend, perhaps by suggesting that she made such racist comments in brincadeira, or joking, or by saying that it was "just her way of talking."

Overtly racist comments, moreover, may be, in some contexts, relatively easy to overlook because they are situated within a broader discursive tendency to devalue blackness. Everyday discourse, both on the morro and on the asphalt, as I have noted in chapter 2, is replete with such locutions as, "He is very dark, but he's a nice guy," or, "She is a pretinha, but she is pretty," or, alternatively, "He is a negro, but he is honest." The possibility of deeply divergent interpretations and the multiplicity of contexts in which both racism and cordiality are practiced reveal the complex and fundamentally ambivalent character of racial ideologies and discourses in Brazil.

Race and Color in Courtship and Marriage

Joia's candid acknowledgment that she consciously sought to marry a man lighter than herself may have been unusual, yet the notion of *clareando a familia,* or lightening the family, is a thoroughly familiar one in Morro do Sangue Bom. While most of my informants professed themselves to be against such a notion, a number of people, particularly women, told me that they had been exhorted to seek lighter partners by their mothers or other relatives. What emerged in my interviews was a picture of contradictory yearnings, fears, and assumptions about race and color as they relate to courtship, marriage, and children. While much Brazilian scholarly and popular literature would lead one to believe that marriage between people of different colors is not only considered natural and without significant conflict, but is, in fact, celebrated, my informants suggested that the issue (and the experience) can be saturated with social and emotional difficulty and danger. Such difficulty may be described as occurring within the ostensibly private intimacy of a heterosexual relationship; but, more commonly, the objections of parents, of the community, or of society are called to account for conflicts between women and men of different colors.

It is evident that in the arenas of courtship and marriage, color differences, and not merely the differences between the bipolar extremes of black and white, do, in fact, become significant—despite the coexisting claim that all people of color are members of the *raça negra,* or black race, and are thus equal. The phenotypical differences between Joia and Daniel, which I had at first failed to recognize as notable, were in fact significant enough for Daniel to become, in Joia's eyes, an especially attractive mate—and significant enough in the eyes of Daniel's mother to make Joia an especially unattractive daughter-in-law. In the arenas of courtship and marriage, it appears, the notion that all Brazilians of African descent are negros and thus equal is sometimes suspended.

To a certain extent, the issue of mixed marriage and courtship is influenced by stereotypical notions about sex, sexuality, and race, yet my informants neither indulged in nor talked about such stereotypes as much as the literature on race and racism in Brazil would lead one to expect. None of my informants introduced such stereotypes in interviews, and while this may have been the result of etiquette, I was left with the impression that they were entertained neither as seriously nor as obsessively as many publicists and interpreters of Brazilian culture (including anthropologists) would suggest.

Dona Janete, however, was well aware of such stereotypes, and she believed they influenced heterosexual relations.[3] Our interview was somewhat unusual in that I invited Dona Janete to comment on sexual stereotypes to a greater degree than I had with most of my other informants. Our conversation thus focused more on her general impressions of the roles of race and color in relations between men and women than it did on her personal experience. I began by asking her, however, if her parents or others had ever given her specific encouragement in seeking a white husband. She replied, "No, I never felt that they did. What was important was a good worker. I never sought wealth, but, thank God, I have never gone hungry." I asked her, "And this thing of marriage more generally, do you think there can be problems in a marriage between a person who is lighter and a person who is darker?" Dona Janete paused and began, "Yes. For the most part, no. Well, I haven't had [problems]. Thank God, up to now, I haven't had [problems]. When [my husband] says something to me, it is in joking. But it exists. There are [problems] in the home. Sometimes the woman has a good job and the guy takes advantage of the escurinha (little dark woman). He doesn't work."

I asked Dona Janete if white men were more likely to engage in this sort of exploitation than black men, and she answered in the affirmative. She had illustrated the notion that black women are viewed as workhorses (whose labor is exploited by whites), and I pursued the issue of such stereotypes by asking, "And what about the idea of the mulata?"

"The mulata is first in everything," Dona Janete responded. "The mulata here has rights. You don't see a mulata who is lost. . . . She is always accompanied by a good gentleman. . . . The white men, they look more for the mulata . . . because they are pretty, they samba, they have more opportunity, more of everything." I asked Dona Janete if this might be a kind of sexual exploitation, and she responded, "It could be also, this could be the case—because the heart of another is such that no one can enter it. Here they are with the mulata, but out there in front, they're with a blonde. [Laughter] He marries the blonde, but in the place of samba he is with the mulata. So the mulata must be exploited, right? Because these men [go out] with them [and] they naturally dump the mulata at the exit later."

I began to ask Dona Janete, "And this blonde, is she also courting?" She interrupted,

No, none of that. It's very rare, very rare to encounter a blonde with a dark man. You encounter more often a mulata with a white man. In my going through life, I have seen the mulata with the white man much more than a white woman with a mulato man, right? I think the woman has more—she is more exploited. She also wants it. Or rather, she doesn't want the negro, right? The mulata herself doesn't want the negro. It's very rare. When you see a blonde with a dark man, she must not be from here, from Rio, or she isn't Brazilian. I've seen a lot of this. They aren't Brazilians, they come from outside to be with a dark man. The dark men, they have shame. They're too timid to seek a white woman. They are restricted from seeking a white woman.

In many senses Dona Janete had reproduced the familiar discourse on the white man's pursuit of the beautiful mulata, the mulata's rejection of black men in her pursuit of a prestigious white partner, and the foreigner's pursuit of black Brazilian sexual partners. Like many stereotypes, such notions are, in fact, played out, to some extent, in observable behavior in Rio de Janeiro— which is, arguably, the national epicenter of these particular stereotypes. An extremely important issue remains largely implicit in Dona Janete's comments: the fact that such stereotypical notions and the patterns of behavior associated with them bring class as well as color into play. The white man who marries the blonde while courting the mulata has more money. The dark man she refers to is of a lower class than the blonde woman, and his shame is related to class as well as to color.

In reality, cross-class courtship appears to be rare in the lives of people in Morro do Sangue Bom. While I knew that some domestic servants had had sexual encounters (apparently both coercive and consensual) with their white middle-class patrões, such relationships were, with very rare exceptions, concealed by the men and never even emerged into what Dona Janete called "the place of samba."[4]

The marital trajectories of people within Dona Janete's own network (as well as her own marriage) contradicted her comments, and many of these trajectories were informed by a far more complicated set of racial assumptions than her astute but brief summary of classic stereotypes allowed for. Her own son, Jacinto, for example, far from being too ashamed to approach a white woman, was married to Marlene, a branca who was born and raised on the hill.

Although of different colors, Jacinto and Marlene shared the same class background. Their courtship, which occurred about eight years before the period of my fieldwork, had caused considerable discord within Marlene's family. Marlene is what many would be apt to call *branca mesma*, or really white, as is her entire family, which includes seven siblings. Like Jacinto's parents, her mother and father were born in the state of Minas Gerais and had come to live on the morro before Marlene was born. At the time of our interview, Marlene's father had been deceased for several years and her mother suffered from Alzheimer's disease.

When I asked Marlene about racism, she told me about her own family: "Yes, my parents. So, they were racist, you know? Prejudice against people. They said that the children, that their grandchildren would be completely black. They said, 'What neguinhos they will be!' They were racist, my father and my mother. They said I should get a white husband. So, when I began to go out with [Jacinto], they never liked him, right, because of [his] color. But I said, 'I don't see it like that. I like him and his color doesn't make any difference.' But they stayed against it, right? Because of color."

I asked Marlene if there had ever been an open dispute between Jacinto and her parents, and she continued, "No, [Jacinto and my parents] never fought, you know? I argued with them over color. But they never fought. They would always throw it in my face: 'That guy is preto!' You know? But [Jacinto and my parents] never fought; they just said it to me. [They said to me,] 'You have to look for a better person,' right, 'a white person, because the preto, when he doesn't shit on entering, he shits while leaving,' right? But [color] has nothing to do with it."

Marlene went on to tell me that she had been the first in her family to marry a preto. Later, five of her siblings married people of color. When I asked Marlene if her parents had come to accept her marriage to Jacinto and their grandchildren, she answered equivocally, "Well, there was no way, there was nothing they could do about it."

In a separate interview, Jacinto also told me about the courtship: "Her mother and father, well, her father died, but he was racist. Oh, they didn't like me, no! And when we started to go out together, her mother said, 'You're going to marry a negro! You're going to dirty the family! You're going to go hungry!' . . . Never in front of me, no, only behind my back." I asked Jacinto how his mother, Dona Janete, had handled the situation: "My mother always liked [Marlene] but she was like, a little nervous because of that business. [She said,] 'If [Marlene's mother] doesn't like you, let it go, give it up.' I said, 'No, Mom, she doesn't like me but I am going to marry [Marlene], and later, the family will come to respect me.' She thinks what I think now. She was never against Marlene. She was worried because of that business, that I would get married and they would mistreat me because they didn't like me. All mothers worry, right? Because of color, because of color."

These narratives suggest that some white parents in Morro do Sangue Bom are outraged when their children fail to choose mates from among the relatively few white families in the community. Nearly all the people I knew who were of my own generation had married within the community; in this sense, Marlene's trajectory was typical. Jacinto's parents—themselves a mixed couple—were steady, full-time workers until Dona Janete's disabling stroke. As Dona Janete said herself, they were poor but they "never went hungry," and they were known for their generosity, amiability, and humor. Despite the good reputation of Jacinto's family, Marlene's parents predicted doom and the racial "dirtying" of the family.

Susana, Joia's half-sister, also had a great deal to say about relationships between men and women of different colors. Our interview began with a story about a friend and neighbor of hers whom she called a mulata. Her friend was twenty-three and had been dating a twenty-four-year-old man who was darker than herself. Susana said, "I have a friend and she likes a dark guy. And the mother doesn't. [My friend] is a mulata. And the mother [said], 'Why did you choose a negro man?' She is mulata, and the mother also. He is super dark, quite dark. So, the mother, I think she has [racism]. So, she gave him the boot and it ended. It ended because the mother wanted it to. . . . [The daughter] was wanting to marry him, she liked him very much, but the mother wouldn't permit it." I asked Susana why the woman was, in her opinion, so disapproving of the courtship. She continued, "I don't know. It could happen that later there would be children and the children would come out preto, you understand? . . . So, I think that's it, that she didn't want to have preto grandchildren. . . . And she likes pretos, the daughter. But her mother has this thing in her head. She might converse with me because I am an acquaintance, right, but perhaps she doesn't like me very much because of my color. But she doesn't want [pretos] in the family!"

Susana herself is married to a white man. I asked Susana if she thought the kind of discord over mixed relationships that she had described was common, and she responded, "No. If my mother-in-law didn't like me, she wouldn't have given me this house. I've never had problems with his family." It is no doubt true that many such relationships are permitted to develop without interference, yet in the midst of our interview, Susana recalled an experience from her own youth:

> Oh! I had a boyfriend whose mother didn't like me. His mother beat him so he would leave me! He was lighter, from the north. And his mother didn't like me. She liked me for friendship, but as a daughter-in-law, no, no! She beat him! So I left him. He said to me, "Shit, my mother keeps fighting with me over my relationship with you." So, I left him. I was nineteen. . . . I felt humiliated, humiliated, down low! I felt really low. Shit, because of my color!? I am human, right? . . . I

told my mother. She said I should leave him. If [his mother] didn't want it, I should leave him, so I left him. . . . But he was so good!

Although public discourses repeatedly affirm the notion that Brazilians are all mixed, that interracial relationships are common, approved, and even celebrated, and that the members of Brazilian families span the color spectrum, all of these narratives suggest a set of contrary assumptions that generate discord within the community. Conjugal relationships between men and women of different colors may not only raise a few eyebrows but may provoke censure and harassment.

As she had for other topics, Analucia commented on the issue of interracial relationships in a particularly cogent and epigrammatic manner:

> There are problems because of prejudice. No one accepts it. The prejudice that the white has about marrying a negro, they think it's a mixing of races. . . . Most whites don't accept the negro because of prejudice. And there are many who like negros but they can't marry negros because of the society. Because it is the society that discriminates. Do you understand? When you marry a negro [people say], "Oh, this fool is going to marry a negro!" So there comes a time when you are uncomfortable in sleeping with a negro. And it is society that makes you uncomfortable. And you can see that there are many couples in which a preto is married to a white. And [these whites] are discriminated against because they are married to negros. . . . Do you understand? I mean, [they say,] "Why is that white woman going to accept him?". . . There's a lot of this. You know, I myself have a friend who says she has never courted a negro, nor married a negro, because of the prejudice. Other people don't accept it. I myself, when I was courting my husband, [people said,] "What is this, girl? That negão, you're going to marry that ugly negão?"

Such narratives suggest what might be called Romeo and Juliet scenarios in which impassioned couples see beyond color and attempt to weather the storms of familial and community censure, or the disapproval of society. They may succeed, as did Marlene and Jacinto, or such relationships may collapse under the weight of a mother's pressure, as happened in Susana's youthful romance. In some cases, however, it may not be outside pressures alone that impart a fragility to romantic relationships between women and men of different colors; more private conflicts can occur. In my interview with Rosa, I broached the topic of such relationships by asking, "Do you think that marriage between white and black—?" Before I could finish, Rosa replied:

Doesn't go well. There are problems. My nephew courted and
married a girl who is light like you. Oh, she fought with him. She
threw right in his face [words like] "monkey," "crioulo," you
know. . . . They stayed together for more or less a year, truly married.
After that, it was hell—throwing things in his face, calling him a
crioulo. She began to betray him with a boy of her own color and
then she left him. Her family spoke against him and she herself spoke
against him. So, this experience is in my family. I think that preto
and white doesn't work, you know, because of this. Not all of them,
there some whites who marry pretos and it's fine. But most are going
to throw it in your face, just like that girl. . . . So, I think that to
marry, you have to marry one of your own color. Because most black
and white couples separate, they don't stay married for very long.
Because there is always something to throw in the other's face. "Why
did I marry you? You are preto!" You know, always some little thing.
So, in my opinion, it doesn't go well.

In saying that "there is always something to throw in the other's face,"
Rosa suggested that mixed marriages tend to be fragile not because of racial differences that are somehow inherent or natural but because what may begin as
a relatively ordinary marital squabble may come to be articulated within a
vicious racial idiom.[5] Because racist epithets and the familiar assumptions on
which they draw their power resonate so deeply, one imagines that neither
love, nor passion, nor affection can long survive such an assault. While Rosa's
close-up view of a marriage gone awry and her inclination to generalize may
have led to her to an unusually pessimistic view of such relationships, all of the
narratives I have quoted suggest that underneath the public surface of roman-
ticized visions of interracial love, there are stories of interracial wounding.

This does not mean, of course, that all such relationships are doomed
(despite Rosa's comments to the contrary); nor, indeed, does it mean that
Brazilians' vision of themselves as antiracist is pure mythology. The celebration of miscegenation is culturally meaningful and it does allow a space—
which is supported by the rhetoric of democracia racial—in which many
people of different colors can achieve intimacy and form durable relationships. Yet they do so in a cultural context of mixed messages and, potentially,
deeply personal danger. It is no wonder that Jacinto said, "All mothers worry,
right?"

As I suggested in the introduction to this section, such mixed messages
and conflicts are not limited to courtship and marriage between whites and
people of color. As in Joia's case, there may be conflicts between people who

are da raça, or of the race, yet of different skin colors and hair types. The notions of "lightening the family" and "improving the race" frame color and not merely race as significant attributes in a mate.

Branqueamento, the idea of progressive lightening, inevitably pits people of color against one another as well as against whites; such an ambition suggests a kind of game in which there are winners and losers. While José Veríssimo, a turn-of-the-century literary critic, argued that "the white man, harboring no illusions and with some insignificant exceptions, welcomes, esteems, and joins with" people of color (qtd. in Skidmore 1993a, 73), it is evident that not only whites but also some Brazilians of African descent have a tendency to reject potential partners who are dark-skinned. Just as those who are darker may cherish the notion of lightening the family through succeeding generations, so whites and lighter-skinned people of color hope to maintain their "white blood" or continue the lightening process. While many Brazilians say that "negros are attracted to whites and whites are attracted to negros," the hyper-valuation of whiteness tends to prevail, especially in relation to marriage and family. Those who are darker may thus be vulnerable to the discourses that emphasize a hierarchy of color and encourage lightening, yet they are likely to be rejected by the very people such discourses urge them to pursue.

Although the notions of lightening the family, improving the race, and cleaning the color are familiar to everyone in Morro do Sangue Bom, it must be noted in concluding that they do not always go unchallenged. In my interview with Paulinho, he included the following description as one of many he used to illustrate the pervasiveness of racism:

> And another example was with a friend of mine, right, a preta woman. Her daughter was courting a white boy. And she said it like this: "Paulinho, thank God, my daughter is going to marry a white man to clean the color." [And I said,] "To clean the color?! No, my dear! Our color is clean! She is going to marry the guy because she really likes the guy! Do you understand? I don't think you have to clean the color. There is no such thing as 'cleaning the color.' The color of the white is clean and the color of the preto is also clean. . . . There's no preto; there's no white; there's no moreno; there's no pardo; there's no mulato. Do you understand?" . . . This is what I said to her.

What merits emphasis here is less the fact that Paulinho and his friend disagreed, and disagreed fundamentally, about the meaning of race, but that their argument proceeded according to discursive formulations that were very familiar and deeply resonant to both. Both drew from discursive universes that offer ready-made vocabularies and narratives that support both racist and antiracist ideologies.

"We Had Poverty, as God Wills It": Racism in the Family

One would like to assume that when women and men of different colors begin living together and have children, the censure of relatives, if it has been expressed, ceases and is replaced if not by complete approval, then at least by acceptance. Marlene's mother's compromised mental state did not allow one to determine whether or not she had warmed to her grandchildren, who looked, as some people said, "moreno, like little Indians." For the most part, I believe that familial bonds and interdependence tend to supersede the more extreme forms of concern over color. This is not, however, always the case.

An articulated acknowledgment of color differences within families definitely occurs, and such color differences are the rule rather than the exception. Although parents tend to say that their children "lean" or "pull" toward the color of one or the other parent, color differences between a mother and father need not be dramatic in order to produce children of different colors, features, and hair types.

Although it is not so openly acknowledged, one senses a kind of anticipation and concern over color before the birth of a child. Without a doubt, friends and family make frequent remarks about a baby's color in the weeks and months after it is born. Visitors in the house of a small baby often pick up the child, and color terms are often included in the affectionate crooning and baby talk of the adult. Words like moreninha (little brown one), pretinha (little black one), and clarinha (little light-colored one) are often intoned, sometimes in spontaneously coined rhymes.

Neither color nor hair texture tend to be stable in babies of any color, and a number of informants made comments about the lightness of themselves or their children during infancy and early childhood. "When my daughter Tininha was born," Joia's aunt Natalia told me, "she had fine straight hair, just like yours, and the same color." Natalia excused herself for a moment and returned with a plastic bag filled with important family documents. Among them was a lock of Tininha's hair, cut when she was still a small child.[6]

The darkest children in the family are often the butt of ribbing and brincadeira, or joking, as Tiago was. While one is expected to take such ribbing in good humor, I had the impression that it is difficult to do so. Tiago never laughed at the jokes that were put to him but simmered with his eyes narrowed and his arms folded tightly across his chest. Similarly, a woman in her thirties told me that as a child she had had to endure constant brincadeira on the part of her father and siblings about her darkness. "It was always in the form of joking," she told me, "but I never liked it. My own family! My own father!"

Adults can also be subjected to such brincadeira by their children. While I was having lunch with Dona Janete's family one day, her son Efraim called his mother "you negra." It was a kind of brincadeira, yet it was a brincadeira with unmistakable overtones of callous disrespect. (Recall that Jacinto, Efraim's brother, accused Efraim of racism, and it is possible that he did so for other reasons besides his arrogant manner.) While I tried to pretend that I had not heard Efraim's "slip," I could not help noticing the dismayed and hurt expression on his mother's face. Dona Janete is, needless to say, the darkest in her family.

Those who are the lightest in the family, on the other hand, are often seen as the most attractive and perhaps even as the most intelligent, and while I have no truly solid data on which to base such a conjecture, I often had the impression that parents and other extended family members have higher expectations for their lighter children than they do for their darker children. I found it difficult to broach such a painful topic with those I was close to in Morro do Sangue Bom, but John Burdick reports that "stories about parents giving preferential treatment to lighter-skinned children are not hard to find" (1998, 43). He cites, for example, a story of twin girls, one of whom was dark, the other light-skinned. The dark-skinned girl, as a neighbor told Burdick, was "treated like a servant in the house," while the other was pampered and allowed privileges (43).

The favoring of lighter family members, whatever form it might take, extends backward, in fact, to the ways in which people tend to describe their genealogies. On the morro, people of color who had white or Indian ancestors placed special emphasis on the fact. Daniel, for example, must have told me a half dozen times at least that his grandmother was an Indian woman. Although he had no photographs of his other grandparents, nor of his own parents, he kept a photograph of this Indian grandmother in his home and showed it to me on numerous occasions. Susana also had an Indian great-grandparent as well as African great-grandparents who were slaves. When I asked her if she had heard stories about slavery when she was a child, she told me, "No, my mother only told me about the Indians. [My great-grandmother] did not like Brazil because she was really an Indian, an Indian of the forest. But about my [great-] grandmother who was a slave, she didn't tell anything."

Even fleeting romantic encounters with whites may be recalled as special occasions that cast a glow whose significance may grow with time. When I was interviewing a very old dark-skinned man who was considered a respected elder in the community, he excused himself, went to his house, and returned several minutes later with a very worn photograph (probably taken in the late fifties) of a dark-skinned man and a white woman. "You see, my own brother has danced with a white woman!" he exclaimed triumphantly.

Recitations of family history that invoke *mistura*, or mixture, are often framed as dramatic narratives in which color and race may be figured as defining motifs through which deeply personal conceptions of family and self are construed. These narratives, I discovered, were sometimes offered as explanations of one's success or failure in the world and, just as often, as burdensome secrets that could not, despite one's intentions, be forgotten. The role that color and/or race played in stories of one's ancestors and one's family was usually a deeply tragic one.

The story of Dona Beatrice will serve as an illustration of the ways in which race can play a pivotal role in family and personal history and how that role might be narratively represented. Dona Beatrice was a woman in her sixties who many years before had immigrated to Rio from her home state of Bahia. I met her briefly very early in my fieldwork, and over many intervening months, I reminded myself that I must return to pay her a more extended visit. When I finally did so, Dona Beatrice welcomed me, put coffee to reheat on the stove, and insisted I sit on the only stuffed chair in her tiny, cramped home. The chair startled me, however, for when I sat down, the springs seemed to bounce of their own accord. Seeing my expression, Dona Beatrice began to laugh. I looked under the chair and saw a tangle of kittens raucously playing with each other and the underside of the chair. When I looked to Dona Beatrice, I saw that the mother cat had settled on her lap. Our conversation began with an exchange of comments about the sad failure of most people on the hill to recognize, as we both did, the value of a cat's companionship.

Dona Beatrice's unusual fondness for cats may have been partly due to the fact that, for all intents and purposes, she was without family. I began our interview with my survey questions, and when I asked her how she described her own color, she launched upon a wistful description of the world from which she had come. Despite the tragedy of her story, nothing she told me was a secret, nor did she suggest that there might be others who could be wounded or unwillingly exposed by its telling. Her story, in fact, revolved around the sense of anonymity that permeated her adult life. To be without family, she seemed to imply, was to be permanently adrift and somehow unknown. "My color in my land," she began and paused for nearly a minute. She seemed to be looking inward. Knowing she had my full attention, she continued: "It's not preta, no. Preta is like him [gestures towards her companion, who was sitting outside the house]. My color is *fula*; it is *canela* (cinnamon). It is neither white nor black, nor is it mulata, nor is it *sarará*. It is cinnamon. I am from the interior of Salvador (Bahia), a plantation called Calandro. My parents were *sarará*. I am the granddaughter of a captive, from negros, from the people of the time of captivity."

Dona Beatrice spoke in a mesmerizing rhythm. "From slavery?" I asked. "From slavery. I am the granddaughter of a slave. I am the granddaughter of a Portuguese woman. My grandmother—my great-grandmother—was white, white with green eyes—like yours. Because when the captivity ended and the negro had freedom, my [great-] grandfather married a Portuguese woman. Now, my parents—well, I have two qualities. [My family has] whites with green eyes, with their hair flowing down their backs—the same as yours—and it has negros with kinky hair also. One part came from within the captivity of slavery and the other part comes from the Portuguese."

Dona Beatrice's description of her familial origins sounded like a classic Brazilian narrative of race mixture. Although she stressed the existence and whiteness of this single Portuguese woman within her family, I was, at the moment, more interested in hearing anything she might have to say about slavery. She told me truncated but very vivid stories that she had heard about gruesome tortures and exploitation. The slaves, Dona Beatrice explained, were forced to carry the brancos (whites) about on their backs, as though they were beasts of burden. Those who collapsed in exhaustion or despair were beaten mercilessly. "But," Dona Beatrice intoned, "it does no good to hold rancor."

Later in our conversation, I asked Dona Beatrice to tell me again about the Portuguese woman. She continued,

> Yes, I knew her, my grandmother and my great-grandmother, who was
> very old. I was a child, and she was white, hair the same as yours. . . .
> After [her] there was my grandmother, who was a mother, and the
> daughter of my great-grandmother on my father's side. [My family]
> had hard hair, [they were all] preta, because they leaned to the side of
> my mother. And [there were] other cousins, of a very fine family with
> green eyes and good hair. And why did my cousins lean that way?
> Because they leaned toward the side of their grandmother, of their
> father, who was the son of my grandmother, [who was the daughter]
> of my [white] great-grandmother. So, there was a mixture. The
> Portuguese with negro, negro, negro, negro, negro.

I took a deep breath and asked Dona Beatrice, "Do you think this side with the descendants of the Portuguese woman had more value in the opinions of people back then?" She replied, "Yes, they did, because of color. Yes, they spoke like that. . . . Because they had money, they were fine people with good hair and green eyes, blue eyes. There is like this—a racist color complex (*complexo de racismo pela cor*). So, we lived on one side, in the middle of every-one, and we didn't run along behind them. Each was left to themselves, right? And we didn't bear any rancor towards them over this. And they had pride because they had good hair, they had green eyes, they had money. And that's how they lived. For our part, we had poverty, as God wills it."

Dona Beatrice's recitation of her family's history was not only classic but, in the end, sadly predictable. Class and color followed typical trajectories such that the white side of the family achieved economic success while the dark side of the family, unable or proudly unwilling to "run along behind," struggled in poverty.

Dona Beatrice's narration of her own life history was also classic, uncan-nily reminiscent of Gilberto Freyre's literary scenarios; and like the story of her ancestors, it is also, in the end, both predictable and tragic.

As a child, Dona Beatrice lived and worked with her parents and eight siblings on a traditional plantation so large, she told me, "that you didn't know where it ended." The property still bore the ruins of slave quarters and the stocks in which slaves had formerly been tortured. At the age of twelve, Dona Beatrice continued, she had "lost her honor" to the plantation owner's asthmatic son, who was then in his late twenties or early thirties. I asked Dona Beatrice if she had been afraid of this man, so much older and more powerful than she. "No," she replied wistfully, "later we lived together."

She described her relationship with the plantation owner's son, a rela-tionship that continued for another six or seven years, as one of love and mutual concern. Dona Beatrice bore three children in a small house the man built on his family's property. Her own mother evidently supported their rela-tionship, while most of those in her companion's large family did not, because, she told me, "he mixed the negro family with their white family."

When her companion became extremely ill and was hospitalized for an extended period, some of the men in his family came to Dona Beatrice's small house, threw her violently to the ground, and set her house afire. Dona Bea-trice fled in great fear to her mother's house. When her companion returned from the hospital he "nearly died from crying," as Dona Beatrice put it, and he sent her to work as a maid in a residence in a nearby town "until he could build another house." Things "did not work out," however, as Dona Beatrice, still only a teenager, was sexually harassed by her new patrão. Her companion's rel-atives apparently continued to threaten her, and in the end, at her mother's urging, she fled to her sister's home in the distant city of Salvador. From thence she went to Rio, leaving her three small children in her mother's care.

She arrived in Rio, entirely alone and without social contacts, at the age of nineteen. "I didn't even know what a morro was. I didn't know anything," Dona Beatrice said, describing her first days in the big city, more than a thousand miles from home. "My suffering was so great that I slept in the woods and awoke to find rats biting my feet." She wound up, like so many immigrants from the northeast, in a shantytown in Copacabana. She found work as a domestic servant, maintaining the homes of various white families. Her youth, whatever was left of it, was quickly used up.

In the 1970s, her community was razed to make room for middle-class housing, and after another period of homelessness, Dona Beatrice moved to her present home in Morro do Sangue Bom. Looking about me as Dona Beatrice told me her life story, I could see that the home in which she had finally settled, after all those years, was no more than a tiny shack with a dirt floor.

During her early days in Rio de Janeiro, Dona Beatrice wrote a letter to her sister. It was returned with a stamp saying "address unknown." "I almost cried blood," she told me. Dona Beatrice had not heard from her family, nor have they had any news of her, in over forty years. "No one knows if I am even alive," she said with resignation.

Dona Beatrice's story was so dramatic, so theatrical, in fact, that I rolled it back and forth in my mind for months, wondering if her life had really imitated the tragic shadows of the Brazilian literary imagination. Perhaps the story was an embellishment, a fantasy even, of her life before she arrived in Rio, where she remained without family, unmarried and childless, liked and respected by many on the hill but, in many ways, very alone as she approached old age. Perhaps, I reflected on the other hand, it had all happened just as she had told it. I realized, finally, that it did not matter; stories that resonate so deeply are always, on some level, true.

Dona Beatrice's narrative articulated and circled back upon scenarios in which she had been both embraced and loved by whites and left behind, cast out, and rejected by them. They were her family. Her life and the trajectory of her family, whether composed within the imagination or within the concreteness of lived history, were, in this sense, quintessentially Brazilian.

Other stories that I heard about family articulate with the often deeply ambiguous meanings attributed to race and color. It is within racialized idioms that scenarios of hope and despair, pride and shame, mobility and poverty are sometimes implicitly and sometimes explicitly construed. It is part of the nature of democracia racial, combined as it is with narratives of interracial love and racialized hierarchies of power and exclusion, that makes the white world simultaneously seductive and rejecting for people such as Dona Beatrice. Many of the narratives I have quoted in this chapter concern family, those who share blood—people who continue, unlike Beatrice's more fortunate cousins, to live in similarly disadvantageous circumstances. Yet white domination often remains as a kind of protagonist—even when a distant one—in intimate, homebound stories.

I was struck by the historical continuities that some of my informants wove into their narratives, a compelling sense that the volatile mix of intimacy and exploitation—a mix that was formed in the context of slavery—continued to animate and shape contemporary constructions of relationships with whites. Racism is far more complex than cultural survival of archaic arrangements, of course, for it is driven by a racially bifurcated social structure that supports the labor requirements and political economy of contemporary capitalism. Yet, these cultural continuities, defined as both narrative and lived experience, inform the shape, the tone, and the texture of Brazilian racism. Brazilians of all classes and colors speak in metaphors of mixture, blood, and union; and in some senses, their suggestion that they all belong, ultimately, to the same family is true. Like all families, perhaps, theirs is shot through with ambivalence, but it is an ambivalence of a particularly deep and painful sort. It is undoubtedly significant that when my informants in Morro do Sangue Bom spoke most movingly about racism—when their words were not a litany of familiar and predictable complaints, but offered a heartfelt sense of wonder and distress about what we call the human condition—they described not distance and mutual incomprehension but yearning, intimacy, rejection, and betrayal. Dona Beatrice's story is metonymic of both the social divisions and the ambivalent communal sentiments that inform the unique character of race relations in Brazil. Such is the shape of life under the contradictions of *democracia racial*.

Chapter 6

Whiteness

Middle-Class Discourses

In 1983, WHILE AN undergraduate, I conducted research on the maintenance of elite status among the affluent youth of Campinas, a provincial city in the state of São Paulo. Over a sixth-month period, I stayed, for brief periods of time, in the homes of several of the city's elite families. During those times, the only people of color I interacted with were the empregadas who worked in these homes.

When I began my research in Campinas, I was not particularly concerned with the issue of race. It continually emerged, however, as a persistent subtext in the discourse and behavior of elite Campineiros, the vast majority of whom were white. Sometimes references to color were more than a subtext. I overheard, for example, crude piadas, or jokes, about people of color. In the case of one family, my host, a wealthy landowner, had adopted a black child, whom he punched, threatened, and berated. He justified his abuse with constant claims about the supposed inherent racial inferiority of his adopted son, saying, "What can you expect with a person of his color?"

For the most part, however, the issues of color and race remained at a subtextual level, just as people of color, in many senses, remained hidden from view. They were not to be seen at the watering holes that were frequented by the city's well-to-do youth, and they were barred, as everyone knew, from joining the elite clubs where my informants spent their weekends trading business and political information and riding horses. Racism, as a social or a political problem, was never explicitly discussed. Comments about color were occasional, and sometimes they referred less to a preoccupation with blackness than with whiteness. When I attended a birthday party for a woman in her early twenties, for example, one of the guests asked me, as if in challenge, "People in your country think that all Brazilians are negros, right?"

During my fieldwork in Rio de Janeiro, my encounters with middle-class whites were less frequent. Informal encounters—that is, those not directly related to my research—were apt to happen while I was traveling or during carnival. Several months after my arrival on the hill, for example, a white American friend visited me during the week of carnival. Avoiding the touristic and prohibitively expensive shows held in the Sambodromo, we frequented the Avenida Rio Branco. There, competitive *blocos*, or small carnival groups, many of them based in Rio's many morros, paraded throughout the night in what seemed a listless and disorganized fashion. The overwhelming silence surrounding the issue of racism was abruptly broken by a troupe of men passing by who bore a banner reading, "There is no difference save for the color of our skin." They quickly passed into the shadows at the end of the avenida.

Middle-class white Cariocas tend to eschew the carnival of their native city, saying that they deplore the noise, the disorder, and the shameless promiscuity. Huge numbers of them flee the city, destined usually for mountain or seaside resorts. Some remain, however, and their numbers are swelled by foreigners and Brazilians from other cities, who come seeking the very things that the Cariocas disdain. It was on the Avenida Rio Branco that Varena introduced me and my visiting American friend to Sergio, whom she called her *namorado do carnaval*, or carnival boyfriend. He was a white middle-class man from one of Brazil's southernmost states, who had stopped to play the Rio carnival enroute to an overseas engineering job. He was accompanied by a younger man, Felipe, also white and middle-class, but a native of Rio.

Together, Varena and her *patrão* were operating a concessionary stand on the Avenida, and they had set up several tables where their customers could rest and drink beer. Tomas and several of his musician friends had brought their drums and guitars down from the morro, taking advantage of one of the rare moments in which they might enjoy the respect and feel the unreserved pleasure of outsiders. I conversed with Sergio while Felipe attempted to flirt with my friend, who understood very little Portuguese. Sergio told me, in rather excited terms, that his wife and daughters had "exactly" my "coloring"—very pale and freckled, with light brown hair. "They aren't like me," he told me at least three times. "They are very, very light, as white as can be. Just like you!" When Sergio referred to his own color, his tone seemed slightly disparaging, yet he was unambiguously white.

During a pause in our conversation, I overheard Felipe's tortured and increasingly aggressive attempts to engage my American friend. He seemed to hope that by speaking loudly he could overcome her inability to understand Portuguese. "We whites have to stick together," he said, leaning toward her conspiratorially and waving his arm toward the crowd of people on the avenida, most of whom were various shades of black and brown. "What did you say?" I asked Felipe. "Be careful, she's an anthropologist!" Sergio immediately warned him. I insisted that I was merely curious, an obviously mendacious claim, for I had blurted the question in an abrupt and startled fashion and had utterly ruined Felipe's attempts to fabricate a sense of intimacy between himself and my friend. I could not persuade Felipe to repeat the remark, and he eyed me warily during the remainder of the conversation.

My description of these encounters helps to introduce some of the common themes whereby middle- and upper-class whites tend to articulate a sense of their own identity and their relationships with poor people of color. They serve, in addition, to illustrate some of the difficulties involved in what Nader (1974), arguing for the need for ethnographies of dominant groups, called "studying up." My attempts to contextualize my research on the morro by generating an understanding of the ways in which their middle-class white neighbors talked about color, race, and racism was the most difficult aspect of my research in Rio.

Like middle and upper classes everywhere, those in Santa Teresa tend to socialize behind closed doors. Privacy, which seemed to have little meaning for people on the hill, appeared to be something of a strategic and conspicuous commodity among their middle-class neighbors. High walls, into which jagged bits of broken glass had been set in the cement, and heavy iron gates often fortified their homes. Zealous doormen scrutinized visitors, and prior communication by telephone was absolutely requisite. Protection against crime and a symbolically emphatic separation of the public world of the street and the private world of the home went hand in hand (DaMatta 1985). Many of Santa Teresa's middle-class residents are well traveled and educated; and foreigners, whether researchers, tourists, or expatriates, are hardly novel to them. As in the experience of all anthropologists, my positioning and the prestige that I was assumed or not assumed to represent were interpreted in profoundly different ways by informants who occupied different locations within locally and transnationally constructed status hierarchies.[1]

When I did meet middle-class whites informally, whether in the neighborhood of Santa Teresa or outside of it, I often told them, in the course of what began as a friendly conversation, that I was an anthropologist studying issues related to race and racism. Sometimes those I met changed the topic of conversation rather abruptly. Often, they insisted that while there was some racism in Brazil, it was, as the entire world knew, far worse in the United

States; I would do better, some said explicitly, to study the issue in my own country. When middle-class people referred in a facile and generalizing way to the people of Rio's many morros as *marginais* (people who make their living from crime) and asked me to lament with them "the ignorance in which those people live," I flinched inwardly.

When I did succeed in recruiting middle-class informants for interviews, I was often disappointed in the results. I had become accustomed, in my interviews with people on the hill, to a narratively constructed sense of escalating exposure and drama. I was comfortable with my role as a rapt pupil who needed to be informed about racism in Brazil because I was a foreigner and because I was white. My queries, people on the morro suggested, might be difficult and even awkward at times, but they were directed toward something that was significant in their lives, something that they could, without a doubt, speak to with unassailable authority.

For the most part, my middle-class white informants were bored by my questions, and I wondered if my apparent failure to elicit what I considered interesting material was a result of my fear of offending them. I was relieved by the fact that none of them expressed interest in my research in Morro do Sangue Bom. I was never called upon to express the opinions and impressions that I had formulated while living there, and although I occasionally played, as politely as possible, something of a devil's advocate in my interviews with them, this fact allowed me to avoid disruptive and confrontational conversations. It was only after I left the field that I came to recognize the fact that it was the very flatness, awkwardness, boredom, evasion, and vagueness that characterized so many of my interviews with middle-class whites that constituted, if incompletely, the very ethnography that I had despaired of grasping and describing.

In one sense at least, those who told me to study my own world were right. I could not at first see whiteness as a territory partly because I had always lived within it. I had forgotten that in the restricted American world from which I had come, as well as in the tightly bounded world of Santa Teresa that I entered so incompletely and ambivalently, racism is always someone else's problem, and its pathos, whether constructed through rhetorical artifice or lived as a part of everyday life, is rarely if ever felt. I had encountered the articulation of a kind of indifference that should have been immediately and entirely familiar to me.

These comments are partly addressed to a growing concern within anthropology: the ways in which ethnographic encounters are negotiated and the insistence that these negotiations often spell out the very boundaries of power and identity that we attempt to investigate through more conventional ethnographic means. In a more direct way, however, I intend them to illustrate the difficulties involved in studying whiteness, the subject with which this chapter is centrally concerned. These difficulties, whatever their personal, reflexive dimensions, are most constructively viewed as symptomatic of the peculiar forms of practice and self-representation that characterize the dominant: the assumption of cultural normality and racial neutrality, the location of the self within a symbolically elaborated and ostensive (but taken-for-granted) mainstream, and the largely unconscious construction of boundaries that insulate those who exercise privilege and power from a confrontation with their effects on the nondominant.

Dominant Discourse and Whiteness

As in previous chapters, my presentation and analysis of the discourse of my middle-class informants is based upon what I take to be the central themes, preoccupations, and rhetorical strategies that were introduced by informants. The chapter is nevertheless informed by several literatures, and it engages, at a more or less implicit level, a number of theoretical and analytical concerns, chief among them the identification and definition of whiteness.

Narratives of racism produced by people of color, and analyses of such narratives, are, as I have noted in chapter 4, relatively scarce. There are several literatures, spanning a variety of disciplines, however, that are devoted to the issue of white racism. Some of this literature is implicitly, if not explicitly, concerned with discourse. Particularly in the 1950s, 1960s, and 1970s, social scientists within a variety of disciplines were preoccupied with prejudice, discrimination, and intergroup conflict. Most of these works did not focus on racism within specific local arenas but rather examined prejudice and/or discrimination in more abstract and often typological terms. Concern with these issues continues into the present decade, as is evidenced by recent books based on public opinion polls (e.g., Sniderman and Piazza 1993), social-psychological analyses (e.g., Lott and Mauluso 1995), sociopolitical analyses (Omi and Winant 1994; Winant 1994), and interdisciplinary collections (e.g., Goldberg 1990), to cite only a few.

Literatures that concern white racism in Brazil are also fairly extensive. The UNESCO-sponsored ethnographies, for example, were explicitly concerned with race relations. As in the case of early discussions of racism in the United States, these and similar studies tended to focus on the sociological categories that were popular from the 1950s to the 1970s: white's "attitudes," "stereotypes," and "prejudices" regarding blacks (see, for example, Bastide and van den Berghe 1957; Bastide and Fernandes 1955; Cardoso and Ianni 1960;

Wagley 1971; for reviews of this complex and influential literature, see Fontaine 1980; Saunders 1972; Winant 1992). Although these studies do not explore everyday discourse in a systematic fashion, they often include the quotation of colloquialisms and similar discursive evidence of derogatory stereotypes of blacks. Read from a presentist perspective, the more dated studies of racism often invoke, at least implicitly, the problematic of discourse and silence, and they provide historical evidence of a remarkable stability within Brazilian whites' discourses (subsumed within the analytical categories of attitudes, stereotypes, and prejudices) about blackness (see especially, Bastide and van den Berghe 1957).

More directly relevant is the currently expanding area of discourse analysis and its application to the study of white racism (e.g., Billig 1988; Goldberg 1990; Smitherman-Donaldson and van Dijk 1988; van Dijk 1992, 1993; Wetherell and Potter 1993). These works have grown out of a larger literature that concerns the intersection between discourse, ideology, and power (e.g., Bakhtin 1981; Bourdieu 1991; Foucault 1972, 1980; Fowler et al. 1979). Focusing primarily on First World countries, studies on discourse and discrimination emphasize the fact that racist discourses and/or practices have become, during the last decade especially, increasingly covert. They have, in related terms, become more contradictory as well. In *Elite Discourse and Racism*, for example, van Dijk focuses on the "more subtle discursive dimensions of modern elite racism" within Europe (1993, x). Although driven by very different histories, the Brazilian discourses of democracia racial bear striking similarities to the more recently elaborated discourses of racial and ethnic tolerance in areas such as the United States, Europe, and New Zealand.

Especially relevant to my analysis is the recent concern, primarily located within the disciplines of anthropology and cultural criticism (Crapanzano 1986; Delgado and Stephancic 1997; Hill 1997; Frankenberg 1993, 1997; Joseph 1994; Roediger 1998; Sacks 1992) but also within history (Roediger 1991; Ware 1992), sociology (Alba 1990; Wellman 1977), and literary criticism (Morrison 1992; Mullen 1994), with the social and cultural construction of whiteness. The racism of dominant (white) groups is at least implicit in this concern, yet it incorporates the larger issues of identity, discourse, power, and social location.

The belatedness with which scholars have turned their attention to the cultural construction of whiteness is, of course, no accident. It is directly related to extremely pervasive assumptions about the nature of ethnicity and the exercise of racialized power. With the exception of "ethnic whites" and elites, about whom there is a voluminous literature, whites who are members of modern middle-classes have been implicitly treated as a kind of "default" category. Whiteness is rarely problematized. Whites have been figured as a norm, as representatives of the mainstream, as a people devoid of the invented traditions, strategies, and self-conscious cultural embodiments that the term ethnicity has come to connote for a variety of disciplines. "Naming 'whiteness,'" Ruth Frankenberg has noted, "displaces it from the unmarked, unnamed status that is itself an effect of dominance" (1993, 6).

The novelist and literary critic Toni Morrison is similarly concerned with unmasking whiteness and its largely implicit assumptions. In *Playing in the Dark,* her reference to slaves and masters is both metaphorical and literal when she writes: "It seems both poignant and striking how avoided and unanalyzed is the effect of racist inflection on the subject. . . . The scholarship that looks into the mind, imagination, and behavior of slaves is valuable. But equally valuable is a serious intellectual effort to see what racist ideology does to the mind, imagination, and behavior of masters" (1992, 11–12).

As Morrison suggests, the absence of scholarship on whiteness mirrors a lack of critical self-reflection within middle-class white groups themselves. Unlike the members of nondominant groups, whites do not measure themselves against others but are themselves a standard by which difference and otherness are calculated. Whiteness often seems, above all, to be defined by a peculiar insularity that is manifest in cultural practice as well as within the discourses through which whites define (or fail to define) and describe themselves.

In somewhat paradoxical terms, Brazil and other Latin American nations may differ from other countries in the extent to which whiteness is consciously constructed, symbolically located, and maintained. Felipe's comment to my white American friend, "We whites have to stick together," far more than a pick-up line, is premised on a transnational and deeply racialized notion of shared whiteness. His own and my American friend's whiteness, he intended to suggest, transcended national and ethnic boundaries. Felipe was certainly aware, moreover, that the Rio carnival is stereotypically associated with eroticized interracial mingling, and I believe he also meant to invoke the presumed necessity of carefully preserving whiteness as a highly exclusive, superior, and possibly threatened resource. The young Campineiro's question ("People in your country think that all Brazilians are negros, right?") clearly articulates a preoccupation with white Brazilians' membership in what might be called a transnational racial elite. She implicitly invoked the notion of a first world–third world hierarchy in which national wealth and power are associated, sometimes in causal terms, with the racial composition of national populations. It was not this notion that she resented but rather the possibility that North Americans might lump her with her darker brethren and thus repudiate her culturally elaborated claim to transnational whiteness.

Galen Joseph (1994) emphasizes this preoccupation with whiteness in her analysis of middle-class whites in Buenos Aires. Porteños, she argues, have "a diasporic consciousness" that highlights whiteness and asserts a privileged kinship with Europe and white Europeans. Such notions, I believe, may be common to dominant groups throughout Latin American countries that display ambivalent and contradictory preoccupations with unique and often miscegenated and hybrid national identities while preserving, for their white elites, an extra-local yet highly exclusive sense of racial identity and belonging.

The insularity of middle-class white Brazilians is thus not as totalizing as I have suggested. They envision their whiteness as existing within and, in some senses, measured against a transnational standard. This standard may be a largely imagined one (Anderson 1991), yet it reflects and buttresses objective structures of racialized power, structures that transcend national borders even while maintaining First World–Third World and North-South global hierarchies.

The focus on whiteness de-centers and thus expands our understanding of both the cultural and the moral dimension of racialized oppression by shifting attention away from the notion that racism is a so-called problem of blacks and directing it toward what Morrison calls the "mind, imagination, and behavior of masters" (1992, 12). The "urgent anthropology" suggested by Nader's call for an "understanding of the processes whereby power and responsibility are exercised" (1974, 308, 284) is refigured through the project of unmasking whiteness, which is concerned not only with the mechanics of structural domination but with the culture of dominance.

White Space

Merely asking middle-class whites about their opinions and views on issues related to race and racism is, as I immediately discovered, unlikely to produce the kinds of extended commentaries, personal observations, anecdotes, and descriptions of experience that such direct questions tend to elicit on the morro. Although none of my white informants denied the existence of racism in their country, their descriptions of racism tended to be brief and tempered with a variety of insistent qualifications.

The Brazilian news media—to which all of my highly literate middle-class white informants were exposed—frequently covered events and issues related to racism in countries such as the United States and South Africa. During the period of my fieldwork, for example, the beating of Rodney King in Los Angeles and its explosive aftermath were repeatedly profiled in newspapers and nightly news shows. Coverage of events explicitly related to racism in Brazil was a rarity, however, and the dearth of such reports was taken as evidence that racialized forms of discrimination are themselves uncommon.

Relatively speaking, Brazilians have no sound bites, news reports, editorials, courtroom dramas, docudramas, public policy debates, racialized and controversialized celebrities, or similar representational media by which they might frame an evolving set of everyday public discourses about racism in their country. This fact, combined with whites' lack of direct experience with the consequences of racialized oppression, contributes toward their lack of fluency on the topic.

Virginia, a woman in her mid-thirties, was my first middle-class white informant; my interview with her was, in many respects, typical. It took me a matter of minutes to walk from my house close to the top of Morro do Sangue Bom to her high-rise apartment building, which I will call Edifício Silvestre, situated on the asphalt just below the hill. The building filled much of the foreground of the view seen by those living at the top of the hill, and many who had apartments in the building had, for their part, a clear and practically intimate view of the irregularly tilted, russet-colored homes that crowded the hillside. Virginia's apartment was very spacious and airy, full of plush couches and chairs. Despite its proximity to Morro do Sangue Bom, I had entered a different and separate world.

Repeating what I had told Virginia on the phone, I explained that I was a doctoral student conducting research on race and racism. I began by telling her that, as a foreigner, I was trying to grasp the local vocabulary of race and color, and I asked her to list all of the words that she could think of that were used to refer to a person's race or color. She provided eight terms, the same average that people on the morro had listed, but unlike those on the hill, who often forgot to mention branco, or white, Virginia provided three terms that describe the varying hair types and skin tones of white people. I told her that I was under the impression that many people considered the term negro offensive, and she agreed with this. I asked her if she thought the same was true of other terms, such as preto. She replied, "I never refer to people this way, so I never thought about this. I think all of these words are racist. I have always been concerned about not categorizing, with not treating people in this way, do you understand?"

Striking out in what I hoped might be a fairly general direction, I asked Virginia if she had any memory of her first awareness of differences in color. She paused and responded, "No, I don't remember, no. I never concerned myself with this. It wasn't an important thing for me. I don't remember."

There was in Virginia's voice a hint of what sounded like defensiveness, a suggestion, perhaps, that the question itself was gauche and inappropriate.

She brightened somewhat when I asked her if she recalled when she had first become aware of class differences: "I think so. I think that this was more important for me, when I entered the department, the university. . . . I had contact with the student movement, people, right, who were poorer. I think it was more or less then. Consciousness of class. I was eighteen years old."

To clarify, I asked, "It wasn't when you were a child?" She confirmed that it had not been. "And when you were a child, were there people of color in your school?" I asked. "No," she answered. "This was in São Paulo. I came here when I was twelve, but there weren't any here either. It was a Catholic school, of the upper middle class." I asked Virginia if her family had had an empregada when she was growing up. A number of empregadas had worked for Virginia's family, she told me, including "whites, mulatas, and negras." "We never noticed this either, no," she added. I asked her to describe the relationship between her family and the empregada(s) and her defensive tone returned: "It was normal! It wasn't a relationship of slavery. She was always treated humanely. . . . She took the weekends off. She was always well paid, well treated. There wasn't discrimination in terms of food. It was just normal."[2]

Virginia, it appeared, was not comfortable talking about race and racism. Her comments that she "never concerned" herself with issues such as racial-color terminology and her statement that "it wasn't an important thing" and, further, that her family "never noticed" the color of their empregadas have a dual dimension. These aspects of Virginia's discourse resemble patterns in the United States, for as Frankenberg notes, "For many white people in the United States . . . 'color-blindness'—a mode of thinking about race organized around an effort to not 'see,' or at any rate not to acknowledge, race differences—continues to be the 'polite' language of race" (1993, 143). Frankenberg adds that "color evasion actually involves a selective engagement with difference, rather than no engagement," and she suggests that it is associated with the "corollary of power evasion"—a failure, that is, to recognize the racialized nature of white privilege and power (143).

When I asked Virginia to comment on her impressions of the social relations between the residents in her building and those in Morro do Sangue Bom, her vagueness dissipated. "I can speak for myself," she said, warming to what was, for her, a more concrete topic:

> I hardly know anyone [on the morro]. I don't want to know them! I am afraid, like—I am afraid. And it's not a question of prejudice. Quite the contrary. It's because I have had some people from the morro working here in my house and it was very uncomfortable. They steal. They dissimulate. Do you understand? They are dishonest in the relationship. It's a horrible thing of dispute, of not being

friends, of gossiping when they leave here, speaking ill [of me]. The
people there talk behind your back. They arrive one day, you think
everything is fine, and then they leave your house and they go saying
horrible things about you. And for me, these people have very bad
characters, very low-level, untrustworthy, so they are people that I
don't want to involve myself with. And I even sense a great beauty in
black people, in poor people, with the popular movement.

Virginia's notion about the "great beauty in black people" was not an
uncommon one among Santa Teresa's more liberal residents. Such abstract
ideas—like the larger one of democracia racial—seem to have little bearing
on Virginia's facile characterization of the residents of Morro do Sangue Bom
as "these people [who] have very bad characters."

Benedita, a woman in her fifties, lived very close to the morro in a large
apartment complex that I will call the Plazaflor. In our interview she emphasized her regional origin and identity as a Paraibana, or native of the northeastern state of Paraíba. I asked Benedita to describe the area where she had
spent her childhood and adolescence. She first told me that her town had a
mixed population, yet as our conversation continued, she told me that there
were only two black families in the immediate area. Descended from slaves,
they remained very poor, in contrast to most of the townspeople, who,
Benedita told me, were plantation owners. Benedita recalled, however, that
there was a small town nearby that contained a large number of black families.
She knew very little about this town and had never been there herself. Sometimes, people from there or elsewhere passed through her town: "When a
negro appeared, he was remembered as someone who was impudent (safado),
someone bad, you know? If someone passed through the region who was a
negro, people didn't trust them. . . . If a negro appeared, he must be bad. Right
away, being preto, you were obliged to be bad. Do you understand? . . . It
was—how do you say this? There wasn't a defined consciousness about it. But
when a person was there, in the presence of the negro, this consciousness
appeared, you understand? There were very few negros."

Benedita's family later moved to a more urban area within the state of
Paraíba when she was a teenager, and there she had a black classmate. It was
in this context, she told me, that she first became aware of her father's racism:

I remember a [black] friend that I had. . . . On Saturdays and
Sundays, we would get together to study, in a group right? And I was
behind in some material, and I arranged for this [black] friend to
come to my house. . . . And I would serve a soda then, right? So,
when I went to serve my friend, who had arrived, right away, my
father said, "What are you giving to that negro?" . . . My father was a

businessman. He didn't have a consciousness of this, you understand? He just repeated things without thinking. Later I had a discussion with him, after my friend left. I argued with him, and he said things like, it's fine for him to be the friend of my brother, to go out with my brother. But to be my friend, to be my boyfriend, [that was different]. . . . I couldn't court him; that wouldn't do. I was seventeen years old.

In describing her father's racism, Benedita introduced two themes that were common to most of my interviews with white middle-class informants. Although most of my informants, like Benedita, described insular worlds in which they had extremely limited opportunities to interact with people of color (outside of the employer-servant relationship), the issue of sexual or romantic liaisons with them seemed to be a recurring, if abstract preoccupation.

Benedita's comments also resembled those of others in the way she referred to her father's racism as a kind of knee-jerk reaction: "He just repeated things without thinking." As will become clear, many of my white middle-class informants referred to racism, particularly the racism of their own parents, as a kind of unconscious discursive reflex, something that should not, finally, be taken too seriously.

Gilberto, a man in his late forties, made the most explicit, if ambiguous declarations about the difference between "discourse" and "treatment." He also lived in the Plazaflor, close to the morro. He had grown up in a more urban setting, in a small city in the interior of Rio de Janeiro. During much of our interview, Gilberto made a distinction between what he called "ideological and cultural racism." The precise parameters of this distinction were never entirely clear to me, yet for the most part it seemed that he defined ideological racism as a conscious, heart-felt conviction of the inferiority of people of color, whereas cultural racism was constituted by a traditional, knee-jerk discourse within which people of color were derogated.

When I asked Gilberto if he had interacted with people of color during his adolescence or if he ever discussed the issue of racism with his friends, he described the street on which he had lived as a youngster:

Now, close to our street there was a tenement building. It was a residence of the last class before the favela. So, it was close to our house, this building, and it had a family of negros—not really poor negros, they were educated. And they were well received on our street. Now, this was between us children. . . . There were families of the middle class, of the upper middle class [that had] this discourse of racist people [but it] wasn't ideological. They were well received in most houses, I mean—it was neither an ideology nor a disposition. On the contrary, it was joking around.

After Gilberto told me that this single "family of negros" had been well received, his comments became garbled by conversational repair work and incomplete sentences. Having introduced the distinction between ideology and brincadeira, or joking, he continued:

> For example, there were three brothers from this building. The oldest was [called] "Midnight," the next was "Eleven-thirty," and the other was "Eleven O'clock." Those were their nicknames. There was an even stronger nickname; one of them was called "Monkey." But it was because he resisted this relation, right, the joking of the whites. . . . But back then, there was no black consciousness. I'm talking about things of thirty years ago. So, Midnight was even an affectionate way [of addressing him]. Now, the one who resisted this, who was offended, was called "Monkey." So he fought with us, and we wanted to offend him by calling him "Monkey." But the others didn't complain. "Hey, Midnight!" [we would call out.] So, it was easy.

Although Gilberto attempts to assert a kind of innocence in the scenario he describes—one unsullied by "black consciousness"—the easy joking of children serves to guard the borders of whiteness. The fact that one of the brothers resisted what appears to have been the constant marking of his racial status does not lead Gilberto to question, in a truly reflexive sense, the micropolitical implications of such forms of joking, nor does it lead him to wonder about the extent to which it is either accurate or appropriate to suggest, twice in fact, that the family was "well-received."

Heloisa, a woman in her early forties, also lived in the Plazaflor apartment complex. Like Gilberto, she had grown up in an urban area. "We were between the middle and lower class," she explained. When I asked Heloisa if there had been any people of color living on her street or in her neighborhood, she told me that pretos lived in her own building. She apparently did not think of them as neighbors in any but the most technical sense, however; her building was enormous, with twenty apartments on every floor. Despite what might have been a somewhat insecure class position, Heloisa attended a private school, and this fact in itself isolated her from her neighbors and from people of color generally.

Heloisa's mother evidently wanted her to remain within an exclusively white world. She told me that her mother was "racist in the extreme," and I asked her how her racism manifested itself: "It was declared! Declared! [Laughs.] [She would use] expressions—we have these expressions here in

Brazil, [for example,] 'The preto when he doesn't shit on entering, shits while leaving.' Have you heard this? [Laughs.] And the sort of thing, if I was going out with a guy who was brown from being on the beach, she [would say], 'Crioulo! You can not [date him], my daughter!' "

Her mother, Heloisa continued, not only forbade Heloisa to date boys who were very tanned from having spent time at the beach, but she insisted that Heloisa was not to become like them: "She didn't like me to stay on the beach. She wanted me to stay very white, to characterize my Aryan race, right? To stay white. I didn't go to the beach so that I wouldn't get dark like other people."

The term "Aryan race" would seem to be peculiarly out of place in Brazil, yet this was not the first time I had heard it spoken by a white informant. Other informants besides Heloisa, in addition, referred or alluded to a preoccupation with whiteness as a physical and, indeed, aesthetic attribute. They might feel, as one informant clearly did, that when they traveled in Europe, their tanned skin branded them as inferior; they were not white enough. Too much time on the beach could also lead to ribbing by their professional colleagues in Brazil, who might jokingly call them *crioulos*.

As an adult, Heloisa remained, like most of her neighbors, within an exclusively white (and middle-class) social world. In describing racism very generally, she told me, "There is that classic thing, that you can't imagine that [a black person] could be the owner of a car."

Because Heloisa had expressly told me that she had always had an antiracist sensibility, I asked her, toward the end of our conversation, if she had an opinion on Brazil's black movement. She knew almost nothing of it and associated it with art and music, but she said that, generally, it "would be great if someone did something against racism." I asked her if she would attend an antiracist demonstration, and she responded, "I wouldn't go; I wouldn't go because, in the first place, I think—I don't know. I'm going to try to be honest, okay? [Laughs.] What a horror! [More laughter.] Because, in the first place, there would be many pretos there—because, look, do you want me to be sincere or what, Beth? The preto, he has a different smell. It is very strong, right? This makes me uncomfortable. Not the pretos, but their odor."

This was not the first time I had heard about the infamous *bumdum*, the unpleasantly pungent smell that was reputedly unique to negros. I had only heard about it from white people, however, and during all the months that I lived on the morro, I had failed to detect its existence.

During our interview Heloisa told me that her fifteen-year-old daughter, Maura, was racist. She added that her ex-husband, David, was also racist and said, "Perhaps she gets it from him." During the day of our interview, David was visiting Maura and Heloisa in their apartment in the Plazaflor (where he had previously resided with them), and Heloisa encouraged me to interview him as well.

A man in his forties, David, like Benedita, had grown up in a more rural area, what he called a small city in the state of Minas Gerais. He described his family as "upper middle class"; they had been "plantation owners and administrators." I asked David to describe the town in which he grew up and whether any of his neighbors were of color. He responded: "It is a small city and today it is more mixed, but before it had a town center with richer people, plantation owners, right, and on the periphery there were black (negro) neighborhoods—really negro, including neighborhoods where only negros lived, the descendants of slaves. There were families [in which people had actually been slaves], grandparents, great-grandparents. They worked on the same plantations and they are still there today."

David added that there had been no students of color in the school he attended in the town. His description reminded me of Dona Janete's depiction of the world of her youth, where as a small child she helped her parents in the cotton fields of Minas Gerais, close to the original site where her great-grandparents had labored as slaves. Class and color it seemed, fit together with nearly perfect symmetry in the rural world from which both had come.

I asked David if his parents or other relatives ever made comments or conversed about either race or racism. "My family is a family that, like—has something racist," David began hesitantly. I asked him to continue: "I remember that when I was very young, there was a girl who was a mulata, and someone said, right—and I liked her a lot and wanted to play with her—so someone said that I should be more careful because one day I would wind up having sex with a negra."

David had evidently grown up in a very insular world. During our conversation, he told me that he had changed, in many respects, as he grew older. When I asked him to explain, he told me that he had formerly "imagined that the world was for me, as I wanted it." Later, however, he discovered "that there is a mixture of races, of customs, a great number of things." He became comfortable walking through rough neighborhoods in Rio. He could stroll through Lapa, for example, one of the streets of which is known as a red light area. "I can walk through the middle of the transvestites, of the prostitutes. . . . I can see how their life is," he said. He also told me that he had discovered that he had "the capacity to make love with a negra." He described himself as less prejudiced and fearful, more able to move through the urban environment in Rio.

David described these experiences and other places he had apparently visited, such as "the neighborhoods of Jews, the neighborhoods of negros," as exotic, almost otherworldly. "Each place has it's own interest, and if that weren't the case, I wouldn't go," he told me. He had conquered the geography of Rio, and its diversity was laid out before him, somewhat like a museum display. His description of the city and his ease of movement within it immediately struck me as remarkably unlike the descriptions of the asphalt given by men of color on the morro. David seemed unaware of the possibility that his sense of freedom and invulnerability were related to his identity as a white middle-class male.

Celso, a man in his forties who lived in the Plazaflor, was one of only a few informants who seemed to have a sense of how his whiteness constructed his relationships with people of color. Unlike others, for example, he acknowledged that the employer-empregada relationship might be, in some sense, "unnatural" and could lead to a distortion, a perversion even, of what he called "humanistic relationships." Like David, he grew up in a town in Minas Gerais, within what he called a "very rural culture." Without specific prompting, he said, "Look, in my town, I was born in the interior where the relation with the negro was almost a relation of slavery." He told me that children of color were adopted as *criados* by some families, but that they were treated like "adopted animals." When I asked if his own parents had ever made racist comments, he responded, "No, it was more subtle." He reversed himself, however, for he explained: "There was an unreserved attitude. . . . This discrimination was part of the everyday world. It was part of the everyday world, even from the point of view of the people who [made racist comments] but who had strongly humanistic relationships. But it's like the negro wasn't a person."

Celso told me that as a child and an adolescent, he was brought up with the notion that a negra, a black woman, "could only be an empregada or a prostitute." He suggested that although he intellectually rejected such notions, they remained implanted within his psyche. Many of his comments had a distinctly psychoanalytic bent. "I blame myself," he told me. "There is a guilt, I criticize myself over it, for my discrimination."

Eliza, a woman in her early forties, had grown up in the large, stately house where we conducted the interview. She lived there with her husband, her children, and her mother, Dona Margaret. Unlike the Plazaflor and Edifício Silvestre, Eliza's house was situated a short bus ride from Morro do Sangue Bom. It was, however, very near one of Santa Teresa's other large morros. Eliza and her mother were directly descended from an elite family of nationally known statesmen.

Eliza opened her interview by telling me that her husband's great-grandmother had been a negra. Her husband, however, was unambiguously white.

"But this mixture," she gushed, "I think it's incredible, isn't it?" She began to talk about the private schools she had attended (which were among the very best in Rio), and I asked her if she had had any classmates of color. She explained: "There were orphans there, who worked in the school and who studied with us. But I never felt that there was any discrimination in the school. . . . There was equality between everyone, [racism] didn't exist. Since I was little, I always played with the empregada, who had a child."

Eliza, it soon became clear, was concerned with demonstrating that she had grown up in an integrated world and had developed an antiracist sensibility. Unlike Virginia, however, she was an effusive interviewee and there was no hint of defensiveness in her voice. Because she had abruptly brought up the issue of the empregada, I asked her to continue:

> ROBIN: And tell me more about this. Your family had an empregada?
> ELIZA: Yes, we had many empregadas! And a nursemaid. My nursemaid
> is my mother's empregada even now. She has been with my mother
> for thirty-seven years. She is a negra. She was a second mother to
> me, a person whom I adore tremendously. But we had a nursemaid,
> a cook, an empregada who served at the table, a washerwoman, all
> that. This was when I was little. Later things were worsening,
> worsening, worsening in the economy, so it's no longer like that.
> My father was a medical doctor, a very good doctor. . . . Our
> empregadas were negras. We had a few whites and many people
> from the north worked here who were mixed, mulatas, right? But
> the good ones were negras, you know. They stayed longer and we
> always had a good relationship.

In transcription, Eliza's exclamation that her family had many servants appears to be tinged with the nostalgia and braggadocio of the formerly wealthy. During our interview, however, I was struck by what sounded like a kind of innocent, unabashed enthusiasm, propelled, it seemed, by fond memories of a previously bustling and lively household. Eliza was neither defensive nor terse in her responses, yet, as she continued, it became clear that she, like Virginia, was never struck by the juxtaposition of certain forms of intimacy with enactments of extreme inequality. Both were very much part of an insular and taken-for-granted world:

> ROBIN: And did they [empregadas] live close by?
> ELIZA: They lived here in the house! They would stay fifteen days
> working directly, and every fifteen days they would go home on the
> weekend and return on Monday.

ROBIN: And they had families also, children?

ELIZA: They did. This one, my nursemaid who is still with my mother, she never married. But there were others who had married and they had grandchildren who would come here to play with us. They lived over on the morro, you know, and they always played with us. . . . So during our childhood, in my relationship with her, my mother always left us with her. In fact, I don't remember playing with my mother. But I remember playing with the nursemaid, I remember this. We liked her a lot; I mean, we learned a lot of the simple things from her, the things of humble people. . . . like music. We liked what they liked, do you understand?[3]

I asked Eliza if she had a consciousness of race or class when she was a child. She replied,

I think I had a consciousness of this later. Because we stayed here all the time, we didn't go out much, do you understand, and our friends came here more because it is a bigger house, you know? I know that where we would go we had many friends [who lived in other neighborhoods], and that was another thing. There we played with people of our own level, you understand, and here we played with people from the morro, right? . . . Now, I really only had this consciousness later. When I was little I didn't have this—I never saw—I had—I didn't have this conception. I don't remember; I don't remember.

My question had been jarring for Eliza; it had interrupted the flow of her nostalgia, the images of equality and togetherness that she had woven. Her playmates from the morro, it seems, brought neither their world nor their sub-jectivities with them but were recast within, even swallowed by, the insularity of the big house, an insularity that was echoed within Eliza's adult discourse.

Eliza put considerable emphasis on the fact that her husband had a black grandparent, yet she seemed somewhat startled when I asked her if she had ever had a black boyfriend. She replied, "No, no. There wasn't, there weren't any—I didn't interact with any—I didn't interact with any negros." Her com-ment represented an abrupt departure from her description of the world of her childhood. "And if there had been, what might your mother and father have said?" I asked. Eliza seemed embarrassed when she responded after a pause, "Perhaps they wouldn't like it. I don't think they would like it, no. But never during my adolescence, I never had a single contact. In my relationships, there was never a negro."

"So, when you were very young, a child, you played with—" I began. Eliza responded, "Yes, then I played [with people of color]. No, later, no. They, well, each one went to a different—each went their way and it wasn't, there weren't—I never, never. There were some whom I knew in the university . . . there was a black professor, you know. But to date [a black man], I never thought about it. Nor was I interested in it."

As Eliza's hesitant and startled response suggests, my question had been an absurd one, given the racially bounded contexts in which Eliza had spent her adolescence and adulthood. Concluding her comments, Eliza said, "But if something had happened, I would have been fine with it, you know? I don't have any problem with it, you know?"

Her earlier description of an intimate life populated by people of color was abruptly qualified by the fact that "each went their way." After her nostalgically constructed childhood had passed, she entered more fully into the processes of elite socialization, which virtually guaranteed not only that she would not date a black man, but that she would never think about it, nor be "interested in it." Her childhood playmates remained on the morro and took jobs as empregadas, while she attended elite schools, completed a degree at the university, and traveled in Europe and the United States.

Much later in our conversation, when Eliza told me more about her family's illustrious history, I asked her if her family had had slaves during the last century. I expected that her genealogical reckoning would be fairly extensive and that her family's history would be extremely well known to her; official versions of this history are, after all, a matter of public record. She replied, however, "Look, no, no, no. I don't think, so. I don't know." Eliza's evasiveness did not seem calculated, and I asked in surprise, "But didn't anyone talk about it?" She replied that no one, in her memory, had spoken about the issue and then added, "I think that if they had slaves, they didn't treat them badly. I think, I believe—well, I hope, right?"

I later interviewed Eliza's mother, Dona Margaret. A woman in her seventies, Dona Margaret was far more laconic, and at the same time frank, in her responses than her daughter had been. As the child of a French mother and a Brazilian diplomat father, she had spent her childhood moving between Europe and Brazil. When I asked her whether her family had owned slaves, her response was also hesitant but far more matter-of-fact than her daughter's had been. "Well," she said, "the great-grandparents probably [had slaves], right?" "But you aren't certain?" I asked. She replied, "I am certain, because it was normal. It's just that my mother didn't talk about it also, because she was in [Europe]. But everyone, right, who was wealthy had slaves."

Dona Margaret's relationship with the servants who worked for her family during her childhood was far more circumscribed than the relationships that Eliza had described. Her own nursemaid was evidently a European woman, although the family had had servants of color during the years they resided in Brazil. I asked Dona Margaret to describe her own relationship with the family's servants:

ROBIN: And did they actually live here?

MARGARET: Yes, they lived here; they always lived here.

ROBIN: Did they have their own children living here with them?

MARGARET: No. Only once, there was one time; there was one who was married, a washerwoman who had a child. Later she left. Her son . . . was born here. But, generally, no.

ROBIN: And did this child play with you and your siblings?

MARGARET: Oh, no! No! No way! [Chuckles.]

ROBIN: Because your parents would not allow it?

MARGARET: I remember until now, yes, yes. I remember this story. . . . There was a little child, a baby, and he was separated [from me and my siblings], right? And I thought he was beautiful, right, and one time I picked him up and put him in my lap. "Oh, what horror! Margaret! Margaret, what are you doing!" . . . Until now, I remember this.

ROBIN: Your mother said this?

MARGARET: Yes. She was a very open person, quite liberal, but in this, no.

In the end, Dona Margaret said very little about her first years in Rio after an adolescence spent mostly in Europe, and her grasp of Brazilian history seemed very thin, particularly given her own family's salient and well-documented role within it. She was educated in France, she explained, and only knew the history of Brazil through a few books that she had read. Protected by the insular embrace of an elite family, it seems, Dona Margaret's passage from Europe to Brazil broadened neither her perspective nor her experience. While she proudly identified as Brazilian, she continued, like many members of Brazil's traditional upper class, to identify with the elite cultures of Europe.

As the comments I have quoted above suggest, my white middle-class (and upper-class) informants grew up in environments that were highly segregated in terms of both class and color, and this was true whether they lived in urban or rural areas. These informants thus lived and continue to live, like people in Morro do Sangue Bom, within highly racialized structures. As Virginia told me, referring to people of color, "The reality is that they are not normally incorporated into your life; they are not in your social circles." For the most part, they describe these structures as part of a normal, taken-for-granted world, constructed not through personalized forms of agency, but through history, culture, and society—abstract and, as it were, natural forces.

Silvia and Aninha: Crossing the Color Line

Two of my middle-class white informants, Silvia and Aninha, shared experiences and articulated a sense of themselves that differed in fundamental ways from those of my other informants. It is precisely the fact that their stories were so atypical that makes them helpful in illuminating the social geography of whiteness.

Silvia, a woman in her early forties, was comfortably ensconced in a middle-class apartment, but the view from her verandah, as is so common in Santa Teresa, looked out upon one of the district's larger morros. During our interview, I asked Silvia very few questions. Issues related to race and racism were central in her life, and with considerable relief, I allowed her to determine the topics and direction of our conversation. I began by explaining the nature of my research and noted that "some people feel that racism does not exist in Brazil." Silvia interjected, "You just have to open your mouth to say that racism doesn't exist and you are already being racist." Without pause, she continued:

> I was always a woman who followed the pattern of a rebellious
> woman, of a marginal woman, at the professional level, at the level of
> posture, of life, in terms of divisions in the world. . . . I did theater for
> many years; I've experimented with all kinds of drugs; I lived my life
> through that. I don't have like—I'm not a person with this family
> discourse. . . . I have an identity of marginality. I was always a woman
> who liked the street. I was always a woman who liked the night. I
> always wanted to be where there was a lot of movement. And negros
> have a lot of movement!

From the first moments of our interview then, Silvia located herself outside of many of the conventions that characterized the constricting world of her youth. She constructed much of our interview, in fact, as a series of stories that depicted her attempts to escape from that world. She continued:

> For example, I have a very strong history with negros, really very
> strong, right? I have a negro son; my son is an African, right? [His
> father is Senegalese.] I was born in Bahia, right, where the majority
> of the population is negro, right? The woman who took care of me
> when I was a child, who was a black woman, she is very strong in my
> memory, and she was very much loved, including by my father. She
> was taking care of my father since his childhood. She was a

nursemaid. She was a negra, so I have—she was a very strong person in my life, even spiritually. Really, I mean, I was a child and when, after she died, I communicated with her. She appeared to me, as if alive again. So it is a very strong memory. Until now she is appearing. She had died, but she appeared at night so that I could see her, to tuck me into bed, doing the same things she did when she was alive. . . . I was not troubled because it was always a very close relationship, right?

While Silvia's experiences were unusual, she drew from a well-worn discursive repertoire in which people of color are figured as more attuned to the spiritual side than are whites. Silvia engaged in a type of racialized objectification, yet it was clear, in the larger context of our interview, that she had spent too much time in the intimate company of people of color to be entirely comfortable with generalizations. Her romanticism did not blind her to the complexity within her husband's, friends', and son's experiences.

Later in our conversation, Silvia described her relationship with her ex-husband, a widely traveled, politically engaged Senegalese man:

He was very aggressive in his relationship with me because everything that he went through outside [of our relationship], everything that he went through on the street, that he assimilated from racists, right—he had a tendency to throw these things at me. [He would say,] "Oh, because you're white, you are blah, blah, blah." So he threw it all at me. . . . The society is so conflicted, it is a society so full of conflict that this one with whom you live is going to suffer the first punch, right, because it seems that [he or she] is barring you. . . . You're from the world of the oppressor, the completely prejudiced world. . . . You have that image and you represent that world. . . . So, there are perceptions, because every person of any color perceives [racism], right, but to be close to all of this, in a strong relationship—so, it's very different, you begin to see that racism really exists, that it is very strong, right, and that it has been functioning for a long time.

Silvia's comments engaged a kind of shifting perspective. Throughout most of our interview, she remained anchored, like other informants, within her own vantage point and her own voice and referred in a fairly abstract and generalizing manner to "the negro." When Silvia said, however, "This one with whom you live is going to suffer the first punch, right, because it seems that [he or she] is barring you," her vantage point shifted, in a dramatic and obvious way, to that of her ex-husband. She imagined what he might have felt and thought during the progress of his relationship with her. It was precisely the experience of seeing her whiteness reflected in her husband's eyes, Silvia suggested, that taught her about racism as a profound and totalizing form of entrapment that poisoned even the intimate space of marriage. Among all of my white middle-class informants, only Silvia and Aninha (who had also married a black man) engaged in this empathetic shift of perspective and expressed a preoccupation with how they might be represented by people of color. They had a consciousness, in other words, of their whiteness.

Aninha, a woman in her thirties, lived in an apartment in Edifício Silvestre, the large building situated just below Morro do Sangue Bom. My first interviewee, Virginia, was her neighbor, and she told me that because Aninha was married to a black man, she might be interested in talking to me. Aninha led me to a couch in the living room, where we began our interview. Aninha began to talk generally about racism in Brazil and pointed out that although many people denied it, prejudice and discrimination were rife in her country.

Several minutes after we had begun our interview, Aninha's mother, whom I had not even known was in the apartment, burst into the room, shouting, "Aninha! Aninha, that is not true!" This woman—she never introduced herself, but I will call her Dona Regina—began a twenty-minute tirade in which she argued that blacks were far more racist than whites and that they were, by nature, "impudent," "lazy," and "belligerent" people. It was time they stopped "bellyaching about slavery," she insisted, and got over their *raiva*, or rage, toward whites. There was nothing covert or concealed in Dona Regina's impassioned outburst. She never lowered her voice to conversational tones but shouted from across the room. She referred over and over again to the relationship between *nossa raça* (our race) and the *raça negra* (black race). Black Brazilians were poor, she told me, because, like their African forebears, they were naturally "indolent."

"Indolent! Indolent!" Aninha shouted, trying with very little success to make herself heard over her mother's shouting. "What a racist thing! Look at that racist discourse!"

Whites had always dominated blacks, Dona Regina argued, pushing on, because blacks had allowed them to. What galled her most of all was the "impudence" with which they treated her:

> I've already heard it; the negro himself has prejudice! A lot of
> prejudice! They have rage. . . . I myself, I have already gone around
> and they say to me, "You *brancazeda* (sour white)! You *branquela!*
> Brancazeda!"[4] Do you understand? [They say to me,] "If there is a
> revolution here, if we have one, you will be the first to catch fire!"
> They have said that to me! Because I am this type [I appear to be] a
> foreigner, a gringa, so they say, "You gringa, I'm going to throw you in

the fire!"[5] So they have so much rancor, so much hate. . . . I think that people have to work in order to get ahead. . . . Now, most of them are indolent, lazy. . . . All I want is to make you see that [racism] doesn't just exist on the part of the whites. It exists on their part also.

When Aninha did succeed in shouting over her, Dona Regina reverted, for the space of a breath, to the discourse of democracia racial. "You think your culture is better!" Aninha shouted. Dona Regina insisted that she believed that "everyone is equal" and that "the only difference is the color." Illogically, however, she returned to her denunciations.

To devote too much space to this exchange would perhaps distort as much as it would reveal. I do not doubt that Dona Regina's beliefs—that people of color are indolent, that they are impoverished because they do not want to work, that they bear a hatred and rage toward whites—are held, and at least occasionally expressed, by other middle-class whites, including those I interviewed in Santa Teresa. In a very real sense, Dona Regina's words represent a subterranean text upon which a palimpsest of ambiguous, often polite, and liberal discourses is imposed. Nevertheless, the intensity of Dona Regina's outburst is unusual. Denial, dissimulation, ambivalence, indifference, and silence remained the predominant modes through which middle-class whites communicated their beliefs about race and racism to me. For the most part, I believe, they are similarly restrained in one another's company.

After her mother left the apartment, Aninha rolled her eyes and sighed. She returned to her discussion of various aspects of racism, using, on occasion, her mother as an example. "When she says these things happen to her," Aninha said, referring to her mother's description of the hostility that was directed against her by people of color, "I think it's this posture that she has—'I am better; I am white; I am a queen'—so people feel this and they attack her."

Like Silvia, Aninha had been involved with the black movement. Her marriage to a man of color and the fact that she had three children of color had sharpened her perception of racism, such that it appeared to have become one of the central preoccupations of her life.

Needless to say, Aninha felt that she had moved, ideologically speaking, to a position very different from that of the exclusively white world in which she had been raised. I asked her if she had any sense of why she was different in these terms. "I think that there are many people who have a consciousness, right, that people are equal," she began:

> I've always had this. It's a thing that I've had since I was twelve years old. The other day my grandmother was saying that when I was twelve years old, I said to her at the table, "You are racist and I am

going to give you completely mulato grandchildren!" . . . I always
thought it was absurd. . . . My grandmother has this thing, like she
doesn't want to give a kiss to an acquaintance of hers because, as she
tells it, she "doesn't feel right because she is a negra." I mean, I never
understood this! For me, it was never—this has always bothered me,
people making this segregation, right? I think there are some people
who are like that, right? I think that I am equal, completely equal to
a person who is a negro.

According to public discourses, Aninha should have remained a typical
Brazilian, the predictable product of a world that not only permitted, but celebrated miscegenation. On the contrary, however, after her marriage to a
black man, Aninha became alienated from her family. She began speaking of
her mother:

It's this kind of thing, I don't know, in her head; she would want me
to marry another type of man, right, who would be a prince, an image,
right, of the successful white man, who fits into the pattern, right? She
never adjusted—and the whole family! So, I became isolated. Because
they didn't accept it. . . . People don't say anything openly. She and
some of my siblings . . . who don't accept it, they give other excuses to
camouflage their racism. They don't say that it's because he's a negro,
they say other things: "Oh, it's because he doesn't earn a lot [of
money]; he doesn't push himself." . . . And I myself, after a certain
period, I didn't connect to it, this thing of the big family. I didn't
participate. I was imagining another nucleus, other people who had
other codes . . . because I'm not going to hang around with people
who won't have anything to do with negros! So I got out, I got out.

In referring to "people who won't have anything to do with negros,"
Aninha, like Silvia, highlighted the naturalized arrangements within which
her family and most middle-class whites construct their lives. She confirmed
my point that discourses of "camouflage" are the norm, rather than her
mother's impassioned tirade. In the following section, I focus explicitly on the
ways in which my middle-class white informants reveal, and at the same time
attempt to conceal, their discomfort with the transgressive scenarios that the
adult biographies of Aninha and Silvia suggest.

Whiteness and Racial Transgression

As is clear, many of my middle-class white informants appeared to be somewhat preoccupied with the issue of interracial marriage and/or sex, although
only a few (besides Aninha and Silvia) knew interracial couples or had them-

selves dated people of color. Heloisa's and Eliza's suggestions that they had never socialized with black men, were never "interested," and/or had "never thought about it" accurately reflect the racialized structure of the world in which they live. Despite the fact that sexual or romantic relationships remained an abstraction in the lives of most of my informants, a number of them spoke more volubly about this issue than any other.

When I asked Virginia if she felt there was prejudice against color, her first example concerned interracial dating. "For example, if you have a negro boyfriend, no one is going to like it," she said. "Who wouldn't like it?" I asked. "The family!" she exclaimed. "Mixed relationships!" Heloisa's first example of racism also concerned mixed relationships: "When you see a person, generally a preto, with a blonde woman, you stare."

During the first several moments of my interview with Gilberto, he told me, "Racism even exists in a strange form. For example, a mixed-race couple is a thing that obviously calls your attention, and that's natural, because it isn't very common. But besides calling attention, it causes commentary like, 'Hell, how can that pretty woman be going with a negro' or 'How can that good-looking guy be going with a negra.' Right?"

Gilberto's comments clearly contradict the frequently expressed notions that relationships between men and women of different colors are very common in Brazil and that they represent, in fact, the greatest evidence of democracia racial. Gilberto's description of the commentary that surrounds such couples as they walk down the street is accurate. My informants on the morro not only mimicked such discourse for the purposes of my research but participated in it themselves.

Although Gilberto had intended his comments as a critique of racism, at a later moment in our interview he made it clear that he himself did not approve of such relationships. Gilberto's greater concern seemed to be with what he called the "perspective of the black woman." "You well know how negras relate to white men in an affective, sexual relationship," he continued. He suggested that black women were manipulative and calculating, seeing in the white man "the possibility of socioeconomic ascension." "This discourse is stronger among black women," he continued, "upward mobility through a relationship with a white man, right?"

Celso's comments about black women and the way in which white men related to them were very different. For him, the white man was inevitably the sexual aggressor, and the black woman a passive object. It was this scenario that most troubled Celso, and the one for which he "blamed" himself. As I have noted, he told me that he had grown up with the notion that "a negra could only be an empregada or a prostitute." He elaborated:

And the thing of sexual initiation itself was often with a negra, very often with a negra, with the empregada. When I was an adolescent, this initiation was in the red light area [with prostitutes] or with an empregada. The empregada, in most cases, was a negra. These were the first sexual experiences, right? And you didn't have to—you didn't have to marry them. There wasn't such a strong association [of sex with marriage]. . . . It was that kind of business. And wet nurses—in my infancy there were a lot of wet nurses, that whole slavery thing. "The negra is good in bed and good in the kitchen." "They have an odor; the negro has an odor called 'bumdum,' a strong odor." Right? I think that's all [I can remember]. [Pause] "Indecent negro." Because they dance, they express a lot of sexuality in a more open way. "Indecent negro" or "animal." These things . . . I think it's not just in Minas [where I grew up]. There isn't a person in the whole society, principally the society—I don't know, I don't know. . . . This colonialist society, right, colonial, has a lot of this thing. . . . I don't remember anything else.

My assigning of quotation marks to Celso's comments is interpretative; it is difficult to determine the extent to which he was speaking in his own voice or was quoting the voices that compose a public repertoire—which he seemed to summon as if from a psychoanalyst's couch. When I asked him to describe examples of racism, he told me, "It is an internalized thing, culturally internalized. . . . I even feel I have a consciousness of this in my relationship with a negra. And in a relationship that I have, I pay a lot of attention to this. But deep down, I feel that I'm somewhat racist." Celso was far less fluent in describing the multidimensional consequences of racism for his neighbors who lived on the morro.

As I have previously noted, David, also from Minas Gerais and a resident of the Plazaflor, told me that as he grew older he changed and discovered, among other things, that he had "the capacity to make love with a negra." Later in our conversation, I asked him, "If your daughter were dating a negro or a person of color, what would you think?" His response was halting and awkward:

Oh, who knows? [Pause] My upbringing is like that. You have to marry a person who is your equal, right? That is what you seek. For example, if this guy was above her, if he was a guy who was cultured, if [it was a relationship] of affection, of love—it's difficult, right, these days, for someone to have this pure thing of love—if this person had these things, then it's not important, right—their color. But he would have to be very good, and this is something—I think it would [depend] on her luck, for her to have a negro person, but one with ability. . . . In truth, for me now, if he were a totally obnoxious crioulo, then I would be appalled! I would become really appalled with the guy!

David's use of the term "crioulo" was equivalent to a slip of the tongue. He may have felt that my question was somewhat impertinent—although it was a natural, even an expectable one in the context of a conversation that he himself controlled to certain degree—but I had the sense that he was struggling toward candor. As was the case with all of my informants, David had far less difficulty discussing the racism of his relatives and others than he did in describing his own views. I asked him, "And your own parents, what would they say?" He replied, "Obviously they wouldn't say anything; they are educated. But naturally they wouldn't like it. They would accept it, but they would say, 'What a shame that he is preto.' That's what they would say. And it's true what they would say!"

For David, there is no contradiction between his comment that he has "the capacity to make love with a negra" and the horror with which he would view his daughter's relationship with a black man—even one who is "cultured." Envisioning such a relationship for himself, he relies on notions of masculine prerogative and the certainty that such a relationship need not disturb the racial status quo. Envisioning a very different relationship for his daughter, he is confronted by the collapse of racial boundaries, the specter, really, of equality between himself and his daughter's hypothetical boyfriend. Lurking within this, of course, is the additional specter of racial "pollution," the inverse of the whitening ideal to which my informants on the morro were subject. As my two informants who had married black men informed me, the birth of their children (whom they both referred to as negros) was initially greeted with consternation on the part of their families, and it led to an escalation of their sense of alienation from parents and siblings. Whiteness, I would suggest, is viewed as a genetic resource as well as a racialized form of cultural capital.[6]

Both David and his ex-wife, Heloisa, encouraged me to interview their fifteen-year-old daughter, Maura. As had other informants, Maura herself raised the issue of mixed relationships when I asked her to describe examples or incidents of racism with which she was familiar: "When a person says, 'Oh, here is my boyfriend,' and they present a preto guy, and you're white, and you have a preto boyfriend, [they say], 'Oh, you're going out with this guy, how disgusting!' A friend of mine went out with a preto guy and everyone gave her hell for it, saying that he was ugly and all that."

Her friend's relationship, Maura told me, had been very brief. I asked her, "And you, I know it depends a great deal on the person, but would you date a preto?" Her voice was very barely audible when she replied in the negative. "Oh, because of the discrimination," she said in explanation. "Against me and him there would be heavy discrimination."

Dona Margaret also brought up the issue of relationships between men and women of different colors. She did so, in fact, during the first moments of our interview. Before I had even turned on my tape recorder, she confessed to me—in barely audible tones—that she disapproved of, and was uncomfortable with, the notion of "relations between blacks and whites." I immediately gathered what she meant by "relations." Speaking once again, more directly than her daughter Eliza had, she told me that if one of her daughters had had a black boyfriend, she would have been deeply disturbed.

I briefly acknowledged Dona Margaret's comment, set up my tape recorder, and asked her to describe her family and her childhood, for I did not want to begin our interview with probing questions that, more likely than not, would dampen her generous inclination to respond candidly. Later in our interview, I returned to her remark. "And more general things now. You said that if your daughter showed up with a black boyfriend, you wouldn't like it?" Lowering her voice to a whisper, Dona Margaret responded, "Oh, no, no, I wouldn't like it, no! This is so deep in me and even I think that it isn't . . ." Although I had leaned forward, the better to hear Dona Margaret's breathy whispering, her voice faded to an inaudible murmur. I pursued the issue:

ROBIN: Did it ever happen?

MARGARET: No, no, no! Never! Thank God! What a problem that would be! My lord! I think that—no, no, thank God!

ROBIN: And did you say anything to them—

MARGARET: No.

ROBIN: At any time?

MARGARET: No, never.

ROBIN: Do you think they know that you feel this way?

MARGARET: I think that it was a normal thing, right? I never thought of saying anything about this, no.

Through various discursive and prosodic means (including her tendency to whisper), Dona Margaret implied that she had an awareness of her own racism. She never tried to convince me that her horror of interracial sex and marriage was either logical or justified. As had Celso and David, she presented her attitude as one that had simply been internalized. She would not even describe the content of her assumptions but only alluded to their existence. She seemed to be aware on some level that she was entrapped by the things that were "deep in" her, but she sought no escape.

Racism: Narratives and Erasures

Generally speaking, all of my middle-class white informants acknowledged that racism exists in Brazil. In describing examples of racism, most tended, perhaps naturally, to speak not in terms of its effect on people of color but from their own vantage points. Most of my middle-class white informants, in addition, offered various types of qualifications when they discussed racism in their country. Their comments seemed to turn upon an ambiguous or contradictory logic.

Most of my informants, as I have already noted, were more comfortable talking about class than they were about race and/or racism. They tended to follow a very public script that emphasizes what is generally called *discriminação social*. In Brazil, the term "social" is a gloss for class and the structures, behaviors, and beliefs associated with class. Although the consequences of class, or, specifically, of poverty, are often figured as inexorable in Brazilian society, the role of race and/or color is typically underplayed. Most of my informants, moreover, qualified their descriptions of racism by stating their belief that the behaviors and attitudes associated with racism were progressively decreasing.

I asked David if he believed that racism exists in Brazil, and he said, "Yes, I think so." When I asked him if he could describe some examples of racism, he began, "There are people who, depending upon their origin—there are some who have better conditions than those who have different origins, such as favelados. [Favelados] can be discriminated against. When you hear, 'He is a favelado,' it is [said] in a very pejorative way."

Because I had specifically requested information about racism, I asked, "And the favelado is generally associated with color?" He continued, "No, no, people with condemned social conditions. It's not the color of the skin, right? The person is discriminated against socially, right? There are whites in the favela also. And they are favelados like the negros."

By the time I conducted this interview, David's response was extremely familiar to me. Living so close to Morro do Sangue Bom, David no doubt noticed that a clear majority of people on the morro were of African descent whereas nearly all of the families living in the Plazaflor were unambiguously white. Yet the existence of poor whites is often summoned as evidence that "it's not the color of the skin" that is associated with discrimination against Brazilians of African descent, but what David calls one's origin, by which he means, in this particular context, class.

Up to this point, David had sidestepped my question. I persisted by asking him, "But do you think that there is racial discrimination here, besides—" David interrupted, "There is; there is, yes. Brazilian society is from Europeans. This puts a division in society. Because the Europeans are racist. We have here

Portuguese, and the Portuguese is racist. The Spaniard is racist, and the Germans in the south. So, I think, yes, there is a discrimination of race, of color, really."

It is hard to be certain what David means by "the Portuguese." His reference is an abstract one, similar to the hypothetical Portuguese who figures in Brazilian ethnic jokes as racist and stupid. Although David began by saying, "Brazilian society is from Europeans," he does not seem to suggest that Brazilians have learned racism from their dominant European ancestors but rather that racism is primarily practiced by foreigners and immigrants.

David had still not responded to my initial request that he describe examples of racism in Brazil. I reiterated the question and he responded:

> There exist families in which if your son or your daughter is having a relationship with someone—until now, they keep observing their origins, the color of the skin. They observe this, right, and when the person is a mulato, or a mestiço, or a negro, it is really commented on. "My kids are going around with negros, with crioulos," and this [is said] in a very pejorative way. I notice this a lot. There are other aspects too. There is preference for more attractive people, right? And here, people choose in a way that conforms to this, those who have a better look. . . . So there are many cases, but we don't remember. I don't remember. But I notice these things, I notice.

David's description of racism, such as it was, required considerable prompting on my part and weary of pulling teeth, I decided to change the direction of my questions. I asked David if he ever discussed the issue of racism with his friends. He replied, "No, no. I don't talk about it, no. I don't know. There isn't space for us to comment on this. When we have an opportunity to discuss things in a group, we talk about other situations, right, more important things that are happening, right, our impoverishment, our difficulties. So we talk about these things. We don't remember this racial difference that exists between us. Because here, it's very mixed; there is mixture."

I asked David if he knew anything about Brazil's black movement. He told me that he knew that it existed. He was more aware of labor movements and demonstrations by favelados. In general, he suggested, such militant movements were positive, in that they were aimed at securing rights that would "benefit everyone, negros, mulatos, Indians, whites." When I asked him if he would attend an antiracist demonstration, he replied, "No. I don't think anyone would go. Because here in Brazil, no one would go; [only] a few people would go. It's very rare. I don't know. . . . We don't go. It isn't racism that's so widespread. You have seen racism. . . . Over in the nightclubs, pretos can't go in; mulatos can't go in. I know that. But this is a thing that is a class problem, right? . . . So when you're poor and [you say], 'Let's have a demonstration against racism,' the problem is poverty, right, hunger, right?"

David's comments, it seemed to me, were based upon an increasingly procrustean logic. The exclusion of people of color from nightclubs, hotels, and expensive restaurants is frequently offered by those who acknowledge the existence of racism as a classic, even stereotypical example of racialized discrimination. If patrons of color have the pecuniary passport to purchase what such places offer, why are they being held up at the door? Yet even this example, which David mentions as a proleptic aside, is glossed as a class problem. The impulse to offer rhetorical qualifications to the acknowledgment of the existence of racism, it seems, is constant and irresistible.

When I asked Gilberto if he thought there was racism in Brazil, he said, "There is, clearly there is." Unlike many of my other informants, he did not require additional prompting before adding, "But racism exists; I think it exists almost in the entire world, right? . . . Your work is about racism. What is more graphic than racism is social discrimination, right? This is stronger than racism."

Gilberto then proceeded to describe the familiar scenario in which doormen required people of color to take service rather than social elevators, even when they were people "of distinction." Throughout our interview, as I have noted, Gilberto suggested that Brazilian racism was "cultural" rather than "ideological;" and, like David, he continued to acknowledge the existence of racism while denying its significance. "Social discrimination, economic and social discrimination," he said, "leaves this [racial] question nebulous." Gilberto pointed out that neither whites nor blacks "touch on the subject of racism."

"They certainly don't!" I exclaimed. Gilberto continued, "This is data that could even prove right, it would prove—it's good information, right? It could prove that racism really isn't important, that the racial question is not important. Because discussing this discourse, the negro as much as the white—I think the negros are much more racist than the whites. I see a greater racism among the negros than among the whites."

Somewhat later in our conversation, I returned to Gilberto's comment that the subject of racism was rarely touched upon. "So you feel that this is because racism is not an important thing?" I asked. He responded,

> Yes, that's it really. I think that racism is not so important . . . even
> among the negros. The black movement is what? What are they
> mobilizing? Nothing, nothing, right? The militants have not
> mobilized the negro masses. It's because it is not important, not even
> for negros. The negros do not defend their rights as negros, because
> the negro doesn't feel so discriminated against for being a negro.
> Deep in his subconscious, perhaps, he perceives that he is

discriminated against because he is poor, not because he is negro, right? And I think that people don't discuss racism for this reason.

Gilberto evidently felt compelled to repeat his assertion that racism is insignificant in Brazil: "Racism is a crime now; racism is a crime, but how many people go to the police station to register a complaint of racism? When this happens, it becomes news. . . . When it happens that someone seeks out the police because of racism, it becomes news. This is the impression that I have. It becomes a report on the television, on the radio, in the newspaper. It becomes news because it is rare!"

I told Gilberto that I had spoken to people who had gone to the police station to report incidents of racism. "I was told that the police do nothing," I said. I could not press the logic of my point without appearing argumentative, and shortly thereafter I brought the interview to a close.

The rhetorical strategies that both David and Gilberto used to qualify and, ultimately, undermine and even erase their acknowledgment of the existence of racism were echoed by other informants. What they did not say, would not say, and/or simply did not know was also reflected in my interviews with other middle-class white informants. All of my informants, for example, were able to describe a limited number of examples of racism, but their descriptions, like David's and Gilberto's, tended to be very brief and often required specific and persistent prompting.

Eliza told me that her empregada occasionally expressed anger about racism. This disturbed Eliza, who believed it was better to not *ligar*, or connect, with the issue. I told Eliza that I had the impression that many Brazilians did not like to talk about racism. She responded, "I have never—it's really a subject that we don't converse about. I am conversing like this with you today, but it isn't a subject that one converses about. I—when I am with my friends, we don't talk like this about racism. We don't talk about it, you know? I think that this could even be on the part of the negro himself. . . . I have this impression that he himself doesn't like to talk about it."

Dona Margaret suggested that there might be a somewhat different way of explaining the infrequency with which the issue of racism is discussed in middle-class circles. At the midpoint of our conversation, I asked her, "Have you heard other examples of racism? Of any sort, people talking, in the newspapers?" She paused and said, "No, I don't see much in the newspapers. You know, for me, it's a thing that shouldn't exist." At this point, Dona Margaret had once again lowered her voice to a near whisper, and I leaned forward and asked her to repeat what she had said. Still speaking in hushed tones, she said, "It shouldn't exist. So I don't—it isn't a subject that I talk about much. If I told about something like that, it would call more attention to it, right?"

Dona Margaret's remark about calling attention to racism confirmed my impression that she resisted my attempts to elicit information because she obeyed the dictates of what Frazier called an "unexpressed understanding" not to discuss racism (qtd. in Hellwig 1992, 131). In this succinct comment, I believe, Dona Margaret articulated something fundamental about the ways in which many middle-class whites approach the issue of racism and discourse about racism.

Dona Margaret did not have an intimate, fully conscious knowledge of either racism or its painful consequences for people of color, yet in accounting for her own silence, she seemed to echo my informants on the morro. Talking about racism, she suggested, magnifies it. In a certain sense, her comment represents an extreme form of "color evasive discourse" (Frankenberg 1993), one that attempts to erase the significance of racial constructions in the service of a spurious liberalism. In the context of democracia racial, however, it is far more than that.

Clearly, there are important differences in the ways in which middle-class whites and poor people of color account for the silence surrounding racism. The most evident of these differences, I believe, resides in the fact that people on the morro articulate a profound sense of hopelessness, if not complete resignation, when they account for their silence. They say it is best to simply let it go. Middle-class whites, on the other hand, tend to assert that the issue of racism has little or no importance in their lives and it is, besides, rapidly fading into the shadows of a history that is best forgotten.

Nevertheless, I would speculate, the examination of racism among middle-class whites might evoke a kind of pain that overlaps with, without being penetrated by, the pain expressed by people on the morro. Although I have asserted that Aninha and Silvia took the tenets of democracia racial to heart in a way that is uncharacteristic of many middle-class whites, Dona Margaret, and probably a majority of my informants, really did believe that racism shouldn't exist. Many who critique democracia racial as a very simple mystifying ideology would argue that in the mouths of people like Dona Margaret, such comments are mere rhetoric. There is, however, a perceptible if unexamined degree of passion under this rhetoric.

Although Benedita did not describe racism in contemporary Rio in much greater detail than did my other informants, some of her responses to my questions, while terse and even deceptively simple, seemed to underline the significance of Dona Margaret's comment. Regarding the relative silence surrounding racism in Brazil, Benedita told me, "It's like they want to obfuscate it, right? To obfuscate the history of the country, the history of slavery, of the Indian. Because it causes suffering. It causes suffering. When you have a consciousness of it, it causes suffering; it requires work. . . . People know this, that it requires work to become aware, you know?"

We had been talking very specifically about levels of awareness of, and discourses about, racism in present-day Rio de Janeiro. It is notable that Benedita located illusion, lack of consciousness—that which is obfuscated—in the ways in which Brazilians conceptualize and talk about (or do not talk about) history rather than in the ways in which they construct the present. Ironically, her critique of false or incomplete consciousness and the will toward obfuscation is spoken at a safe remove from contested understandings of contemporary social relations.

The suffering that Benedita refers to is more, I would argue, than a sense of personal or private guilt. If guilt does play a significant role in this suffering, it must be noted that it is not limited to middle-class whites but is, no doubt, shared by poor people of color who also engage in racist discourses. While the notion of guilt captures something of the fundamentally moral nature of Brazilian discourses on race and racism, it elides the articulation of this suffering with the collective orchestration of more complex, culturally elaborated sentiments. The discourses of democracia racial embody a utopianism that goes to the heart of Brazilians' historically entrenched visions of themselves and their nation. In saying that racism "shouldn't exist" and in explaining that she avoids talking about it because it "calls more attention to it," Dona Margaret implicitly acknowledges the fragility of these visions and her own and others' investment in them.

The suffering of middle-class whites, as their comments suggest, does not incorporate an awareness of the very different forms of suffering endured by their neighbors in Morro do Sangue Bom, nor does it challenge, in any way, the structural and discursive bases of their indifference. Dona Margaret's comments suggest, nevertheless, that there is a subterranean level at which there is another kind of indifference; it is a studied, even contractual, and morally freighted one, and it is based as much on a culturally produced reticence in looking at what is *embaixo do pano* (under the concealing fabric) of democracia racial as it is on the mechanics of insularity. It is the pano, the gently, graciously concealing cloth itself, that defines everything that is most deeply Brazilian, in one's own spirit and in the nation. To look at what lies underneath it, to comment on it, to engage with it, to allow it to be real by calling attention to it—these things, it is suggested, are undisciplined, un-Brazilian crudities, and they are a betrayal of an unspoken but universally understood etiquette. Not even negros, so many of my middle-class white informants clearly believed, want to have their wounds pointed out to them.

Chapter 7

Blackness

Militant Discourses

I am told that two years ago, a Negro who had got his freedom took to preaching in the Victoria Parks of this place, in black slums and other places where black men most do congregate; that he mounted his barrel, and spoke with the greatest of fervour and eloquence, repeating chapters of the Bible to the people (who of course are ignorant of it) and expounding it with great wisdom—a real Negro Luther, unmerciful to sins, hypocrisies, and frauds, and telling the black man that he was his own slave, as well as the white man's. He was followed by great crowds, and began to be called the "Divine Master." At length the government information laid against him, as for fomenting political sedition—which everybody knew was false—so he got condemned to three years' imprisonment, or banishment, or—nobody knows what and has not been heard of since.

—c. b. mansfield, Brazil and the Platt

THE ABOVE PASSAGE was written by the British traveler C. B. Mansfield in 1856, thirty-two years before the abolition of slavery in Brazil. Although his story comes from the northeastern state of Pernambuco, it could have been told virtually anywhere in Brazil, and the events it describes could have occurred as easily in the post-abolition era. Yet Mansfield reveals the naiveté of a foreign visitor in his suggestion, however sympathetically motivated, that this "Negro Luther" was not fomenting sedition.

"Telling the black man that he was his own slave, as well as white man's," was and remains, more than one hundred years after abolition, a culturally seditious act in Brazil. Contemporary militants, who refer to themselves as negros or Afro-Brasileiros, like the preacher described by Mansfield, are still confronted by the puzzles of *consciencia negra,* or black consciousness, and their *luta,* or struggle, remains one in which angry words are pitted against what appears to be an overwhelming passivity, complacency, and silence. Also like the preacher, who manipulated the rhetoric of the master's religion, contemporary militants are attempting to manipulate dominant discourses, even while struggling to break free of them. To a far greater extent than is the case in countries such as the United States, I would argue, black militancy in Brazil requires, paradoxically, perhaps, that many of the battles of political activism be fought in the metadiscursive arena. Many of the forms of entrapment that I have described in previous pages become clearer through an examination of the discourses and metadiscourses of the activists who so generously served as my informants and, in some cases, as my field advisors during the months I spent in Rio.

My intention, while in the field, was not to delve very deeply into the complicated histories and politics of Brazil's black movement, which is often called, for good reason, a consciousness movement. Undoubtedly, the movement represents an extremely fertile field for research and scholars in a variety of disciplines. For example, Andrews (1991, 1992a), Burdick (1998), Butler (1998), Fontaine (1981), and Hanchard (1993, 1999)—to name the most recent, major English-language sources—have written well-informed and provocative accounts of various aspects of the movement.

My aim in this chapter is a more limited one: to offer the reader a sense of the tone and content of contemporary discourses among some of the members of Rio's more prominent black movement organizations and to present the autobiographical narratives by which they account for their personal involvement in the movement. In addition, my quotation of black militant discourses echoes and in a number of instances clarifies, confirms, or offers a commentary on my own analysis of discourses in both Morro do Sangue Bom and the white middle-class neighborhood of Santa Teresa. Although there is, in truth, remarkably little interaction between these three groups, the juxtapositioning of their understandings of democracia racial, racism, and identity—and the language and discursive strategies they use to articulate those understandings—provide a valuable frame for exploring the diversity of vantage points from which racial meanings are constructed in Rio de Janeiro. Moreover, should the perspectives and discourses of black militants gain increasing salience in the years to come—and there is some indication that they may (Hanchard 1999, 14–15; Roth Gordon 1999; Winant 1999, 111–112)—the examination of those discourses might point to future shifts in the mainstream currents through which racial meanings can be publicly renegotiated.

Black militancy in Brazil has a long and ideologically complex history. Although numerous small, loosely knit organizations emerged in the first half of the twentieth century, none endured more than a few years and only a few achieved any prominence. The most notable of these early movements were the Frente Negra Brasileira and the Teatro Experimental do Negro.

The Frente Negra Brasileira (Black Brazilian Front) was founded in 1931, one year after the collapse of the Republic, which had operated as a one-party system. Beginning in São Paulo, the movement spread rapidly to other states. While dedicated to black empowerment and the denunciation of racism, the Frente Negra quickly aligned itself with Integralism and the burgeoning fascist ideologies then current in Brazil, as elsewhere (Butler 1998, 115–128). Within a few years of its founding, many of the Frente Negra's moderate and left-leaning members left the movement. One year after registering itself as a political party in 1936, the Frente Negra was dissolved by the Vargas regime, along with all other political parties.

The Vargas regime, while stifling political opposition, instituted labor legislation that benefited people of color, many of whom were, of course, members of the working classes. Their incorporation into populist parties, combined with the articulation of discourses of democracia racial, further undermined the development of explicitly political forms of black activism. As Andrews notes, "The result was that the black organizations of the 1946–64 period were almost exclusively cultural in their orientation, focusing on literacy and other educational projects, the fostering of black literary, theatrical and artistic activities" (1992a, 162).

The Teatro Experimental do Negro (TEN), founded in 1944, was just such an organization. Initially formed to provide opportunities for actors of color who were denied work in white-dominated theater productions, TEN also attracted a wider group of intellectuals and artists, both black and white. However, TEN was even less successful than the Frente Negra in attracting large numbers of African Brazilians; this was due not only to the prevailing cultural forces which continue to operate against racialized political mobilization, but also to the essentially elitist character of the organization (Hanchard 1994a, 107).

The military coup of 1964 initiated what was to become the most repressive and dangerous period for black activists. Political activism was officially defined as a threat to state security. Black militants were tortured and jailed. Even those not directly involved in activism, such as the social scientists Florestan Fernandez, Octavio Ianni, and Brazil's current president, Fernando Henrique Cardoso, were forced out of their university positions, at least partly as a result of their critical research and writing on race relations. During this period, what had before been a cultural and ideological form of censorship was now officially and strictly enforced; newspapers, television programming, and cultural activities were all closely monitored by a state determined to silence all public discourse on racism.

As government restrictions on political and cultural activities began to loosen their grip in the late 1970s, new forms of black activism emerged, especially in the states of São Paulo and Rio de Janeiro. Inspired by the civil rights movement of the United States and the anti-colonial movements of Africa, black militants began to craft a more directly political critique of Brazilian racism. Discourses on the systemic relationship between race and class, for example, took center stage. Unable to organize their strategies around the issue of legal segregation as American activists had, they denounced *racismo mascarado*, or masked racism, and the de facto segregation of African Brazilians in the urban periphery and the favelas. To a much greater degree than they had in the past, black militants of this period aligned themselves with leftist political concepts and discourses and, in many cases, with specific leftist political parties.

The Movimento Negro Unificado (Unified Black Movement) was the most visible black movement organization of this period. As several scholars have argued, the MNU and other organizations that began in the late 1970s and early 1980s received their impetus not only from the *abertura*, or democratization, of political process in Brazil, but also from the frustration and disillusionment of university-educated African Brazilians who were unable to secure the jobs, income, and status promised them by democracia racial (Hanchard 1994a; Turner 1985).

The Movimento Negro Unificado was founded in 1978, with the ambitious aim of unifying black militants throughout the country under one ideological and organizational banner (Gonzalez 1985). The MNU was, and continues to be, explicitly Marxist in orientation. Its members, however, certainly refute the notion, common among Brazilian leftists, that race and racism are largely irrelevant epiphenomena of class, and define them rather as functional products of the transnational, historically situated operations of capitalism. Despite its ambitions, the MNU has been unable to significantly effect electoral politics, nor has it succeeded in becoming a highly organized, national movement.

During the 1980s and 1990s several state agencies were formed that explicitly focused on "the conditions of the black community" (Andrews 1992a, 166), and as Hanchard has recently noted, Brazil's current president, Fernando Henrique Cardoso, has publicly acknowledged the need for "state activity around and recognition of racial inequality" (1999, 14). Although these state-level activities represent milestones of a sort, this recognition has been slow in building and many militants continue to view those governmental agencies that do exist as "purely cosmetic entities with no real political influence or significance" (Andrews 1992a, 167).

Contemporary black activism in Rio de Janeiro appears, above all, to be highly splintered and factionalized. Some Rio-based organizations exist primarily or purely to promote antiracist activism and/or black consciousness, while other, more explicitly cultural (and often transitory) groups and associations, such as samba schools, Candomblé *terreiros, blocos afros* (musical and/or dance troupes), and various religious organizations (Burdick 1998), serve as sites for the development of black solidarity and consciousness.

My own research focused on nonreligious organizations of long-standing in Rio de Janeiro—those with a more or less permanent membership, elective offices, regular public events, and permanent housing. Most of my militant informants occupied positions of leadership within these organizations, and most were male—a fact that reflects the dominance of men in Brazil's black movement.[1]

João, the activist informant with whom I spent the most time, was one of the most visible of Rio's self-styled black activists. He habitually wore a large beret with the African national colors, as much to conceal a receding hairline, perhaps, as to announce his political disposition. During the time of my fieldwork, he served as the director of one of the nation's oldest surviving black movement organizations, which was founded under deliberately false public pretenses in the tortured years of the seventies.

João made a successful living as an artist, but most of his energy, it seemed, was devoted to the movement. He was practiced in the arts of oratory, and his comments were almost always embroidered with rhetorical flourishes, illustrative asides in which he mimicked everyday discourses, and bursts of ironic laughter in which he invited his interlocutor to wonder at the myriad forms of dissimulation that animate *democracia racial*. João was known as something of a provocateur, and he often offended delicate sensibilities— never a difficult task when discussing the issue of racism in Brazil.

João described the disagreements within the movement, while emphasizing its very general and shared direction:

> In reality [disagreements] exist, yes. We define the project in a
> general way. If you go to any entity of the black movement, you will
> see that there is only one project: that of the struggle to combat
> racism, the struggle to change the [social] structure, the struggle for
> society, the construction of *our* society. Now, what we haven't yet
> defined are the methods. So, each one thinks he has a viable way of

doing this. Some think that it is through culture, that culture is
sufficient. Others like [this organization, here] think that besides
bringing culture in, it is necessary to have [political] participation,
training, [work on] self-esteem, and so on. So, there are divergences
within this process.

João's description of the historical division between primarily culturalist
organizations and those that are principally political organizations has been
strongly emphasized by Hanchard (1994a) in what remains the most thorough
examination of contemporary black activism in southern Brazil. Whereas in
previous periods these orientations have shifted from one historical period to
another, both orientations currently coexist in Rio and in Brazil generally.
Those organizations that define themselves as political tend to focus on
human and civil rights, legislation, and, to a certain extent, electoral politics.
Culturalist organizations tend to concern themselves with the redefinition
and politicization of what they call *cultura Afro-Brasileira*, or African Brazilian
culture. In essence, theirs is a movement of cultural reappropriation and rein-
vention. Carnival performance groups, dances and music, and even beauty
pageants are recrafted to *valorizar*, or valorize, Africa and African Brazilian
history.

While the political organizations accuse the culturalist groups of "folk-
lorizing" and reifying culture, the culturalists charge the political organizations with ineffectual elitism and a failure to "speak to the masses in their own
language." Although some organizations do, in fact, fit this dichotomous
model, my own research suggests that others are attempting to straddle both
orientations. Moreover, as João implies, black movement militants, whatever
their organizational affiliation, share common understandings of Brazilian
racism. Although they might appear to "have little political coherence or
relation to one another" (Hanchard 1999), they are all, in fact, engaged in the
common project of developing a discourse about the causes and consequences
of racism in Brazil. This project is, without a doubt, a critical one, given the
overwhelming silence surrounding the issue of racism in Brazil.

Despite the fact that black movement organizations are unified in their
dedication to exposing racism and shattering the silence in which it is
cloaked, one of the most salient features of the movement has been its failure
to attract a truly broad-based following. Many factors have been brought to
account for this failure. Some have argued that the emphasis on color distinctions and branqueamento, or whitening, have discouraged people of color
from identifying as black and, by extension, from joining a movement of black
solidarity (Hanchard 1994a; Hasenbalg 1994). Many have emphasized the
mystifying thrust of democracia racial and the fact that Brazilians of all colors

tend, in public discourses at least, to attribute discrimination and inequality to class rather than to race or color (Hanchard 1994a; Twine 1998; Wagley 1963b). Added to these explanations are the more prosaic ones suggested by my informants in Morro do Sangue Bom: impoverished Brazilians of color have neither the time nor the energy to engage in political activism. Other explanations for the black movement's failure to attract the masses focus on inadequacies within the movement itself. Hanchard (1994a), for example, emphasizes the movement's lack of a national center or focus, its internal schisms, and its general disorganization. Burdick (1998) has recently argued that the movement's tendency to espouse an antireligious stance has alienated large numbers of people (especially Catholics and Protestants) who might otherwise be sympathetic to the cause. I would add that a pervasive cultural censorship has suppressed everyday discourses about racism and has, in many senses, made the experience of racism appear to be a private burden for which no public solutions exist. Silence, especially when it represents a historically entrenched cultural etiquette, may not preclude an awareness of oppression, yet it is very difficult to break.

Undoubtedly, all of these factors play roles in limiting mass participation in antiracist and/or black solidarity activism in Brazil. Black militants, of course, have their own explanations, and much of this chapter will concern, both implicitly and explicitly, those explanations. Before focusing on militant discourse, however, I will briefly revisit Morro do Sangue Bom and what some of my informants had to say about their own lack of involvement in black activism.

The View from Afar: Black Activism as Seen from Morro do Sangue Bom

"You know what I think is the best part of Brazilian history?" Joia said one evening as she, Daniel, and I stood drinking beer at Joãozinho's, the little hole-in-the-wall bar near their house. "When Princesa Isabel freed the slaves, that's the best part."

Joia repeated the simple story that all Brazilian school children hear: that in one abrupt, shining moment in May 1888, the slaves were liberated by a signature from the hand of Dom Pedro's generous daughter, Isabel. What Joia and other Brazilians were not taught in school is that by mid-century the slavocratic society of the sugar-producing region was quickly expiring and in the southeastern region, of which Rio de Janeiro is a part, slave insurrections and escape were so frequent that planters had begun not only to despair of maintaining a sufficient labor force, but, in many cases, to fear for their lives.

Princesa Isabel had merely recognized the inevitable. People on the morro, like most Brazilians, seemed unaware of the myriad forms of resistance practiced by slaves throughout the era of slavery.

Daniel, however, expanded on Joia's story and told a bit of subversive gossip. "It was because of this guy named José do Patrocínio," Daniel put in. "He was a preto and Princesa Isabel was in love with him." "So he put her up to it?" I asked. "Yes, he made her do it," Daniel said with a chuckle.

Whether Daniel's story is true, I do not know. José do Patrocínio was a mulato journalist and vociferous abolitionist who no doubt did mingle with the elite movers and shakers who attended balls in the imperial palace. What the story illustrates, however, is the abiding tension between the hegemonic reading of slave history and what might be called the muffled impulse, on the part of people like Daniel and Joia, to subvert that reading. In telling a tale about the secret love between Patrocínio and Isabel, Daniel gave voice to the notion that interracial *paixão*, or passion, is always a more powerful force in Brazil than interracial conflict. While Patrocínio may figure as a certain kind of trickster, who sexually charms the white princess for the benefit of the raça negra, his script fits neatly within the confines of a larger national mythology about interracial tenderness, attraction, and harmony. More frequently than not, it seems, contradictory dominant mythologies remain one step ahead of subversive tales in Brazil.

As I have noted, most of my informants in Morro do Sangue Bom had, if anything, only a glancing awareness of the existence of a black movement in Rio or elsewhere in Brazil, just as they had very little awareness of the true history of slave resistance. My attempts to understand their positions on such explicitly political issues, then, tended to involve entirely hypothetical scenarios. I often asked people, for example, if they would go to a *manifestação*, or political demonstration, intended to protest racialized discrimination and prejudice. Many people expressed trepidation at such a notion. Tomas, for example, told me that if a street march were held in the city, people would throw things at the protesters. "It would be better to have it as a party," Tomas said. "Then everyone would go. As a street march, it wouldn't do, no way."

Dona Janete had never heard anything about the black movement. Her response to my question about a attending a protest demonstration was extremely ambivalent:

> Here, marches never end the way they begin. You fall on the ground;
> another tramples you; another kicks you; the police give you a
> beating. It never ends the way it began. Now, if it were a thing of
> defense, I would go. Because I have to defend my side. I am dark!
> Right? . . . People take a long time to do anything, but when they do

it, it is a rebellion. . . . There needs to be some kind of protest march that says that everything is wrong. . . . We don't have any rights, not even to our salaries. We don't have anything. Children are going hungry; there is this hunger in general. We almost don't have anything to eat. With all that, you have to protest! But one goes to protest, and the other doesn't go. They are afraid!

When I asked Guilherme if he would go to a demonstration, he shook his head dismissively and said he would not. "It's not worth the trouble," he responded. He paused for a moment and said with a sly smile, "But I would go to a riot!" I had difficulty imagining Guilherme, an extremely mild-mannered young man, participating in a riot. I thought he was probably joking, making a point about how ineffectual a street demonstration would be in the face of such deep prejudices and the structures that reflect and create them, but I was never certain.

Only a few people, such as Analucia, told me that they would certainly go to a demonstration protesting racialized discrimination. "Racism is not going to end," she explained, "and it is a thing that my children should understand." When I asked Rosa if she would take her children to such a demonstration, she said without hesitation, "Of course! All my children are negros."

There were a few people who had some knowledge of the movement. Marluce, a dark-skinned woman in her thirties, was one of the few people on the morro who constantly engaged me in political discussion. Although a supporter of Fidel Castro, Marluce, like many Brazilians, was extremely cynical about homegrown politicians and activists in her own city. Hearing that I had interviewed a particular black movement activist, she burst out angrily, "Oh, he talks about the people this, the people that, but he is only in this for his own gain, for money. Do you understand? All these black movement people are a bunch of opportunists!" I was surprised by Marluce's invective and her facile dismissal of the movement and its personnel, but I shouldn't have been. Like all Brazilians of her class, Marluce was schooled in political betrayal; like others, she had listened to rhetoric and promises, been briefly uplifted in hope, and inevitably, it seemed, bitterly disappointed. With a degree of justification, no doubt, Marluce believed that activists, like government politicians, used politics as a ladder for their own upward mobility.

Neusa, a woman in her late twenties, was also dismissive of the movement, though for different reasons. Although Neusa was not an official member of the directorate of the residents' association, she had voluntarily and rather aggressively taken over many of its functions, particularly those that involved mediation between the community and outsiders. She was very ambitious, people said, and she "messed around in everything." Because Neusa had many connections outside of the community and a special penchant for the social and intellectual activities of local politics, she was more aware of the existence of the black movement than were most people on the morro. She believed that if the movement were to become successful, it would create a situation in which "whites and negros would be completely separated as they are in the United States." "I have many white friends," she added.

The comments that my white middle-class informants made about the movement tended to be dismissive. Many suggested that racism is a false problem, for it is class alone and not color or race that is linked to oppression in Brazil. Like Neusa, middle-class whites suggested that any black movement would be, in principle, racist and anti-Brazilian. Some middle-class whites, particularly the women I interviewed, expressed sympathy for the movement, but they believed it to be a purely cultural movement, directed toward the artistic development of African- and reggae-style music and dance forms. The braids, the Bob Marley T-shirts, the kinte cloth, the beads, and all the obvious, fashionable accessories and accouterments that they associated with the movement were thought to be hip and "very cool."

The Discourse on Racism: Otavio's Introduction

I met Otavio at a primarily political organization associated with the black movement in the Centro section of Rio de Janeiro. The organization is housed in a nondescript building located on a dusty, deeply pitted side street; no sign or banner announces its existence to the passerby. More formal, in fact, than other organizations I visited, this one did not seem to invite impromptu visits. Otavio was in his thirties and his manner was businesslike. He was the director of one the organization's permanent programs, and as such he responded to requests from outside organizations and individuals for information on everything from the torture and murder of Rio's homeless children to the sterilization of women of color—the latter of which, many in the movement argued, had been forced on them by coercive doctors and privately funded programs.[2] Throughout most of our interview, Otavio spoke in a manner that seemed simultaneously pressured and rehearsed. When I asked him to comment in a general, open fashion on racism in Brazil, he provided the following, almost, it seemed, without pausing for breath:

> To understand racism in Brazil, you have to understand the Brazilian
> historical process. In truth, when we speak against racism, we are
> speaking of an ideological system which began with the conquest of
> the New World. The New World was "discovered" by the European

who arrived here with motives that were principally economic. And what did he do? He simply destroyed, massacred the people who were different and put them in subaltern positions relative to the European. In this way he created the idea of Eurocentrism, right, that Europe is the center of the world. The European in his art and in his theories, principally in anthropology, [asserted that] the others were savages and that the Europeans were above everybody, as the "civilized ones"—that business of different stages of development, that the negro was less evolved. And this ideology was created to give support to economic exploitation.

So, on arriving here, the European attempted to enslave the Indians, but the Indians did not accept slavery. So the Europeans went to Africa to do the same thing, and the negro became a prisoner of war. This negro, denied the right to practice his religion, denied the right to speak his language, denied the right to maintain a stable family, and denied his liberty—this European, in the name of a civilizing ideology, enslaved the negro in Brazil. The Indians were killed and put on reservations and the negro was enslaved. From that moment, the negro was seen as simply a slave; he wasn't seen as human. He was an object, like a commodity, an exchange commodity.

So the negro became what? He was put in the most subaltern positions and was viewed as an evil element. The negro was always associated with the bad, with the devil. And when England forced Brazil to abolish slavery, what happened? The negros were expelled from the countryside and the Brazilian government recruited European immigrants to take their places, even paying their passage and giving them land. So the immigrants became the specialized workers in Brazil. And the negro? What happened? He cannot own his own land, he is expelled from the countryside, and those who remain in the countryside return to the conditions of slavery, or worse, they go to the urban centers and live where? In the peripheral areas of the urban centers, in the most destitute areas, in the areas with infrastructural problems, in the areas that don't have water, that don't have sewerage systems, that are without access to education— in other words, the favelas. So this negro was segregated within the process of discrimination, and he continues in this situation today.

And he is discriminated against through other means: through the ideology of *democracia racial*, the denial of racism, and [through] the theory that the negro is incapable of occupying a position, of taking advantage of opportunities in the labor market. So, what happens? Racism in Brazil is the fruit of this entire historical process of colonization. It is connected to the international capitalist system. The negro segment of the population still suffers from the repercussions of this historical process; he has been excluded since the beginning and today he remains excluded. . . . As he is marginalized, he is still concentrated in great numbers in the favelas, in great numbers in the prisons, and in great numbers in subaltern jobs, earning a quarter or a half or up to only one or two minimum salaries. He is excluded from education, without direct access to health care.

But today, racism is confounded with and mixed up with poverty. Racial discrimination today is mixed with social discrimination, although they are different. The white, primarily the white from the northeast, and the Indian have also been discriminated against and marginalized. So you note that in Brazil today there is a minority social elite, which is the minority color, that lives a quality of life equal to that of the European elite, or the North American elite, while a large part of the population lives in poverty, absolute misery even. And in an intermediate position, there is the middle class who are neither rich nor poor, and they also struggle to survive, to remain what we call the Brazilian middle class.

But what happened ideologically? The negro himself, because of the way the ideology works, is ashamed to assume a negro identity. The ideology is so deep; it works so well; it is in everything, education and in the concept of beauty. The concept of beauty and everything is associated with the white stereotype. So you have, for example, the Xuxa program on television, and in the favelas they're all wanting to be blonde—which will never happen! The mass communication media, principally television today, are fundamental instruments of this racial ideology, this ideology of racial discrimination—because you can see very well that all the concepts that work, all the images which are put forth, are all stereotypical white images. And the negro, where is he in this question? When they show negros, they are always favelados; they show them doing domestic service, clearly implying that the negro is incapable of anything else. And this ideology also makes the negro judge himself as incapable. It is the function of the ideology to convince him of that. So, many negros don't like the movement, or they don't know it exists, or they don't understand it. The movement itself hasn't managed to attract a large portion of the black population.

I quote Otavio at such length because his comments serve as an introduction to black movement discourse. Otavio, in fact, touches on nearly all of the major concerns of that discourse. The majority of the black movement militants I spoke with defined racism as a historical issue, and while the concepts, words, indeed the general discourse that Otavio uses to describe history may be familiar to most readers, they represent, in the Brazilian context especially, a radical re-envisioning of the history of race relations in Brazil. Otavio intends his words, spoken during the five hundredth anniversary of Columbus's voyage to the New World, not only as an analysis of Brazilian racism, but as a rejection of cultural censorship and a repudiation of the celebratory discourses of the quintencennial in Brazil and abroad.

As I often heard other militants do, Otavio slipped almost imperceptibly from the past to the present tense. History, in Otavio's analysis, is used not only to explain the present but to project the exploitation of African Brazilians as a continuous, seamless process. Those evidentiary claims that Otavio uses—Eurocentrism, the cultural as well as physical enslavement of Africans, the codification of negrophobia and its justificatory function, the recruitment of European labor, the continuing inequity of land distribution, the ghettoing of poor African Brazilians, the false claims of democracia racial, the political economy of globalized capitalism, the exploitation of other minority groups, the racism of the mass media, and the ideological entanglement and sense of shame among poor people of color and their failure to join forces with the movement—are all intoned again and again by black militants in a variety of organizations. Although black militants are often critical of scholars (particularly of anthropologists, whom they see as "treating the negro like a curious object"), many are well read in the history, ethnography, and critical theory of race and racism in Brazil.

Although Otavio's comments seem to suggest that militants might inevitably gravitate toward socialism, João suggested that this is not necessarily the case. Although João championed land reform and argued (less from a position of naive optimism than for rhetorical purposes) that the government should make reparations for the forced contributions slaves had made to Brazil, he professed himself to be a fence-sitter in political terms. When I asked him what type of political-economic system would, in his view, be the most equipped to eradicate racism, he responded:

> Look, I don't know what type of system. I think that we must change the structure of society so that we will have a more just society, a more fraternal society. Now, whether this would be democracy or socialism, I don't know. I do know that I struggle for a society in which I can be judged on the basis of my competence, of my abilities, and not on the basis of my color. I struggle for this society because I want my children and my grandchildren to learn in school about the true history of the participation and contribution of the negro in the

cultural formation of Brazilian society. I want a society which has a
just distribution of wealth. Now, if this is democracy, I don't know. If
this is socialism, I don't know. If it is communism, I also don't know.

As both Otavio's and João's comments imply, the assertion that race and
class are systemically entwined is central to current black movement discourse. This assertion is addressed to a variety of interlocutors. In the public
realm, politicians and political parties, the organs of the mass media, and cultural productions all assert, usually implicitly, at times explicitly, that the discrimination endured by Brazilians of African descent is a result of social, or
class-based, discrimination alone. As I have noted, this assertion is frequently
repeated in the everyday discourses of middle-class Brazilians. Following the
logic of all circular arguments, the evasion of the connection between racism
and political economy is buttressed in the realm of everyday discourse by a
series of tautologies: "poor people of color are poor because they can't get good
jobs"; "they can't get good jobs because they are uneducated"; "they are ued-
ucated because they are poor."

José directed a project in the same organization in which Otavio is
employed. Perhaps because he had spent a number of years working on the cultural front of the black movement, José's comments were closer to the ground,
more illustrative. José, a large man in his forties, had a manner that was
extremely warm. He responded to my more personal questions with both ease
and interest. To an even greater degree than João, he frequently broke off his
discourse to laugh, loud and long, at the ironies and paradoxes of his country.
He emphasized the connection between poverty and racism in this way:

> The majority of negros on the street . . . wind up saying that they
> have never suffered from racial humiliation. Yet each day, every one
> of them is suffering racial humiliation, suffering racism. . . . In Brazil,
> the majority [of them] live where negros live. . . . He lives on the
> periphery of the periphery and works in the center of the city. He has
> to leave his home at three or four in the morning to get to work at
> eight o'clock. He has to get three or four different buses. . . . [The
> place where he lives] doesn't even have the minimum in basic
> sanitation. This is a form of racism. The larger part of the population
> who [live in these conditions] in Brazil are negros. This is all a
> reflection of social exploitation. Even though he says this is an
> economic issue, as many people do, it isn't. It's all a result of the
> process of the false liberation of slaves.

José began with what he sees as the failure of the "negro on the street" to
understand the structural evidence of racism, to connect the daily humiliation

of poverty with racism. Although most people in Morro do Sangue Bom seem to be well aware of the humiliation of racism, José's suggestion that poor people of color tend to interpret their poverty as a class issue rather than as a racialized one is partly true. As I have noted, people on the morro are extremely fluent in discourses that emphasize class-based forms of injustice, and they may evoke slavery when discussing poverty, yet—within everyday discourses, at least—they rarely elaborate on its racialized character.

The organization of which João was the director is also located in the Centro section of the city, on a street graced by some of Rio's oldest and most dilapidated buildings. Busy by day, the area empties out and appears somewhat forbidding during the evening hours, when many of the important events in João's organization are staged. It encompasses both political and culturalist orientations, and it often sponsors public seminars, book-launching parties, and lectures. Just inside the front door of the organization there is a bulletin board, which displays announcements of upcoming events in a variety of black movement organizations, a few rare newspaper clippings detailing police brutality against people of color, copies of threatening and obscene letters sent by an individual or group claiming to represent the "KKK Brasil," and public messages written by members and referring to what appear to be disputes over authority within the organization itself. In one of our long conversations there, João referred not only to the generalized dominant discourse which claims a disarticulation between race and poverty, but specifically to the participation of poor people of color in that discourse. Familiar with my work in Morro do Sangue Bom, he said,

> In a general sense, the population privileges this class issue in
> Brazilian society, and the issue of race is simply put on a second
> plane. If you go up to Morro do Sangue Bom and ask a negro or a
> negra why she is living in that place, why she is living in those
> conditions, she will respond to you that she lives there because she is
> poor.[3] She will never tell you that she lives there because she is a
> negra. . . . It isn't the fact that she was poor that turned her into a
> negra. It was the fact of being a negra that made her poor. . . . Today
> there exists a fundamental issue in Brazil, and that is the issue of
> racism at the structural level. The structure of Brazilian society [sets
> aside] some spaces for the negro, namely, the favelas, the slum
> buildings, the [urban] periphery, and the slave quarters . . . because
> the negro is—we are—second class citizens. So our [restricted] spaces
> are a function of the politics of the developed countries, a function of
> the external debt and of the compromises that the Brazilian
> government normally makes in submitting itself to the World Bank
> and the American banks. What has happened is that this

conjuncture has made whites poor also, and they are living in the
same spaces that were always reserved for negros. . . . So people then
use this conjunctural issue to argue that the issue in Brazil is not one
of racism but that it's a social [class] issue—in order to obfuscate the
issue of racism. . . . But what they forget is that the white is there
because of this conjuncture.

In these comments, João suggests, accurately, I think, that the primary
ideological battle of Brazil's black movement is one of demystification. As
does José, João laments the fact that poor people of color themselves frequently fail to see or consistently draw a connection between poverty, class
discrimination, and racialized discrimination. In bridging this connection,
João focuses not on racist culture(s) but on racist social structures. He brings
dependency theory in to account for the presence of whites in favelas, a fact
frequently brought to bear in the arguments, both popular and academic, that
in Brazil it is only a person's poverty, and not one's color, that provokes discrimination. It is just such facts—that some whites are poor also, that some
negros make it economically, that the middle class also must struggle to maintain a toehold on the dream of financial security—that activists must constantly address in order to make a very simple point.

The "False Discourse": Democracia Racial, Racism, and Consciousness

When I told my activist informants that I had been surprised to find a lack of
everyday discourse on racism in the morro where I was living, they affirmed
my observations largely through comments relating to what they saw as the
problematic *consciência*, or consciousness, of poor people of color. Otavio saw
this consciousness as primarily molded by the forces of what he called conformity and accommodation and by physical repression and terror. Addressing
the issue of the failure of poor people of color to develop or participate in discourses on racism and racial mobilization, he said,

> They are conscious of the fact, in the empirical sense—they suffer in
> the day-to-day sense. But as I said, this ideology is so strong—and the
> church has a big role in this—that there exists a certain conformity.
> There exists a certain accommodation, and besides this, the lack of
> knowledge, right? Also, for the Brazilian people, whenever there was
> a revolt or some mobilization, it was always strongly repressed by the
> dominant elite. It always happened in Brazil that popular movements
> were crushed, with arms, with the military, right? To commit a real
> massacre. So this is also a thing which counts against any type of

mobilization. With the military coup of '64, with the dictatorship and repression, every day the favela population suffered from political repression and from the racist ideology. The negro is on the bus, or in the favela itself, and the police come and harass whomever they want. No one knows what they might do at dawn because anything can happen. So, without a doubt, fear is one of the fundamental factors that can explain this type of behavior; and it's not just this, there are many other things, but the fear, repression, the fear of violence is a very terrible thing, really very terrible.

Many of the militants I spoke with emphasized not physical terror but ideological and, ultimately, discursive manipulation. Mario, a light-skinned man in his thirties, spoke volubly on this subject and others. Although I first approached Mario on a Santa Teresa–bound bus after seeing him at a black movement event we had both attended, he defined himself as "not involved" in the movement. As I later discovered, his disavowal of identification with the movement was based more on a disappointed cynicism toward its factious organizations than on his own politics and activities. Working independently of any organization, Mario taught Afro-Brazilian dance to children on various morros and told them stories related to African Brazilian heritage, such as the legend of Zumbi. He was also involved in efforts to disseminate information on AIDS prevention to centers of Candomblé in the Rio area. When I asked him about the lack of everyday discourse on racism, he said, "People think that racism doesn't exist. They forget history, that we were slaves, that we are slaves even today. They say that racial discrimination doesn't exist in this country, but it reveals itself in society. The negro is always treated differently from the other, the white. So really, the people who say they don't see this don't want to see it. Sometimes I think they just don't want to see it, because racism does exist. I think that saying racism doesn't exist is convenient for the system."

It is notable that Mario moved from the comment that "people think that racism doesn't exist" to statements about what they say and "the people who say they don't see this." He moved, in a sense, from a statement about psychology to one about discourse. In his comment, "saying racism doesn't exist is convenient for the system," Mario refers very directly to the role of the discourses of democracia racial in supporting the political economy of racism. Although Mario seems to suggest a kind of deliberate dissimulation is at work in the discourses of democracia racial, he continues to invoke more directly psychological processes of denial, a communal form of repression. In forgetting history, Brazilians become blind to what Otavio had also described as a seamless, ongoing process of exploitation, the fact that "we are slaves even today."

João spoke directly to the issue of psychological internalization and the lack of public discourse on racism: "You have to understand that it's a thing of internalization (*introjeção*), because it is not a thing that works through an explicit process. It works through a process of internalization and assimilation. This begins in the childhood of the negro; that is the issue."

In describing the problem of consciousness among poor people of color, José emphasized the public discourses of the mass media:

> We can't deny that those who control information, who control the
> media, define a type of culture and wind up determining everything.
> This type of system in Brazil, the communication media, manipulates
> and brainwashes people. And a large portion the negro population is
> being deluded by this false discourse. They dismiss racism in Brazil
> and [seem to believe] that Brazil is living out a great democracia
> racial and that everyone is equal—which everyone knows is not true.
> If you go into any business, you will see two people, one negro and
> other white, employed in the same work, and the white is earning
> more than the negro. So shit, what kind of racial democracy is this?

Apparently contradicting himself, José said that people are "deluded by this false discourse" of democracia racial, yet it is a discourse "which everyone knows is not true." In this comment, he seems to suggest a kind of double consciousness, in which ideological entanglement, or "brainwashing" (or in Otavio's term, "accommodation"), coexists with an awareness of routine forms of racialized discrimination. I was to hear such comments over and over in my conversations with activists. They both echoed and spoke to the very issues that preoccupied me in my research on the morro. Activists constantly invoked the delusion, the Marxian notion of false consciousness, and then, in logical terms, undermined it with references to the true or deep knowledge of racism among poor Brazilians of African descent.

Eduardo, a man in his forties, also referred to this apparent paradox of seeming to accept the discourses of democracia racial while knowing, "deep down," that racism exists. The director of a primarily culturalist black movement organization located in Rio's North Zone, Eduardo was deeply concerned with exposing what he saw as "veiled" forms of racism. His organization was explicitly concerned with the issue of self-esteem among people of color and the work of recrafting a positive negro identity. For him, as for other activists, such work had to begin with an emergence from silence and a recognition of the most subtle and insidious forms of racism:

> In this general way, people wind up accepting [the idea of democracia
> racial] but they know [racism] exists. But [they believe] they have to

stay silent, right, that thing of having eyes but not seeing, having a mouth and not speaking. . . . But they have consciousness, deep down they have consciousness that racism exists. But they think it's not the same as South Africa because, supposedly, no one kills. So they think it's good [as it is]. There's no fighting. There's no war. "It's better not to get mixed up in it." The person doesn't perceive that veiled forms of discrimination are as bad as other forms of open discrimination.

Eduardo's comments obviously have a bearing on the silence and discursive frames through which racism is dealt with both on the morro and, to an extent, among middle-class whites in Santa Teresa. His imagery of people as "having eyes but not seeing, having a mouth and not speaking" reminded me of my own sense of being surrounded by a palpable silence on the morro, and of the simultaneous discomfort and boredom which with white informants so often greeted my questions.

Eduardo was certainly correct when he suggested that so many people associate racism not with the quotidian discourses and practices that surround them but with the violence and representations of violence in and of other countries. "No one throws stones," Virginia, my white informant in Edifício Silvestre, said tersely when asked to comment on racism in her country. "There is no violence, nothing," Eliza, my elite informant asserted. "It's not like the Unites States, you know?" My informants on the morro were certainly aware of the effects of racism in their everyday lives, but exactly as Eduardo suggested, they engaged in a variety of locutions (as well as everyday forms of silence) that insisted, "It's better not to get mixed up in it."

Addressing the issue of the problematic consciousness of African Brazilians from a somewhat different angle, João commented on the processes of internalization at greater length:

> So in this process in Brazilian society, it's not a class issue, but an issue of race, of racial consciousness itself. In the community we receive this very powerful socialization coming from the level of Brazilian society, and this [process] is also impacted by the media. When this mirror appears [before us], it confirms what we are living in a day-to-day sense—being on the street, being a domestic servant, doing the cleaning. So, with this mirror, I only see myself in this form, meaning the mirror doesn't see me as a writer, as an airline pilot, as an engineer. It doesn't see any of that, so I just stay where I am.

It is notable that in his metaphorical framing, João attributes agency not only to the person seeing his or her reflection but to the mirror itself. In another conversation, João told me that "the white man is a mirror." João's language, of course, is Fanonian, and like Fanon's anguished writing, it echoes the insights of Hegel; people of color inevitably see themselves reflected in the eyes of the dominator. These eyes are cold, blind to the humanity of the other, and utterly lacking in imaginative vision. The mirror puts a freeze on intersubjectivity, and the dominated, as João suggests, become entrapped within their own frozen reflections. Continuing in this Fanonian frame, João said, "There is another model that I want to follow, but this model is white. But I am going to try to be white, and trying to be white means that I will forget that I am a negro. What puts me closest to being white is being a mulato, so I am a moreno; I am a pardo. If I am a preto, I will be farther away from [the white]. This is the reality . . . that we call a dominating racist ideology."

Referring to the ideology of branqueamento, João appeared to be concerned less with the issue of interracial marriage and "cleaning the family" in a strictly biological sense than he was with the culturally produced impulse to escape the blackness within oneself. In line with Mario's comments about forgetting history, João said, "I will forget that I am a negro." Both imply that Brazilians of African descent are entangled within a process—perhaps partly conscious and partly unconscious—of repressing the authentic self. At a very simple level, of course, João is referring to what so many people both inside and outside the movement regard as a failure, among poor Brazilians of African descent, to identify as negro.

Eduardo framed the issues of consciousness in a similar fashion: "So, the negro is also a racist; he doesn't want the other negro, because he doesn't like himself. He thinks he is dirty, he is ugly, he is a bad thing. So he thinks, 'How could I want something that is like myself?' So, it's this issue of many negros discriminating against other negros. Because he doesn't feel himself to be a person, he doesn't feel that the other is a person either. And society always uses this argument rather than discuss the [real] racial issue. They are always talking about how the negro discriminates against the other negro."

What Eduardo, João, and other militants seemed to describe was not merely what is usually called "false consciousness" but, even more clearly, a wounded consciousness that seeks to turn away from pain. Eduardo suggested, correctly, I believe, that the moral and political causes and implications of black racism—or wounded consciousness—seem to be lost on dominant whites. "Negros themselves discriminate against each other, so what do they expect from me?" one of my middle-class white informants said.

Mario discussed the issue of the internalization of dominant discourses about blackness in a personal way. He also suggested the persistence of a pained inner dialogue with oneself:

You are brought up and educated within another ideology. It's like
I'm always thinking, I found myself with a black body but with the
ideas of a white ideology. That is something I ask myself about—
because I knew that I had this ideology, but I had this body, this hair,
this skin, which are exterior markers that I am a negro, and there's no
way to change that. . . . So you were brought up with this ideology
from the time you were little. And the heroes that you have, from
history, for example—history doesn't have any negro heroes.
[Although] these days there are Brazilian historians who are trying to
retrace the issue of black history. If you don't have negro heroes, you
don't have anything to identify yourself with this race. . . . So you
have heroes of the other race in order to feel stronger. You use this,
which comes from outside, but it isn't you; it's not of your race. So it
creates conflict. . . . History always told the good deeds of the whites.
The negro is always the poor one, dirty, a pig, a second-class citizen.[4]

Generally speaking, my activist informants articulated a vision and an
analysis of the consciousness of poor Brazilians of African descent that would
appear—in some of their comments at least—to be somewhat at odds with my
analysis of discourses in Morro do Sangue Bom. João's discussion of what he
represents as the pressured, Fanonian psychology that informs the use of terms
such as moreno, mulato, and pardo would seem to represent a fundamental
misunderstanding of what I have called the pragmatic discourse of color—and
a lack of awareness of what I have called the discourse on race. The suggestions of José, Eduardo, and others that poor people of color tend not to be
aware of, or to recognize, various forms of racialized discrimination—from
subtle, supposedly nonviolent forms to the historically entrenched racializa-
tion of social structures—seem to contradict the often richly articulated narratives of racism produced by my informants on the morro. They seem to
assume, in addition, that the silence surrounding the issue of racism is an
empty rather than a very full and meaningful one.

I would argue, however, that my own analysis and that of activists in the
black movement are only somewhat different ways of describing the same
issues. Black movement militants have been accused, in various contexts, of
being out of touch with the problems, experiences, and what might be called
the phenomenological perspectives of poor people of color. Yet, this is hardly
the case. Some of the comments of my activist informants seemed to echo
statements I heard on the morro to a nearly uncanny degree.

As I have noted above, activists tend to suggest, through a variety of
locutions, that poor people of color both know and do not know about the
racialized nature of their own oppression. João told me that "they have a frac-

tured consciousness" both in terms of oppression and in terms of their own identities. His analysis of consciousness was not systematically and consistently discursive, yet it provides a different kind of frame through which to read discourses on color, race, and racism. Ultimately, the metaphors that my activist informants used—fracturing, splintering, entrapment, superficiality, and depth—were immediately familiar to me, and I have used them repeatedly in my own analysis. Narratives of racism can hardly be understood apart from silence. The pragmatic discourse of color cannot be understood without reference to the wounding implications of blackness. The discourse on race is a subterranean one, almost buried by the quotidian performance of euphemism, dissimulation, and avoidance.

Joia's pained comment, "I am know I am a negra, but I'm really morena, right?" aptly illustrates the critical thrust of activists' accounts of Brazilian racism. Although João fails to distinguish between different discursive registers in his account of attempts to approximate whiteness and escape from blackness, Joia's comment reminds us that both the descriptive and pragmatic discourses of color are themselves cultural signs, failed attempts at neutrality and politeness, and they speak to both private and communal forms of agony and entrapment. The pain and shame of blackness that João refers to, moreover, is the same or similar to what I have tried to describe, following the lead of my informants, in chapter 3. Activists emphasize the shadows cast by the performance of what is most quotidian and the implications of what appears on the surface of daily life. My documentation of the subterranean discourses and muffled narratives in Morro do Sangue Bom does not truly contradict activist's accounts so much as it complicates them still further.

The question of the differences between my own and activists' accounts revolves, really, around the problem of describing the entrapment that is racism, and, in even broader terms, how we, as scholars and/or activists, describe or allude to the nature of consciousness. Although my activist informants referred implicitly and explicitly to discourse and silence, they attempted, to a far greater degree than I, to plumb the depths of *consciência*— a word that signifies consciousness, its English equivalent, as well as the supposedly more mundane notions of awareness and recognition. In my focus on what people say and do not say, I have stayed close to the ground and I have tried to maintain the caution carried in Dona Janete's observation that "the heart of another is such that no one can enter it." It may be that my activist informants have gone out on something of a hermeneutical limb, yet as the following section would seem to suggest, their descriptions of the consciousness of poor Brazilians of African descent may also be, at least in part, autobiographical reflections.

Becoming Negro Assumido: *The Discourse of Conversion*

Given the cultural and psychological conundrums that activists describe, how does one break out of the pattern of "delusion" and "fractured consciousness" and achieve consciência negra? Early in my fieldwork, I learned that activists draw a fundamental distinction between what they call the *negro assumido* (assumed negro) and the *negro não-assumido* (non-assumed negro). "No one is born negro in this country," João explained. "One must become negro" (see Sousa 1983).

To become a negro assumido is to reject the polite discourses and miscegenated identities associated with intermediate racial terms (moreno, mulato, pardo, etc.) in favor of an unambiguous, unsoftened, and unqualified negro identity. It is to make a psychological leap into what activists sometimes call "negritude" and to undergo what they describe as something akin to a conversion experience. While there was considerable diversity in the experiences of the activists who told me their personal stories, there were a number of common themes that emerged in their telling. Although neither I nor they can answer, in any simplified, ultimate sense, the question of why some Brazilians of African descent become negros assumidos and others do not, their stories illuminate, if not the path to consciência negra, then the discourses used to describe and, in a more immediate sense, carry the process.

When I asked how and why they became involved in the black movement, and, by extension, how they became negros assumidos, a number of militants began their accounts by describing their personal brushes with racism during adolescence. On occasion, the confrontation with racism is described as producing an abrupt and disturbing sense of revelation or insight. José provided such an account. Brought up in a stable, working-class household in the North Zone of Rio, José, like many boys and young men of his background, was an avid soccer player.

"Look, this is a very interesting thing," he began, referring to an incident that occurred when he was eighteen or nineteen:

> I participated in a club in the Baixada [Fluminense]. I was an athlete. And one time I arrived to take a swim in the pool at the club. But they told me I couldn't take a swim. I wanted to know why. They wouldn't give me a straight answer. They wouldn't tell me a single reason. Later, a close friend of mine said, "Look José, what happened is that this is an elite club and you arrived at an hour during which negros are not permitted to swim in the pool." . . . It was a thing that I hadn't perceived before. I only perceived this racism issue after that. And God, it's really interesting how you start this introspection, how you suddenly become aware that at various other moments you were

discriminated against. Only [when it happened] you didn't have
consciousness, you weren't aware that you were discriminated against.

Referring to comments he had made during an earlier moment of our
interview, he continued, "It's like everything I said before about the issue of
the media throwing all that [at you], making you constantly deny yourself. It
makes you forget that you are a negro. You look in the mirror, but you don't
see your color; you see a person. You think you're above it all. So, after that, I
began to question things."

Thus, when José is told directly that he has been discriminated against
because of his color, he realizes, apparently for the first time, that he is a negro.
As José tells it, only by encountering racism directly—and perhaps hearing
the word "negro" applied to himself—was he able to grasp who he was for the
other and, ultimately, he seems to imply, who he must become for himself.
José suggested that after he had this experience he began to reinterpret his
own past, to perceive meanings that he had not previously recognized.

José's experience of reappraising his past was described by others as well.
Although Eduardo did not describe his coming to consciousness of racism as
occurring in one abrupt flash, he said that his involvement with the black
movement precipitated a reinterpretation of painful events from his childhood. Responding to my question concerning his first awareness of racism, he
said:

> The only thing I remember are some things that happened when I
> was younger. Only later did I go out and struggle [against racism]. . . .
> I began to work when I was only fourteen; I was an office boy. I was
> delivering correspondence to a certain place, and I was looking for a
> certain person. The person who attended me treated me very badly
> because I was a negro. They said that they were going to call the
> police, and I don't know what all. I was terrified and got out of there
> and was even fired from my job because of this. And another thing—
> I took a test to get a job in this store. At that time, I wasn't aware of
> this issue of struggle, I didn't have consciousness. [After I took the
> test] I went back to the store, hoping for a job at the front counter. I
> asked this girl there if there were any messages for me, and she told
> me that there were no openings at the front counter but that there
> was an opening in the stockroom, in back. But she didn't even know
> my name; later she asked me, "What is your name?" So she didn't
> even look [at my test score], but I had already seen the score. I got
> very angry and didn't go back for the opening [in the stockroom].[5]

Eduardo's story about applying for a job in a store is a very typical one.
Although certainly qualified to work with the public and with the cash regis-

ter at the front counters of stores, Brazilians of African descent are routinely denied these positions and are sent to the stockrooms, kitchens, and other backstage areas where they are less visible. "Only after I had gone to the university and got involved in the black movement, where people were talking about the issue of veiled racism," Eduardo continued, "did I go back and question [these things that happened]."

Although some of those in the black movement were, like Eduardo, first exposed to black movement discourse while pursuing university degrees, José suggested that there are other routes to participation in the black movement. After his experience at the athletic club, he felt compelled to discuss the issue of racism with his friends. "They were difficult discussions in the beginning," he said.

> I had the questions, but I didn't have anything theoretical in my head with which to elaborate [on the issue]. It was a very new thing for me. It was difficult with my friends in the neighborhood because they were at the same intellectual level that I was, at the same level of knowledge about the issue. So the discussion didn't grow very much. . . . Then around 1980 I began working at a job in [a certain place] and I made friends with someone who worked in the room across the hall. He was a negro also, and we began to discuss the racial question. Once we started this discussion, other people started to appear, and from there, the discussion began to grow.

José's and others' accounts point, obviously, to the fact that there are no highly developed everyday discourses on racism in Brazil. José's neighborhood friends, like José himself, were unable to generate an effective, sustained discussion of racism and the issues related to negro identity. In finding like-minded friends at least, José was fortunate; generally, the initial attempt to come to grips with racism is described as a solitary, lonesome, and alienating process. "You have to assume your identity individually," as Otavio put it. As José argued, discussion must be actively pursued in order to achieve an understanding of Brazil's contradictory and masked forms of racism. Talking to people—the achievement of fluency in an analytical, unmasking, antiracist discourse—is conceived as crucial to the achievement of *consciencia negra*.

Otavio provided a similar, though truncated account: "It's very, very difficult to get conscientized. I myself came to consciousness only when I began to study better, to talk to people. When I was younger, I was ashamed to go to my friends' houses, which were nice houses. I was ashamed of showing myself there, as a negro. So this process is very violent."

I assumed that Otavio referred to formal (university) study, but he corrected me. "On the contrary, I learned nothing about racial issues in school," he explained. "It was studying on my own and talking to people who were in the movement and others that I met along the way."

Mario, like Eduardo, was introduced to the discourse of the black movement while a university student. However, he described his own coming to consciousness as occurring in the context of visits to the northeastern state of Bahia:

> During the time that I was a student, I began to get involved in the black movement. I wanted to know things about myself that I didn't have answers for, as a negro. So I wanted to be around other negros. Because I had an education—I'm a dentist and I had an elite education. I was the only negro and the rest [of the students] were all white. So, I was more in the white world than in the black world. I absorbed things from both worlds, but I absorbed a lot of things from the other [white] world, because I had to absorb them—sink or swim! At that time, I spent some time in Bahia. And in Bahia, I saw so many negros. Rio de Janeiro has negros, but they're all in the periphery. But in Bahia you even see negros in the South Zone. Negros are on the beach; they're in the bars; negros are everywhere! So it was a very strong thing of identification for me, with them. Their identification was the same as mine. And it made me happy to see this other who is the same, who is similar to me. And there [in Bahia] also I began to get involved in Candomblé, which is specifically [a religion] of the negro population. I went to Salvador a number of times . . . and got to know various people in Candomblé and various people in the black movement in Salvador.

Mario spoke directly to his experience of converting from what was no doubt a nominal Catholicism to Candomblé, regarded as the most "pure African" religion in Brazil. His description is both metonymically and metaphorically related to all of the accounts that I have quoted. The achievement of consciência negra and the process of becoming a negro assumido were described as if they were a conversion experience. Flashes of insight, the adoption of new frames and languages, the reinterpretation of the past (and its association with feelings of shame and ignorance), and the sense of a present position of recognition and illumination from which there is no turning back are all described or alluded to by the activists who responded to my more personal questions.

Once the process of racial conversion begins, the converted, like their counterparts in the religious arena, often feel at odds with those around them. They seem to feel themselves in possession of an esoteric kind of knowledge and understanding that is rejected and dismissed by others. As Mario said,

"Whenever I brought up the issue of racism, people would say the problem was in my head—even my friends and family." The process of attaining fluency in antiracist discourses occurs against a backdrop of silence and denial. As I had with my informants in Morro do Sangue Bom, I asked activists if their parents or other relatives had ever spoken to them about racism during their childhood. This question often produced references to the sense of isolation they felt as adults.

Otavio, who was more comfortable occupying an impersonal spokesperson's role in our interview, responded to my question with distancing generalizations about "poor families." Nevertheless, his comments were among the most moving that I heard, for he described how he had learned to abide the gulf that lay between himself and his parents:

> No, even today my parents don't know exactly what I do. They don't
> have an understanding. And this whole process also, of family culture
> that we have, poor families don't have much time to spend together.
> Work starts very early, and the mother and father go off to work and
> come home late. So that culture of familial intimacy, that gets lost.
> We all care for each other, but that thing of always hanging out
> together, conversing, discussing things, it doesn't happen much in
> families like mine. So my mother and father know that I have
> confidence in myself and that I am doing what I want to do. They
> know that I work with the negro issue, but they don't know exactly
> what that's about. They don't have an understanding of it. And I also
> don't come home and force the issue on them—because the biggest
> problem of the militant is that he arrives home and wants to teach a
> class to his parents, to lecture them, his mother and father, who are
> already forty or fifty years old and have lived a life of oppression and
> repression. I don't want to teach my father and mother. On the
> contrary, I have a great deal of respect for them. My mother is
> illiterate. My father made it only to the junior high. So I'm not going
> to take on this attitude with them. I respect them very, very much,
> for all the experiences they've had, all the suffering they've gone
> through; and frankly, I only talk about these things when they ask
> me. I don't bring it up with them. So this issue is not really discussed
> at home.

Other activists were less sanguine about the lack of open discussions concerning racism at home. When I asked Eduardo if he had ever heard discussions of racism when he was a child, he said, "Never! It's very rare [that people talk about it]. Most people had this other discourse when I was little, that the negro has to progress and marry a white person to 'clean the family.' We discussed that here [in the organization], and everyone [who was present] said

that that [discourse] had occurred in their families! We don't have this discourse of talking about racism because only a very short time ago we came out
of the period of political repression. We didn't live in a democracy. You
couldn't discuss this, ever!"

José, especially, responded to this question in strongly emotional terms:

> No, it isn't discussed. I am the son of humble parents. My mother is
> totally illiterate; she can neither read nor write. My father, no—he
> can read and write. But this discussion never arose at home, because I
> think [the family] was in this process—principally my father—he was
> very much in this process of becoming a middle-class family. And
> from within this perspective, as a specialist worker who was upwardly
> mobile, he didn't discuss these issues. . . . After [what happened at]
> the club, I remembered some things; I remembered the high school
> [that I went to] where I was called names like "monkey," and so
> on. . . . I remember I came home and talked about this. And the
> response was always the same: "Oh, don't pay attention. They don't
> know what they're saying; it's just a joke." You understand—always
> that type of evasion. Open discussion did not exist! If today you got
> one hundred militants together and asked them this question, you
> would find that perhaps one would say that this issue was brought up
> at home! Even today, as a person who has become militant, I have
> great difficulty in developing this discussion in my home. Because the
> people in my family reject it; they don't want to discuss it.

José spoke with pride, however, about his relationship with his young
niece: "I have a niece who is eleven years old, and with her I manage to discuss
it, because I started discussing the racial issue with her from the time she was
three years old. Even though she is surrounded by this type of negra who wants
to be white and all that, straightening the hair, she has a deep perception of the
issue of discrimination and how it can effect her. Now, even though she doesn't
reproduce the discourse [about racism], she is attentive to it. The first moment
something happens to her, she will run straight into militancy!"

Mario, like José, was unable to discuss racism and other issues related to
consciência negra with the adult members of his family, yet he pursued such
discussions with the younger generation: "I tell stories about Zumbi to my
nieces and nephews. I say, 'Look, I have a story, a story that is not told in your
education, in this whitening ideology.' Nothing is written, so I have to tell
this to my nieces and nephews. . . . If you don't hear this history in your family, where will you hear it?"

All of these accounts emphasize the fundamentally discursive nature of
consciência negra. Although in much of their language activist informants

seem to suggest the possibility of an "authentic" identity that has been stolen and concealed through history, silence, and denial, they also seem to recognize the constructed, even invented nature of identity. In saying that his niece does not yet "reproduce the discourse," José highlighted what he himself views as the centrality of subversive talk in the process of becoming a negro assumido. In telling stories to his nieces and nephews, Mario was clearly attempting to invent a kind of oral tradition, almost, it would seem, out of the thin air of silence. Generally speaking, when militants reflect on the issue of self esteem among people of color, they are concerned not only with what is clearly an extremely difficult reappropriation of the term negro, but with highly constructed notions of memory, culture, and the racialized self.

Yet clearly and inevitably, it would seem, attempts to construct a counter-hegemonic discourse of consciência negra sometimes echo, in often subtle but disturbing ways, the shadow of essentialism that lurks in all discourses of color and race in Brazil. When speaking from within the discourse on race, my informants on the morro sometimes referred to sangue, or blood, as the true, authentic substance of race. Black movement militants tend to substitute the notion of culture for that of blood, yet such notions of culture are often articulated from within an essentializing discourse of authenticity—almost as though culture were a dormant substance lodged in the body, one that need only be reactivated through the rediscovery of one's true identity.

Essentialism always shadows any politics of identity, to greater or lesser degrees. What makes consciência negra so interesting in Brazil is the fact that as a set of discourses, it is intended as a countervailing force against what are generally thought to be nonessentialist, fluid notions of identity, notions that are structured around color distinctions. Although many have suggested that militants have imported a foreign politics of identity in a more or less wholesale fashion, it is evident that transnational discourses of negritude as they are articulated in Brazil fulfill different functions, address different issues, and contest different meanings than they do in countries that tend to articulate, through dominant discursive modes, a simple bipolar and dichotomous vision of racial identity.

It is obviously notable as well that contrary to the conventional wisdom on racialized identity in Brazil, poor people of color, such as those in Morro do Sangue Bom, do share, to a degree, the discourses and understandings that divide the world into black and white. In referring to "fractured consciousness" and "deep knowing" among poor people of color, activists signal their awareness of this fact. The emphasis on bipolar visions of identity, it is clear, is constructed less by the transplantation of foreign discourses, or the ideological residue of dominant discourses, than by the raw experience of racism. Black-

ness is an experience of oppression to which all Brazilians of African descent
are subject; the intractability of the material structures that contain it impose
upon color a unifying force.

"For the Totality of the Brazilian Population": *Critiquing the Movement from Inside*

In concluding this chapter, I must note some of the ways in which activists
themselves critique the movement. It is in such self-reflective comments that
the larger social and political context in which the movement operates
becomes clearer. Mario, who characterized himself as outside of the movement, focused on the enormous distance between most of the movement personnel and poor people of color:

> There are many fights within the movement. . . . It's a question of
> power. . . . You have to be very careful with this. Because to protect
> our heritage you have to watch out for this system that has been
> implanted. The black movement says it is against this system, but it
> works in collusion with the system. . . . Where are the negros? They
> are not in the South Zone. They are in the *suburbios*, in the
> peripheral areas, on the morros, in the favelas. They are not in the
> South Zone. We have to speak with them, not just with each other;
> we have to speak with others. . . . But no one wants to go [to those
> places]. Those who don't become part of the system.

Mario referred to what some African Americans have called an "ebony
tower"—the tendency among black intellectuals and activists to remain distant from the impoverished and marginalized sites at which racism launches
its most crushing forms of oppression. Negro elites, however they are defined,
are constantly vulnerable to various forms of cooptation. Mario seemed to
suggest that even activists concerned with consciência negra have allowed
themselves to be seduced by the insularity of middle-class worlds, and like
their white counterparts, they have refused to cross the class frontier.

Mario's critique is obviously well founded, yet the issue is related to far
more than a class-based squeamishness. João told me that it was far easier to
give lectures in universities, even when he was the only person of color present, than to go into poor communities where his racialized call to arms was
met with blankness, cynicism, and misunderstanding. Once again, those who
critique the movement from outside tend to suggest that it is the fundamental
foreignness of black movement discourse, its attempted imposition of alien
models on local realities, that creates this discursive disjuncture. While I have
argued that the discourses of my activist informants and people on Morro do

Sangue Bom are not so distant as they at first seem—not in their content, at any rate—it is nevertheless true that the registers and styles used by the two groups remain very different. It is these differences that activists, who are aware of the discursive gap, tend to emphasize. José was particularly concerned with this issue:

> Another thing which is very complicated and difficult for the
> movement is that it still hasn't found a language with which to reach
> the masses. It doesn't do to have a very academic discourse. You
> know, it's no good to go to the masses and start asserting certain
> things that they don't understand because it isn't their language. As
> it isn't their language, they reject it—it's just "blah, blah, blah." . . . It
> is not a mobilizing discourse; it's a very academic discourse, you
> know? . . . This is a population that doesn't know the reality of our
> history. They don't know the cultural reality. So shit, how are you
> going to say that this population is going to understand and going to
> follow that whole discourse that you throw at them?

José's comment that poor people of color "don't know the reality of our history" would seem, in many ways, to be inaccurate. They are schooled not so much in ignorance and denial as in silence and exhausted forms of resignation. José is probably right, however, in his assertion that an academic discourse cannot and will not penetrate silence and convince the masses that battles over racialized discrimination can possibly be won, now or in the future. The discourse of the movement is a fundamentally analytical and cerebral one; and while people in Morro do Sangue Bom are certainly capable of producing, in their own terms, analytical and descriptive statements about racism, their discourse, as I have argued, is a fundamentally moral one.

As was so often the case, José reversed himself when he continued, "We know how to say that racism exists in Brazil; everyone already knows that it exists. It is not effective to just say Joe So-and-So was discriminated against because he is preto." Here he acknowledged that the problem is not, after all, ignorance. He began to talk of the need for a movement with a broader base:

> It is no longer possible for the entities of the black movement not to
> establish alliances with other sectors of the popular movement. It is
> not effective for the entities of the black movement to continue to
> discuss only the issue of the negro—because we are going to create
> simply a mass of negros who are conscientized. It is necessary to talk
> to [other] people, with the white, about racism. It is necessary
> because most of the time the white is racist even though he doesn't
> know he is racist. It's a question of the cultural behavior that they
> have. So it doesn't do to just have negros talking to negros.

As José continued, I was struck by the degree to which he echoed other activist informants. Superficially, he seemed to be proposing a more viable strategy for recruitment and mobilization, but at a deeper level, he was articulating a distinctly Brazilian vision of change. José, like all activists, knew that many Brazilians, especially middle-class whites, tend to assert that a Brazilian black movement would be inherently racist; it would create separations where none had existed before. Activists such as José, however, often invoke the dream not of a black movement composed entirely of Brazilians of African descent, but of a movement directed toward all forms of discrimination. José continued:

> The black movement wants—it really wants to become a movement of weight, of political weight in Brazil. It has to have a proposal not only for the negro community. It has to have a proposal for the totality of the Brazilian population. . . . In the same way that negros are discriminated against, so the homosexual is discriminated against. The woman is discriminated against. The northeasterner is discriminated against. The Jew and the Arab are discriminated against. . . . I think this discussion has to occur. This is very difficult work; it isn't easy. . . . You have to be aware of that type of thing. And [you have this situation] with the left, that action in which you only organize yourselves if you are in a room discussing political and ideological questions—as if reality isn't really there.

Otavio, who spoke in the most abstract and condemnatory terms against white racism, was also concerned both with broader processes of discrimination and with the divisive, counterproductive dangers inherent in more rigid forms of identity politics. For him as well, the battle lines of the movement should not be drawn between blacks and whites but between racism and antiracism: "And you can't commit reverse racism. This is a great preoccupation of ours, that some in the black movement might commit reverse racism. In Brazil, racism was directed against the Indian, and principally against the negro. If you go to Europe, you see that it is directed against the Turks in Germany. It's not a thing of the skin. It's really a cultural question, fundamentally cultural and ideological."

All of these comments address and speak against the shadows of essentialism, shadows that are present in the discourse of consciência negra. In the midst of a long-winded discussion of agrarian reform (an extremely potent, historically entrenched dream that potentially affects all rural poor and not only those of African descent), João paused and said, "I will tell you that I do not have anything against white people. I don't, sincerely, sincerely. If you ask me if I have three personal motives to not like a white person, personally, I don't have any. . . . Now, ideologically, I combat the system that whites represent, this system that has exploited me, that has exploited my parents, my grandparents, and my great-grandparents."

In this comment, João cast racism into dominating structures and away from notions of naturalized opposition between rigidly racialized individuals. Had João spoken with Neusa, my informant in Morro do Sangue Bom who felt that the existence of a successful black movement would undermine her friendships with whites, he would have reassured her. The true goal of the movement is not to pit blacks against whites, he might have told her, but to unite all Brazilians in the struggle against Brazilian racism and its peculiar forms of silence and hypocrisy. João, as I knew, had been married to a supportive white woman for more than twenty years, and he did not abide color lines and clannishness in his personal life. Although a fully converted negro assumido, he had hardly abandoned the prescriptive principles that constitute the heart of yearning within democracia racial. Despite his calculatedly vociferous rhetoric, so extraordinary and unfamiliar in most of the contexts in which I conducted my research, João projected the same warmth, concern, and humor that sheltered me in Morro do Sangue Bom. Racism in Brazil has never been about simple and stark oppositions, nor will it ever be.

"How long will you be staying in Brazil?" one veteran activist asked me just after we had met for an interview. With a kind of proud confidence, I told him that I would stay for a minimum of a year and a half. "Oh, that is too bad," he said gently and laughed. "This is not a simple problem," he began, and he continued to speak about silence, denial, and hope long after my supply of audiotapes had been exhausted.

There is clearly a sense in which João and all of the other militants I met are subversively dangerous—as they are surely thought to be—yet I remain convinced that their hope is not to turn Brazil upside down and inside out, as their opponents seem to fear, but simply to turn it more fully and honestly toward its own dreaming.

Chapter 8

Conclusion

Dreaming

WHETHER NAMED OR UNNAMED, democracia racial lies at the heart of all discourses on color, race, and racism in Brazil. Its puzzles and paradoxes, as a consequence, occupy the center of my discussion. In this book, I have tried to treat democracia racial as itself constituted by a set of overlapping discourses or, perhaps more properly, as a series of themes that are articulated within a range of discursive registers. While it obviously represents what we generally understand by the term "ideology," I have sought to locate it within the mouths of speaking subjects, to represent it as tangible, concrete, and empirically grounded. Here I would like to pursue a brief but more general and admittedly provisional discussion of democracia racial.

While constituted through discourse, democracia racial is, at the same time, both too powerful and too nebulous to summarize and identify with quotes and quotes of quotes. It resists facile paraphrasing. As an ideology, it is an exceptionally capricious one. Its meaning has always resonated well beyond Brazilian borders, for traditionally, it has been movingly represented as a beacon of hope in a confused and violently divided world. Yet, within the past two decades especially, democracia racial has been insistently called a myth. Although this renaming of democracia racial is sometimes attributed to North American scholars—who are accused of looking down their ethnocentric noses at Brazil—the expression "the myth of democracia racial" is often requisite in Brazilian intellectual circles as well. Explicit debates about the nature of democracia racial have certainly been inspired by extremely passionate forms of nationalism, but the battle lines have never been neatly drawn: at roughly the same time, the American anthropologist Charles Wagley (1963b) championed democracia racial while the Brazilian anthropologist Thales de Azevédo (1975) challenged it.

When intellectuals call democracia racial a myth, they typically invoke political and commonsense understandings of the term rather than traditional anthropological ones. Democracia racial, in other words, is a misjudgment, a fallacy, a deception, a lie, or, in slightly more sophisticated terms, a mystification. What is being referred to is that set of beliefs and discourses that asserts that racialized prejudice and discrimination, to the extent that they exist at all in Brazil, are so subtle and mild as to be practically meaningless and without significant material consequence.

Defined as such, democracia racial represents an especially salient and convenient target for various forms of critique. Democracia racial can be dismembered from within, for as many have noted, it lacks consistency and logical coherence. Nineteenth-century elite discourses of branqueamento, for example, existed alongside those that denied the force of racialized prejudice. As Brazil enters the twenty-first century, the celebration of color-blind love and notions of lightening the family go hand in hand. More to the point for many who have explicitly challenged democracia racial over the last contentious decade of Brazilianist studies is the obvious and enormous hiatus between assertions of equality and what my informants in Morro do Sangue Bom call *realidade*—the concreteness of racialized oppression and its observable consequences. Juxtaposed against this reality, democracia racial appears to be pure delusion, and it lends itself to those forms of critical analysis that highlight hegemonic domination, obfuscation, false consciousness, and directly instrumental forms of mystification.

While I certainly align myself with those who critique the delusional thrust of democracia racial, such a formulation remains incomplete. The incantatory reference to it as a myth may lead us to assume that we understand democracia racial when we have merely glossed it with a label. Even when its internal contradictions are cogently described, democracia racial tends to be figured as monolithic and monological, a single-tongued ideology with a single and entirely fallacious message. As such, references to the myth of democracia racial hardly do justice to the heteroglot, double-voiced, and slippery sites at which it is articulated. The framing of democracia racial as an easily identifiable, monoglot master narrative—as a rather pathetic, if persistent, smoke screen—cannot account for the fact that it flows so easily across the borders of class and color, nor for the fact that Brazilians continue to defend it with a passion that clearly reflects something more complicated than a vulgar nationalism.

At various points in this book, I have alluded to a distinction that other scholars do not make: that between the descriptive and prescriptive claims of democracia racial. Conventional discussions of democracia racial only engage the former claims and ignore the latter. My own focus on the prescriptive claims of democracia racial is directly based on my observations in Morro do Sangue Bom, where the fundamental, inherent, and essential equality of all people is insistently invoked.

One evening I dropped in to visit Marta, and there I found Beto, obviously reeling from an afternoon spent drinking cane liquor. When he was sober, I enjoyed his company, but at times like this he could be irritating. For ten minutes Beto discoursed on whiskey. "Some like it straight, some like it with a little ice, and some have it with orange juice. That is how it is here in Brazil," he said as though coming to the conclusion of his lecture. "And how is in your land?"

I told him that it was the same. "You see!" he said. "Everyone is equal! Black, white, I don't know what, it's all the same. Equal! There are no differences!" These comments too, I want to argue, take their place within the discourses of democracia racial, and as such, they represent an unassailable moral high ground from which Beto could stake his claim to equality. "Of course there are no real differences," I said to Beto, "but there is discrimination." He waved his arm back and forth dismissively. Now he was shouting. "Everyone is equal! Here in Brazil, everyone is equal!"

In Morro do Sangue Bom, insistent claims to inherent equality refer to universal human values, but they are articulated from within a distinctly Brazilian idiom. "We're all going to the same little hole," they say. When they pronounce this judgment before racist whites, they know they are standing on solid ground, that their antagonists will be reduced to stuttering, shame, and, finally, silence. Sem graça, they are stripped naked before a graphically final judgment. There are precious and memorable moments in Brazil when the tables are turned. "The same blood that runs in your veins runs in my veins!" they say. Occasional references to "sangue negro" are nearly drowned out by the much louder and more emphatic chorus, "The blood is the same!" "Nos somos todos iguais!" (We are all equal!)

The finality and the shaming power of these statements resides also in the fact that the hearer knows that the speaker knows that the hearer knows. Poor Brazilians of African descent draw upon an idiomatic repertoire that is embraced not by them alone but by all Brazilians. More than a mere "invention of the people," as Dona Janete put it, it pulses at the center of Brazil and its unique history and, for the faithful, it is given by God. Although these prescriptive claims to a shared and undivided humanity may have a double-voiced quality when they come from the mouths of poor Brazilians of African descent, this quality is not directly addressed to the difference between speakers and hearers, but rather, it summons the collectively held notion of the moral force of a shared heritage, a common family, a unified nation. Racism is repugnant. It is immoral. It is, above all, un-Brazilian. It poisons what is closest to the shared heart, the common spirit of Brazil. Those who practice it, no matter how secure in their presumed superiority, always wind up in the same little hole. No matter how constrained and surrounded by contradiction and cruelty, within the registers through which they are spoken, these are things upon which all Brazilians can agree. Undeniably, this also is democracia racial. To call democracia racial a mere myth-as-smoke-screen is to miss the extent to which it is also a series of heteroglot narratives that are nearly mythical as well as mystifying and that implicitly direct themselves to the future as well as to the past.

Democracia racial is undoubtedly a myth, but it is also, I would assert, a dream. In authoritatively articulating its prescriptive claims, poor people of color are not describing Brazil as it is, but as it ought to be. Despite their resignation and exhaustion, people such as those in Morro do Sangue Bom are clearly among the self-appointed guardians of this dream. Their silence, their apparent passivity, as well as their careful maintenance of a democratic ethos within their own sequestered communities are stances that are informed by defense and a subterranean antagonism, but they are also directed toward the protection of an extremely fragile sense of hope. Their faith is compromised, suffused with cynicism, beset on all sides by the certain knowledge of past and future betrayals, but poor Brazilians of African descent cannot let go of democracia racial because it is a dream that they share with all other Brazilians. In so many ways, it is a dream that is about them, about their citizenship and their humanity, their contribution to their country, first as slaves and then as wage laborers. Democracia racial is, as I have noted, their moral high ground, perhaps the only one they have that is recognized, however incompletely and hypocritically, by their nation.

Needless to say, Analucia's dark-skinned husband, Jair, was profoundly outraged and hurt when he discovered that his white neighbor on the morro had said to another neighbor that if it were up to her, all negros would die. Confronting her, Jair had asked how she could say such a thing when he had always greeted her with neighborly courtesy and warmth. As Jair described it to me later, he felt called upon to defend not only himself, his family, and his race, but also his nation. "Tomorrow," Jair said rhetorically, "you may fall in the middle of the road. And who will go to help you?" He continued: "Before we die, we will have already witnessed so much. Before we die—on our feet, still working, sick and full of worms. But to die? After we die, everyone is equal. There are no differences! Racism should have ended a long time ago because each of us depends on the other. One hand washes the other. . . . No one is better than anyone else. And if we together were a united Brazil? . . . All of us *should* be equal! Because if we were all equal, our Brazil would have a greater force with which to go forward into the struggle."

DREAMS OF A glory that remains just beyond reach have always animated Brazil and its people. They represent an extremely distinctive and undeniably poignant, rather than a generic and thoroughly predictable, form of national-ism. It is not only the content of these dreams but the peculiar passion that underlies them that is constantly referenced and indexed in Brazilian idioms of self-representation, including, naturally, those articulated by the nation's elite.

José Honorio Rodrigues, a revered historian of the traditional mold, is merely one of many Brazilian intellectuals who sought to question those dreams, to assess their potential, and to define their relationship to national character. It is Brazilians' peculiar approach to their own speech, he suggests provocatively, that spells their entrapment, that represents the fatal flaw behind their failure to achieve national glory. It is "rhetoric," he concludes, that presents the greatest "obstacle" to Brazilian "prosperity and efficiency" (1967, 47). While the "liking of rhetoric" and the promiscuous outpouring of an "excess of words" is hardly unique to Brazilians, he explains, their passion-ate embracing of it, and their lack of ironic perspective on it, is the most damning trait of their character (47). Rodrigues apparently did not visit com-munities such as Morro do Sangue Bom—where a taste for irony seems to be one of life's fundamental necessities—but there are Brazilians, principally those of his own class, for whom he speaks.

Whereas "rhetoric is clearly and consciously recognized as such" by oth-ers, among Brazilians, Rodrigues argues, "rhetoric is an integral part of thought and is presented as a solution" (1967, 47). He continues: "Brazilian patriotism is connected with a consciously developed and preserved history. Brazilian national life suffers, however, from a capital defect: the confusion of words with deeds, aspirations with achievements—in a word, verbalism joined with a lack of political realism" (50).

Rodrigues, it seems, fell into precisely the same trap when he wrote of his nation's history that "gentleness in dealing with the Negro slave became gen-eral" and that "miscegenation and the possibility of rising in the world created an atmosphere of peaceful relations and fellowship" (1967, 47). He spoke in the rhetoric of dreaming and did not recognize it as such.

In an extended disquisition on the "psychology of the Brazilian"—another study in national character—José Fernando Carneiro notes, "There has always been in Brazil, the presentiment of a future of grandeur." It is the "idea of unity," Carneiro believes, "that lays the foundation for our hope in the future" (1971, 55). As did Jair of Morro do Sangue Bom, Carneiro refers in large measure to racial unity. This unity was threatened, Carneiro observes further, by the Brazilian "preoccupation with hiding the negro," by the attempt to "flee from the subject," and, more generally, by the "national shame on the question of the black race" (37–38). While implicitly critiquing democracia racial as a specious rhetoric that purports to describe the reality of Brazilian social life, Carneiro argues that national unity might still be built upon a modification of the most fundamental virtues of Brazilian national character: "We have to change ourselves, without abandoning the fundamental features of our character, such as [those of] tenderness, the love of family, the spirit of conciliation. . . . Our substance is very good, but it has been badly used. There is a tiresome preachment of tenderness, which is frequently used as a disguise for a lack of convictions. It is even a lack of character. We need to preserve this tenderness, making it yet more authentic, without ever using it as a smokescreen" (55–56).

Neither Rodrigues nor Carneiro refer directly, in the passages I quote, to democracia racial, but their attempts to speak to the peculiarities of Brazilian national character address the larger understanding of it that I am proposing. The Brazilian dream of democracia racial, such comments might suggest, is indeed fundamentally rhetorical in nature. The "tenderness" that it and related discourses tiresomely preach is often used as a *cortina de fumaça,* a smoke screen. Although undermined by insincerity, inauthenticity, and a "lack of convictions," there is, Carneiro tells us, something in the value given to this tenderness that is worth saving.

The lack of convictions that Carneiro refers to is hardly a unique preoccupation but is one that constantly emerges, in one form or another, in Brazilian discussions of national character. A toleration, to a fault, for ambiguity and contradiction, a kind of cultural and intellectual fluidity and flexibility, and a dread of rigidity, essentialism, direct opposition, and open confrontation are constantly invoked in describing and defining what makes one most deeply Brazilian. For Carneiro, as for others, there is both good and bad to be found here. "From ideological eclecticism," Carneiro laments, "one passes into ideological confusion" (1971, 51). It is this very flexibility of character, however, that feeds the "spirit of conciliation," one of the "fundamental features" that must be salvaged; as Carneiro argues directly, "the traditional Brazilian tendency to flee from the prison of ideologies can be an advantage" (57).

The peculiar nature of Brazilian racism partakes of this contradictory, fluid, and rhetorically constructed character. "The Brazilian is racist," Carneiro finally states, after pages and pages of gently demystifying illustrations. "Only he is not a convinced racist." "Our prejudices," he concludes insightfully, "operate from within a certain moral doubt" (1971, 51).

Democracia racial obfuscates oppression and its moral meaning, it silences the victims of racism, and it proffers a preachy and inauthentic tenderness in place of genuine equality and sincere respect. It is, following Rodrigues, a rhetoric that is not recognized as such, a "confusion of words with deeds, aspirations with achievements" (1967, 50). Yet, it is these aspirations, the tender dreaming that goes on behind democracia racial's prescriptive commandments, that most fully constitute and protect the cultural space of "moral doubt" that Carneiro refers to.

There is, finally, something that is different about Brazil. While typically misidentified, there are moments in which it seems almost real enough to touch. When I left Brazil, I missed it—even though, in the welter of claims and counterclaims that I had heard, I could not immediately name it. A dream is a nebulous thing and we cannot weigh it or measure it, but it is worth something, just the same. That the dreaming is a tiny fire that must be constantly stoked, tended, and defended is testament to the profoundly fragile ground on which it is built—but it surely warmed the voice of a woman in Morro do Sangue Bom when she said, "There is only one race, right? The human race." This dreaming—its ability, no matter how compromised, to throw moral doubt into the rigid face of brutal essentialism, wherever it is to be found in the contemporary world—may be all that is left of the beacon that Brazil holds out to the rest of us.

Epilogue

In May of 1992, the city of Rio de Janeiro moved to complete the last-minute preparations for the International Earth Summit. Heads of state would convene just outside the city, while nongovernmental organizations would meet in the park attached to Flamengo Beach, not far from Santa Teresa. Thirty-five thousand soldiers, deployed more for symbolic than direct military purposes, seemed glad of something important to do. Wearing tight green uniforms and carrying automatic rifles as though they were sartorial accessories, they posed stiffly on every street corner.

Several days before the summit, *Istoé,* a major newsmagazine, finally acknowledged, in one sentence, what people in places like Morro do Sangue Bom had known for several weeks: "For a country that intends to improve its international image in hosting the conference, the guarantee of the smooth functioning of Eco 92 has, however, a depressing price: the image, which will also run throughout the world, of soldiers and tanks pointed at the population on the streets and, above all, at the favelas" (*Istoé* 1992).

People such as those in Morro do Sangue Bom had first looked forward to the summit. The building excitement was infectious and people living on the hills could not help but feel a certain pride in their city and their country. As preparations intensified, however, they were being deliberately and menacingly pushed off the streets and shoved out of the South Zone and the city center. Whatever forms of hospitality and expressions of goodwill they might have extended to the foreigners were not wanted. In the weeks preceding the event, men began to return home directly from work or never left Morro do Sangue Bom at all, while women began to stockpile food, so that everyone might stay in their place, exactly as they were commanded.

Far more ominous than harassment, however, was talk of the *limpeza,* or
cleansing, that was occurring in morros all over the city. That local and federal politicians and men high in the police hierarchy truly believed that local
drug traffickers represented a threat to the conference participants seemed
absurd. That the Earth Summit was being used as an excuse to assassinate certain gang leaders, and thus shift the local ecologies in which rival gangs com-
peted for drug money—while the police skimmed the cream from the
top—seemed so shortsighted as to be unconscionable from any perspective.
Such a scenario was, however, more plausible. The torture and murder of the
city's homeless children, while seemingly routinized, briefly reclaimed its grip
on the city's moral imagination after these children virtually disappeared from
the streets of the Centro district. People in Morro do Sangue Bom began to
whisper that terrible crimes were being committed, far more openly than was
usually the case, on behalf of the delicate sensibilities of the soon-to-be-arriv-
ing gringos.

One morning just before dawn, I was awakened by the angry buzz of heli-
copters flying overhead. It was two weeks before the Earth Summit. I had been
living on the hill for a year and a half. I was ill from a protracted period of par-
asitic infection, and I was growing anxious about my imminent departure from
Brazil. Exhausted, I went back to sleep.

Several hours later, when I emerged from the soothing darkness into the
sunshine, Dona Janete appeared at the window over my door. "They took him
away," she called down with obvious anxiety. "It was very early, and no one
saw, but the police said he broke his leg. They said he was trying to escape and
he fell from a roof. They took him away like this"—she made a slicing motion
in the air with her good arm—"before anyone even knew what was happening." She was talking, of course, about Delson, the boss of Nova Época. There
was real fear in Dona Janete's voice and I absorbed it instantly.

On my way to do errands in the city, I passed by the open area at the bottom of the hill. Several of Nova Época's men stood in an anxious huddle by
the public telephone, broke off to briefly pace in tight circles, and repeatedly
wiped their brows. Others, unconnected to the gang, stood alone or in small
groups as though waiting for something to happen. Looking back from where
I had come, I realized how quiet it was on the hill. "What is it?" I asked a
woman. She told me that the police had taken Delson first to their station
house and then to the hospital. His men were anxiously waiting for news of
his condition. It was ten o'clock in the morning.

When I returned to the hill just after six o'clock in the evening, an enormous crowd was massed at the bottom of the hill. I was struck by the number
of unfamiliar faces—I had come to believe that I knew them all—and how

little noise they made. I found a friend and asked her what was happening. "We are waiting for Delson," she said. "The police let him go, then?" I asked. She looked confused for a moment and said, "His body. His family left in the car to go get him. He will return in a box." She turned away and began to cry.

At about eight o'clock, the crowd parted for only a moment to let the car pass, and more quickly than I could have imagined possible, young men whisked the casket into the association building and slammed and locked the door. Night was falling. We waited, hundreds of us, shifting from one foot to the other and whispering, until finally a line formed. I went in with the second group. With others, I signed my name in a book. His family would keep it, I knew, and years later remember how many had come to pay their respects. Delson's face was nestled in a blanket of beautiful white flowers that concealed his entire body.

"For all we know," Dona Janete speculated that night, "he could have been decapitated." Restricted by her partial paralysis, she had not gone to the wake, but she knew the details well before I came to her door hoping, rather desperately, to find her still awake. People had already begun to suggest that Delson had been a victim of the limpeza. "This man did not die of a broken leg," I said, stating the obvious. "Even if he had had gangrene," Dona Janete added, "he would never have died so fast." "God only knows what they did to him," Seu Arnaldo muttered. Dona Janete sighed heavily and said, "This is what happens to people like him. But he was a leader of our community."

Although everyone had shut their doors and shutters and the morro was quiet, slivers of light peeked out all over the hill until well past midnight. Drinking too much coffee and speaking in hushed tones, Dona Janete, Seu Arnaldo, and their son Efraim told stories about how it had been before Delson and his men had gained undisputed control of the hill. "Not even a word could you say back then," Dona Janete whispered. After Delson had control, there had been six years of peace. The question that hung in the air, unspoken, was, "What now?"

I went to bed knowing the world had changed. I couldn't put words to my feelings, but I could not bear the thought of going home. The fact that Morro do Sangue Bom was, from a different angle, but a small and unknown place of little consequence seemed incomprehensible to me.

It did not become less so when I went, the next afternoon, to Delson's funeral on one of eight crowded city buses that Nova Época had chartered for the occasion. All the way down the narrow back streets of Santa Teresa, people stood by the roadside waving palm branches. The echoing blast of farewell gunshots resounded from the neighboring hills. There had been even more to Delson's reputation and his short life than I had imagined.

For weeks afterwards I pestered my friends for information on who had stepped in to fill Delson's shoes. His death left a vacuum of power, one that might lead to more killing as his men matched their ambitions against one another. Far more critical was the fact that a leaderless and disorganized Nova Época was horribly vulnerable to outside attack. The immediate threat was represented by the police, the more distant one by the Red Command. The truth of the matter seemed to be that there was no one on the hill who possessed Delson's charisma and connections. After several weeks, Nova Época did kill one of their own. Perhaps because the murder followed so closely upon the death of Delson, or because the victim was widely disliked, it caused only a small and brief ripple on the hill.

People put on a kind of cheer that first seemed false and forced, and then, except for the frequent presence of the Nova Época men at the bottom of the hill, things appeared, on the surface, to go on much as before. The borders between the community and the outside world, however, were closed. I had taken to visiting a friend who lived in a small apartment building close to the morro, and I often urged him to visit me in my home. After he was questioned at gunpoint while entering the community to buy a fresh chicken, I desisted.

We both suffered from insomnia and I sometimes returned on foot from his apartment to the morro after three o'clock in the morning. I felt safe making my way up the labyrinthine paths as the world slept, wrapped in a soothing stillness. On one such night, I arrived at the open plateau just beneath the hill and saw a man moving stealthily through the shadows. He appeared to be limping and made a very wide circle around me, very deliberately keeping out of the light cast by a street lamp. I waited for him, certain he would recognize me as a member of the community, if only a temporary one. He very quietly approached my side, one leg held stiff and straight. "What's going on down there?" he asked me.

I told him that I had seen a police car parked on the street at a specific hour much earlier in the evening but that it had since gone. "It is quiet down below," I reassured him. "I saw no one as I was coming up." He thanked me and turned away. I saw that his limp had been false; from behind his leg he swung a sawed-off shot gun onto his shoulder and moved back into the shadows. From that time on, an evidently leaderless Nova Época kept a tense nightly watch.

In the evening, some days later, Seu Arnaldo rapped on his floor (my ceiling) with the handle of a broomstick, a signal for me to come outside where he would speak to me from his bedroom window. "Close and lock your windows and door and don't go out tonight," Seu Arnaldo said. "The X-Nines have been seen." He told me that it was best to put my book down, turn off my lights, and go to bed. If anyone knocked on the door, I was not to open it—even if they claimed to be the police. Because, he explained, they might indeed be the police, but they would be wearing masks.

No one came to my door that night but the hush that settled on the hill had lost its soothing quality.

Before the *despedida*, the going-away party, that was held for me on Varena's roof, I told Joia and Varena that they must not fail to write to me in the coming months. Given the situation with Nova Época, I would worry. Varena insisted that my illness, which briefly improved and then worsened, was caused by my anxiety about leaving. Through nothing more than a simple accident of birth, I kept thinking, I was granted the privilege of abandoning a sinking ship and returning to a world where the fear of calamity was entirely absent and nothing ever seemed to change. There was something in this, as Varena knew, that made me extremely *nervosa*, and she tried to console me by singing the foolish and half-remembered lyrics of a song about Nova Iorque, the glamorous city to which I would be returning. "We know you won't forget us, Beth," she said to reassure me. Toward the end of the raucous despedida, as I was being passed from arm to arm and embraced, I finally allowed myself to cry openly.

I wrote to Joia, Varena, and Jorge a number of times over the next year but received no response. In 1993, a year after Delson's death, I read about the siege of Morro do Sangue Bom in the *New York Times*. The Red Command had arrived. It would be another two years before I would return to the hill and learn the details of the siege—which residents counted as three separate but related wars that occurred over the space of a year—but a colleague sent me news clippings about the first war from the Rio papers.

The events in Morro do Sangue Bom became international news largely because they provided evidence for the fact that groups like the Red Command had begun recruiting men who were, or had been, soldiers in the Brazilian Army. They offered not only additional manpower but more significantly, military training and technical expertise.

Digging trenches around the periphery of the community, the Red Command settled in for a protracted battle that began on a Friday night. They fired upon the electrical transformers, throwing the community into complete darkness. The men of Nova Época and their new leader, Barão, were their first targets. Varena later told me that I had known Barão and "adored" him; but for reasons about which I can only speculate, I could not find him in my memory. Sometime after the sun rose, Barão's body was cut into pieces and his second-in-command, Samuel, was ordered to carry them in his arms to the community Dumpster. After he had done so, Samuel was shot and killed. The

Red Command placed their flag outside the association headquarters in order to "intimate the community," according to the papers.

The message was probably intended, however, for the Third Command, a smaller imperialist gang that had long had it sights on the boca de fumo of Morro do Sangue Bom. Recent police activity on a nearby hill that they had previously controlled led to plummeting drug sales, and they immediately responded to the Red Command's incursion into the most profitable boca of Santa Teresa. For the remainder of the weekend, evidently, the Third Command and the Red Command turned Morro do Sangue Bom into a bloodbath. The victory of the Red Command, while perhaps not yet decisive, appeared inevitable. By Wednesday evening, when the military police finally ascended the hill (after rather than during the war), nine people had been killed and the cement steps were slippery with blood. Leaving with little more than the clothes on their backs, many fled the community, vowing that despite the depth of their roots in Morro do Sangue Bom, they would never return.

When I returned to the hill two years later, only a few of the people I had been closest to were still living there. Among them was Jorge, whose unemployment left him entirely unable to relocate his family. He had converted to the Assembly of God, one of the strictest of the Protestant religions in Rio. He had entirely renounced his previous roguery and neither drank nor smoked nor used the swear words that he had taught me. He attributed his newfound reliance on Jesus to the intense crisis and terror he had experienced after a member of the Red Command had vowed to kill him within several day's time. Overnight, Jorge converted, and his wife, Angela, loyal as ever, followed him into the church soon after.

When I found Jorge, he rushed to tell me, as did every friend that I was able to locate, that Neusa, who always "messed in everything," had been one of the first victims of the war. "I know she was your friend, Beth," Jorge said solemnly. The Red Command had simply knocked on her door, and when she opened it, they emptied a round of bullets into her body, in plain view—as I compulsively forced myself to imagine—of her eight-year-old son.

Although the military police had briefly occupied the hill after the first war, they once again abandoned it to its own devices and the Red Command returned to reinstate its claim. It was during this period that Joia and Daniel's son, Alberto, had a gun held to his head when he was returning to his home after work. No longer a child, Alberto was, like all of the young men in the community, viewed as a potential threat by the men of the Red Command. Having no connection to the hill except a heavily militarized, commercial one, they could not distinguish between lifelong residents, rival gang members, and police informers. Joia was literally sick with fear for Alberto, her body falling apart after months of terror. The doctors, she later told me, could do nothing.

It was only in 1995, after repeated pleas from the community, that the military police began to occupy Morro do Sangue Bom for an indefinite period. I was introduced to two of the officers when I returned. They were cheerful men, and talkative. "Isn't it strange how enemies have become friends?" I later asked Dona Janete, also one of the few who remained stranded on the hill. She nodded but offered qualifications. Many were predicting that they would soon leave, she told me, and, besides, no one really trusted them. They lounged around in the building that housed the residents' association, consorting with God knew whom—for the gang now seemed to be composed of a mixture of local men and outsiders—and freely snorted their cocaine and shared in the profits of its sale. It was because they were high, Dona Janete explained, that they seemed so friendly.

Dona Janete's husband, Seu Arnaldo, had had a stroke, which she was sure was brought on by the fact that he, too, had had a gun held to his head and had been threatened with public execution by a member of the Red Command. After his stroke he retired, and although he and Dona Janete still laughed at the private jokes they had amassed after more than forty years of marriage—they were still making up new ones, in fact—she worried about the blank places in his mind.

Dona Janete took me to her son's house, an unusually large and airy place he had acquired after I left the hill but then abandoned following the war. Everything had been left behind—his bed, the pots and pans, and the refrigerator I had given him when I returned to New York three years before. "Maybe I could stay here, Dona Janete," I said, testing the waters, "just for a week." She smiled but shook her head. It just wasn't safe, she told me, and I knew she was right. Several weeks later, Dona Janete and Seu Arnaldo moved too, relocating to a town in Rio's periphery.

Well before my return, the families of both Joia and Varena had fled the morro and had begun new lives beyond Rio. Joia, Daniel, and their children—the last, a beautiful girl born while I was still living in Morro do Sangue Bom—had set up house in a tiny two-room building on the property of Daniel's sister in Niteroi. They had scrimped and gone without for years to expand their house on the hill and then had to abandon it just before it was completed. They had begun all over again, slowly building a smaller house in a growing working-class neighborhood several miles from Daniel's sister's house.

Although Daniel occasionally got together with old friends on the hill, Joia and Alberto refused to return and claimed that they felt no saudades, or homesickness. "Just for a little reunion to kill the *saudades*," I said. They wouldn't consider it. Only my own memories of the epoca de paz had been left intact, frozen in time by my departure before the war. They tried, rather delicately, to explain it to me—how bad it had been—but they soon gave up. I could only nod uncomprehendingly, both wanting and not wanting to hear.

Varena had purchased a dilapidated and leaky but large apartment in the North Zone, an hour distant from the city. She had failed to make friends in her new neighborhood, where everyone socialized behind the closed doors of second-story apartments like her own. Unlike Joia, she could not repress her homesickness and she visited the hill nearly every week, spending most of her time at the home of Guilherme, Daniel's younger brother, who was now married and a father. Varena and the husband that she had so sorely missed had reunited. Although the family's income increased as a result, Varena worked harder than ever, rising before dawn to make and sell pastries in the city. But she carried on her face and body a kind of contentment I had never before seen there. She had also found comfort and solace within a Protestant congregation. Her descent into alcoholism stopped abruptly and her relationship with her children dramatically improved.

Rosemary, her adopted daughter, quiet but already independent, had stood on the sidelines while her homeless brother was adopted by an American couple amidst international publicity. It was a human interest story. I learned of it before my return to Brazil, when I saw a photo of Rosemary's brother in the *New York Times*. I had never met him, nor even knew his name, but the article mentioned that he had a sister and I accurately read the trace of Rosemary's features in his face. Unnerved by the coincidence, I wrote to the *Times* reporter and tracked his adoptive mother in California. We spoke on the phone for hours. She told me that, yes, she and her husband had met Rosemary, a pretty, soft-spoken girl, poised and mature. Impossibly, I wanted the world to truly be as small as it sometimes seemed, a place where people could meet in any number of strange circumstances and hold on to each other, even across international borders.

Rosemary, I saw on my return, had grown up and left Varena's house to work as a live-in empregada. She came to Varena's home during my visit there, and when the three of us walked down the street together, she and Varena held hands. The grace with which Rosemary carried the profound losses of her young life astounded me.

Although the hill was, as everyone said, *tranquilo*, or calm, for the moment, I had to agree with Joia's explanation for her refusal to meet me there. "Beth," she said, "that community no longer exists. The Morro do Sangue Bom that was is no more. Let it go."

Those who remained on the hill missed those who had left, and rather halfheartedly, they sometimes pretended not to. It was their way of dealing with loss, and after my first visit, I could see that there were things—the war, the exodus, even the future—about which they didn't want to talk. They visited each other's homes far less often than in the past. There were people living on the hill whom no one knew. How and why they had come was something that was best left alone. They were not welcomed, as other newcomers arriving before the war had been.

Those who were born and raised on the hill, such as Guilherme and his wife, spent their Saturday nights watching television with the shutters tightly closed and the doors locked. They were surrounded by empty, boarded-up houses. Guilherme filled me in on the larger picture of his life. The real value of wages had depreciated appallingly, and somehow people had learned to live with even less. Everyone detested the new president, who, Guilherme said, clearly hated the poor, despite his reputation among the middle classes as a man of the left.

Beleaguered, resigned, and struggling both with implacably gruesome memories and an insecure future, many on the hill had turned to either cocaine or religion. Outside of José and Elena's home, which they had long since abandoned—I never did find them—graffiti urged the acceptance of Jesus while mature family men openly sniffled, clearing their nostrils of what had begun as an infrequently indulged recreation and had become, during or after the war, an unconcealed addiction. Others drowned themselves in cachaça and fell on the path, where they stayed, too drunk to get up or to care who might see them. Because so many remained huddled inside with their doors shut, no one came to help them or even knew that they had fallen. The concern with appearances and many other social controls, both too numerous and too invisibly constructed to remember by name, had clearly weakened or collapsed. Joia was right: this was not at all the Morro do Sangue Bom that was, but a different place altogether.

A community is more than a place, more than the sum of those who are left behind, and while outsiders might not notice or care, it can pass into memory. I felt that Morro do Sangue Bom had become, in its desperate, if mostly quiet, forms of mourning, something like the favela of the imagination. It had become history.

Notes

Introduction

1. Morro do Sangue Bom translates literally as "Hill of Good Blood." *Sangue bom* is a slang expression used to describe a person who can be trusted, who does not put on airs, and who communicates in a warm, easy-going, and unpretentious manner. For many people, it is also a favorable reference to people of color. Sangue bom invokes notions of race through the metaphor of blood but inverts the typically pejorative associations of blackness by giving them a distinctly positive spin.
2. See especially Harris 1956, 1964, 1970; Harris and Kottak 1963; Hutchinson 1957, 1963; Kottak 1967; Pierson 1942; Wagley 1963a, 1963b; and Zimmerman 1963. Although these researchers documented the existence of racialized prejudice, they concluded, in the words of Harris, that "racial identity is a mild and wavering thing in Brazil" (1964, 64). Wagley was explicit in his defense of the racial democracy thesis. "[R]acial origin," he wrote, "has not become a serious point of conflict in Brazilian society. . . . Brazil remains a lesson in racial democracy for the rest of the world" (1963b, unnumbered pages, preface). During the same period, a number of researchers working in urban Brazil were more equivocal in their assessments of the racial democracy thesis (Azevedo 1953; Bastide and van den Berghe 1957; Bastide and Fernandes 1951, 1955; Cardoso and Ianni 1960; Costa Pinto 1953; Fernandes 1965, 1969, 1972; Nogueira 1955; Pereira 1967). Fernandes, the most widely read of the Brazilian researchers, argued, however, that racism was little more than a cultural holdover that would wither away with the development of industrial capitalism. For the critique of the racial democracy thesis, see, for example, Andrews 1991, 1992b; Dzidzienyo 1971; Fontaine 1980, 1985b; Hanchard 1993, 1994a, 1994b; Nascimento 1979; Saunders 1972; Skidmore 1992, 1993a, 1993b; Winant 1992.
3. Except when quoting others, I use the term "race" in this book to refer to a cultural and historical construct rather than as a valid biological or natural category.
4. For discussions of the functional relationship between race and poverty, see especially Hasenbalg 1979, 1985, 1994; Hasenbalg and Silva 1990, 1993; Lovell 1989; Lovell and Dwyer 1988; Porcaro 1988; Silva 1985; Silva and Hasenbalg 1993; Telles 1992; Wood 1990; Wood and Carvalho 1988; Wood and Lovell 1992.
5. Recent ethnographies have critiqued the racial democracy thesis, but they have tended overwhelmingly to focus on rural communities and subcultures (Baiocchi 1983; Bandeira 1988; Twine 1998) or the practice and politics of religion (Brown 1994; Birman 1980; Burdick 1993, 1998; Dantas 1988; Hale 1995; Maggie 1991; Shapiro 1996; Vogt and Fry 1996; Wafer 1991). Although these researchers discuss

local and transnational (see especially, Sansone 1992, 1994) stances toward racism, they do not systematically detail the ways in which specifically urban Brazilians of African descent experience, interpret, and talk about (or do not talk about) racism in everyday contexts.

6. See Hanchard 1999; Roth Gordon 1999; and Winant 1999.

7. See, for example, Bakhtin 1981; Bourdieu 1991; Foucault 1972, 1980; Fowler 1985; Fowler et al. 1979; Volosinov 1973.

8. I acknowledge the significance of Clifford's (1983) work and that of others (e.g., Behar and Gordon 1995; Clifford and Marcus 1986; Crapanzano 1977; Dwyer 1977; Marcus and Fischer 1986) in promoting more explicitly collaborative ethnography.

Chapter 1   *The Hill*

1. Although I refer to traditions that continue to be associated with Africa and Africans, many of the cultural elements that were historically associated with African Brazilians have been, as Fry (1982) cogently notes, racially and politically neutralized. As such, they have been harnessed to the service of representing a mainstream, national Brazilian culture.

2. Unlike many who have written about Rio's hillside shantytowns, I tend to follow the usage of those who live in such communities. For the most part, when I use the term "favela," I intend it in the technical and generic sense, as it is used within a particular literature, or, alternatively, to quote or index the speech of outsiders. In this latter sense, it is best translated as "slum," and like its English equivalent, it is, in the ears of those who live in such communities, an extremely pejorative term.

3. Many of the women I knew in the community had their first child at the age of seventeen, but they differed radically from their mothers and grandmothers in their goal, and very often their success, of limiting their families to two or, at most, three children. Although many in Brazil's small black movement suggest that the extremely high number of tubal ligations performed in Brazil represents an attempt by racist whites to control the fertility of poor women of color, my informants expressed anger and frustration at the condescending assumptions and obstacles—particularly the requirements that they be at least thirty years of age and in possession of their husbands' permission—that they encountered in their attempts to arrange the procedure.

4. I attended four beauty pageants during the twenty months I spent in Rio. Notions of feminine beauty are heavily racialized in Rio (see Simpson 1993), and poor people of color often feel that it is necessary to insist that "black women can be beautiful too." Everyday discourses on color and beauty embody striking contradictions for the mulata and/or the morena (browned-skinned or, possibly, black women) as abstract types are thought to represent a uniquely Brazilian ideal of sensuous beauty. The association of blackness with ugliness is, however, no less pervasive in everyday discourses, so much so that the master of ceremonies at a citywide beauty pageant called "Beauty Comes Down from the Morro" reminded the audience that "beauty has nothing to do with color." This comment was, in many ways, the implicit message of the entire event. Beauty pageants that involve poor women of color as contestants involve a peculiar mixture of ideological conservatism and subversion.

5. Antagonism between the city's working poor and the police is historically entrenched in Rio. See Flory 1977; Jakubs 1977; and Holloway 1993.

Chapter 2 Talk: Discourses on Color and Race

1. What might be called the "Brazilian model of race relations" is, in fact, less unique than the literature and Brazilians themselves often imply. Brazil serves as a much-discussed exemplar of cultural patterns that are evident (with some variations, obviously) throughout Latin America and the Caribbean. Although my discussion in not explicitly comparative, it is located within and informed by similar discussions of the discourses and meanings associated with color and race in other Latin American and Caribbean nations (see, for example, Alexander 1977; Godreau 1994, 1995; Khan 1993; Lancaster 1991; Martinez 1974; Rahier 2000; Segal 1993; Stutzman 1981; Wade 1993, 1997; Wright 1990).

2. What I had not expected, given my review of the literature on racial classification in Brazil, was the relatively small number of terms used in the overall sample. In the late 1960s, Marvin Harris (1970) and Roger Sanjek (1971) collected hundreds of terms. A number of factors might account for the remarkable difference between my own and other researchers' data. The most obvious factor is the difference in methodology. Presented with a stack of drawings and asked to define the "quality" or "type" of person represented, it may well be that Harris's informants felt that they were being asked to produce as many distinguishing terms as possible. My informants in Morro do Sangue Bom, on the other hand, understood that I was attempting to census the community rather than to "collect" race and/or color terms. The existence of regional variation in race and color vocabularies is also a probable factor. An additional explanation is the possibility that Brazilian race and color vocabularies may be shrinking through time, as Kottak's (1992) recent work suggests.

3. In Morro do Sangue Bom, the mulata is much less a color or racial category than a sort of cultural figure or icon. The term "mulata" usually describes a curvaceous woman who projects sexual allure; she can be either light- or dark-skinned. The masculine term, "mulato," sometimes connotes an especially handsome man but, unlike the feminine form, it can also be a neutral description of someone of intermediate color.

4. Historically, the existence of mulato brotherhoods and even of a "mulato press" have been documented, and they were based, in large part, on the more favorable economic positions and special concerns of free people of color living in the context of slavery. The institutionalization of such distinctions, and the legal and socioeconomic arrangements on which they were based, had waned, however, by the early twentieth century (see, for example, Andrews 1991; Flory 1977; Russell-Wood 1982).

5. Burdick (1998) has recently upheld the view that there are important distinctions to be made between light- and dark-skinned blacks. I would argue that the conversational contexts in which such distinctions are drawn are critical. Burdick's female informants tended to emphasize differences in color when discussing notions of beauty and courtship. In chapter 5 of this book, I concur with Burdick's point that color may be emphasized in such contexts, yet I maintain that race is conceived as a more fundamental feature of identity than color, and it is viewed as a bipolar quality.

6. There are occasional references to bipolar visions of race in the literature, but they tend to be highly qualified or unanalyzed. Irene Barbosa, in a dissertation about black families in the city of Campinas, S. P., for example, provides a quote from an informant: "Not being white, all are negros; some are lighter, others darker, but everyone confronts the same problem" (1983, 117). The significance of her informant's comment, however, is barely noted by Barbosa.

7. Zimmerman also contradicts the conventional notion that racial identity in Brazil is based solely on appearance rather than ancestry or parentage. Referring to informants in the northeast, he writes, "Family . . . in its genetic sense, becomes important as a race criterion. . . . In numerous instances people who were interviewed said they could not indicate the *qualidade* of some of the people on the list because they 'did not know their family'" (1963, 103).

8. These different emphases are made in standard Portuguese dictionaries as well. In this strictly limited sense, both words resemble their English glosses: black/*preto* (which can refer to the color of an object as well as a person) and negro/*negro* (which refers to a person of the supposed negro race).

9. This response, while cutting straight to the point, was extremely unusual in that my informants on the morro and those in the black movement typically understood that I was asking for linguistic and cultural explication. Most black militants, in fact, prefer to be addressed by the term negro, as will be seen in chapter 7; they are engaged in an extremely deliberate and self-conscious act of linguistic reappropriation. Nevertheless, this informant's response suggests the degree to which my foreignness allowed me to ask—and, with this one exception, to be given patient answers to—questions that Brazilian researchers might feel compelled to avoid.

10. Comments that suggest that the words "negro" and "escravo" (slave) are nearly synonymous were, in fact, ubiquitous, and they are confirmed by dictionaries of modern Brazilian Portuguese. The fifteenth edition of the *Novo Dicionario Aurelio* (a standard dictionary), for example, gives the first definition of negra as "a woman of the black color" and the second definition as "a slave, a captive."

11. In yet another example of the ways in which Brazilianist anthropologists document the existence of the very different discursive registers in which race and/or color terms are used—while persistently asserting that such terms are taxonomical—Sansone writes, "Relations of friendship, but also, fear of gossip can bring a family to *classify* the other neighbor with a term that is taken as positive—above all, moreno in place of preto" (1993, 85; emphasis added). In such a case, I would argue, the family Sansone describes was using a polite and deliberately vague term of reference, an act which is quite different from classification.

12. Debates about the meaning of race and/or color terms and their relationship to the statistics that appear to demonstrate the severity of racial discrimination have been recently revisited by Harris et al. (1995a, 1995b, 1995c); Silva (1996); and Telles (1995). This debate is based on the slippery nature of demographic categories and their relationship to what Harris calls "emic categories." This is not the place to engage this debate, but I would note that my research has some relevance to it, for it clarifies the fact that terms such as "moreno" may be conceptualized by their users not as racial categories at all but as polite ways of speaking. Moreover, I conducted a survey in which I asked thirty informants to provide open-choice race and/or color terms for thirty people in their personal network. I then asked these informants to choose from among four terms ("branco," "negro," "pardo," and "indigena") in describing the same individuals. Most of my informants who first gave intermediate terms translated them into "negro." This supports my contention that racial identity—as opposed to color or the deceptive implications of polite speech—tends to be conceptualized in bipolar terms.

Chapter 3 *Silence: Racism and Cultural Censorship*

1. See Sheriff (2000) for a more detailed theoretical analysis of cultural censorship.

2. Irene Barbosa (1983) based her thesis on the question of whether the parents in

the black families she studied in Campinas, S. P., engaged in practices through which they prepared their children for confrontations with racism. Working from within the limits of a psychocultural model, Barbosa's thesis circles around, without really analyzing, the issues of discourse and silence. She concludes generally that parents tend not to speak to their children about racism. Such discussion, when it does occur, only emerges after a child or adolescent forcefully broaches the issue after a disturbing encounter with racism.

3. Silence between parents and children may often be exacerbated by the type of facile dismissal and apparent avoidance to which Paulinho refers. Barbosa makes a similar observation: "During conversations in which mothers and their children participated, frequently a child or youth would provide testimonies about [racism] with which the mothers were unfamiliar. . . . When they asked, 'Why didn't you tell me?' the response was generally, 'You yourself told me that it isn't good to give importance to these things and I am only remembering now because the [anthropologist] has asked me'" (1983, 106).

4. Those stories I did hear about slavery often involved burning as a method of punishment, and sometimes murder. Dona Janete's grandmother, for example, had recounted to her an incident in which a slave woman was forced to immerse her arm in boiling water. Gilberto Freyre (1986) occasionally departs from what others have called the "myth of the friendly master" and describes the sadism of slave-owning families—which was sometimes extreme.

5. In this comment, Tomas seems to contradict his earlier statement that he did not discuss such encounters with his mother. Some stories are clearly being exchanged in the familial context. I would speculate that Tomas had told his mother about some of his encounters with the police without stating explicitly that he himself interpreted their harassment as racism. Jacinto, similarly, may have told his mother of the events leading up to his dismissal from a job without explicitly referring to racism. Aside from the possibility that stories about racism may be told in a very elliptical fashion, I can only explain these peculiar gaps by suggesting that just as people are motivated to forget and let go of the memory of the original experience, so they may be motivated to forget any subsequent conversations about it.

6. See Burdick 1993 and 1998. The former provides an ethnographic account of religious practices and their political and cultural contexts among Protestants, Catholics, and Umbandistas in Rio de Janeiro's Baixada Fluminense. The latter deals with Anastácia and her relationship to racial politics in more detail; the research on which it is based was conducted in the Baixada Fluminense and the greater Rio de Janeiro area.

7. The eating of dirt, evidently common among Brazilian slaves, was believed to be motivated by a desire to commit suicide by slow degrees. It may be more likely that it was caused by a pica, a nutritional disorder.

Chapter 4 *Narratives: Racism on the Asphalt*

1. This statement requires some qualification. The work of domestic servants does require both skill and training. The labor practices involved in maintaining distinctly middle-class environments are highly specific. An empregada not only must master those practices but also must acquire certain social skills and project a particular type of demeanor. Women constantly exchange information about the conduct of domestic servitude, and teenage girls are typically trained by older female relatives.

2. Twine (1998, 35–38) describes the practice of *criação*, or adoption, in which middle-class families provide room and board to girls and women in exchange for

full-time domestic labor. Adoptees receive no wages, and in some circumstances, it is difficult to see how the practice differs significantly from slavery. True criação appears to be more common in Vasalia, Twine's research site, than in Morro do Sangue Bom. Rosemary was something of a criada in Varena's household, but the contours of their relationship were partly conditioned by the fact that they shared the same class and color positions.

3. Ironically, not only cab drivers but policemen are extremely fearful of entering the area around Morro do Sangue Bom at night. When a friend and I were stranded with a broken-down car close to Morro do Sangue Bom, the policemen who stopped were so noticeably anxious—they clearly expected to be shot at by snipers in the woods—that I felt an impulse to reassure them. At that particular moment, Nova Época and the police, so far as I knew, were observing a truce. Promising to inform other officers of our car trouble, they speedily drove away. On the few occasions when I took a cab to Santa Teresa after dark, the drivers often warned me about the boca de fumo; they did not always believe me when I told them that I myself lived on the morro and was known by the "owners" of the boca.

4. To a certain extent, I believe, men view their reputed fearfulness as laughable. Although it puts them in danger, it may be less damaging, in psychological terms, than the imputation of qualities like incompetence and servility. Men's encounters with racism often entail an attack not only upon one's race but upon one's masculinity. One is constrained from defending one's masculinity, just as one is constrained from defending one's race; and the withdrawal, passivity, and retreat that seemed to characterize the stance of chronically unemployed men was, I believe, conditioned by this fact. Such a stance, I suspect, is experienced as a kind of inner resistance, no matter how compromised (Willis 1977), at the same time that it is clearly motivated by a desire to avoid exposing the gendered, as well as the racialized, self to assault.

Chapter 5 *Narratives: Racism at Home*

1. In February 1996, Jackson and filmmaker Spike Lee filmed a video in a Rio favela, an event that received a great deal of attention in the international news media. City and state officials attempted to prevent Lee and Jackson from portraying the city's poverty rather than its usual touristic sites. They were unsuccessful. Lee and Jackson also incurred the wrath of local officials by making a payoff to the drug lord who controlled the morro where the video was filmed. Jackson's song "They Don't Care about Us" is about the political neglect and social marginalization of the urban poor. Despite the many layers of irony involved, it is a moving video; Jackson has no doubt redeemed himself among at least some of those who live on Rio's morros.

2. I disclaim any support for the views my informants expressed concerning Pelé. In recent years, especially, he has been building a record of public service.

3. My lack of discussion of gay and/or lesbian relationships in Morro do Sangue Bom is not intended to suggest that there were no gays or lesbians in the community or that sexual orientation is unimportant to sexual politics in Rio and elsewhere in Brazil. Color and notions of race, however, appear to play the same roles in gay and/or lesbian relationships as they do in heterosexual ones. See Kulick (1997) and Parker (1991).

4. Goldstein (1999) has argued that some poor women of color continue to fantasize and to joke about forming romantic and economic relationships with a wealthier—and usually older—white man. Whether such relationships occur in fantasy or in reality, they are, as Goldstein cogently argues, based on a pragmatic exchange

in which white men trade racial and socioeconomic status for youth and "commodified sexuality" (1999, 570). Although the discourses of democracia racial thrive on references to interracial relationships, it is the very shape that these relations often take, as Goldstein argues, that spells out the profound ramifications of racialized inequality in Brazil. Burdick (1998) also discusses the ways in which differences in color tilt the power balance in romantic relationships.

5. Twine reports that one of her informants made a remarkably similar comment: "In the hour of lovemaking, everything is wonderful. Afterwards, in the heat of a fight, I believe that the *first* thing that will be said [by the white partner] is 'You black! You nigger! You monkey.' . . . I have seen this occur in other [interracial] families. I know that this happens." (1998, 96, emphasis in original).

6. In an extended discussion, Twine (1998, 127–133) has also noted the ways in which color affects the collection and preservation of family memorabilia.

Chapter 6   Whiteness: Middle-Class Discourses

1. As was the case in Morro do Sangue Bom, there was, of course, a degree of internal differentiation among my middle-class informants in Santa Teresa. Three of my informants characterized their families of origin as lower or lower middle class, and two, a mother and her daughter, belonged to a family that had been historically prominent and very well-known among the national political elite. The majority characterized their families of origin as middle or upper middle class. The current income levels of all of my informants were similar, however; and to somewhat varying degrees, all felt economically threatened by the deepening recession and the austerity measures imposed by the Collar government (see O'Dougherty 1997). Despite that fact, all employed domestic servants. Within the middle classes, the avoidance of domestic labor continues to be regarded not as an indulgence but as a necessity, and it is, in fact, a significant and conspicuous marker of middle-class status.

2. In this comment about food, Virginia signals her awareness of the fact that some middle-class families forbid their empregadas to eat the same food that they eat. In such cases, the empregada is typically provided with rice and beans only; she is forbidden the expensive foods, such as meat or cheese, that are eaten by the family.

3. As Freyre never tires of asserting in his voluminous writings, the hybrid nature of Brazilian culture is given, above all, by the fact that white children are fed the food, told the tales, exposed to the music, and coddled with the sensuousness of black, African-descended nursemaids. Eliza's narrative is an exceptionally conventional one.

4. When I asked the meaning of term "brancazeda" (or the masculine form, "brancoazedo") on the morro, people typically told me that it described a person who was "very white, too white." "Like me?" I asked, holding my pale arm out for inspection. This always caused laughter, and I was reassured that I was not a brancazeda. Its literal meaning is "sour white," and it refers as much to a disposition as to color. Branquelo has roughly the same meaning.

5. Although it has been asserted that the term "gringo" simply means "foreigner" in Brazil, it sometimes has a pejorative thrust, in that it is associated with wealthy, insensitive, and ignorant people who fail to observe, or even recognize, the Brazilian etiquette of cordiality. When I sometimes referred to myself, in a self-deprecating fashion, as a gringa, I was often told, "No, you are not a gringa, Beth, you are an *estrangeira* (foreigner)."

6. Aninha complained, for example, about an occasion on which her mother had surreptitiously taken her daughter—who was only a small child—to have her hair

chemically straightened. For Aninha and her husband, the offense was not only in the fact that her daughter had been subjected to the unpleasant procedure but in the fact that "ideas were put into her head."

Chapter 7 *Blackness: Militant Discourses*

1. There are a growing number of African Brazilian women's groups in Brazil (Hanchard 1999, 19). Galedes, in São Paulo, is perhaps the best known, but like black movement organizations in general, they have had only limited success in attracting a following. See Burdick (1998) for a detailed and cogent analysis of black women's political orientations in the Rio area, particularly as they relate to various types of religious participation and belief.
2. Although I do not doubt that some African Brazilian women have undergone forced sterilization, the male activists with whom I discussed this issue seemed unaware of the fact that women such as those in Morro do Sangue Bom endured intense frustration and unwanted pregnancies because of the *difficulties* involved in getting tubal ligations.
3. João's avoidance of the generic "he" is a conscious one. He often spoke in ways that were intended to show his respect for, and awareness of, the relevance of feminist politics for antiracist politics.
4. Fanon makes a similar point from within a psychoanalytic framework. Referring to his homeland, he writes: "The black schoolboy in the Antilles, who in his lessons is forever talking about 'our ancestors, the Gauls,' identifies himself with the explorer, the bringer of civilization, the white man who carries truth to the savages—an all-white truth. There is identification—that is, the young Negro subjectively adopts a white man's attitude" (1967, 147).
5. In *Veja,* the news magazine I referred to in chapter 1, a journalist remarked on one of the differences between Brazil and South Africa. In South African restaurants, all the patrons are white and all the waiters are black. In Brazilian restaurants, both the patrons and the waiters are white.

References

Abujamra, Wilson. 1967. *A Realidade sobre o Problema Favela*. São Paulo: Industria Grafica Bentivegna Editora Ltda.

Alba, Richard D. 1990. *Ethnic Identity: The Transformation of White America*. New Haven, Conn.: Yale University Press.

Alexander, J. 1977. The Culture of Race in Middle-Class Kingston, Jamaica. *American Ethnologist* 4 (3): 413–435.

Anderson, Benedict. 1991. *Imagined Communities: Reflections on the Origins and Spread of Nationalism*. New York: Verso.

Andrews, George Reid. 1991. *Blacks and Whites in São Paulo, Brazil, 1888–1988*. Madison: University of Wisconsin Press.

———. 1992a. Black Political Protest in São Paulo, 1888–1988. *Journal of Latin American Studies* 24: 147–171.

———. 1992b. Racial Inequality in Brazil and the United States: A Statistical Comparison. *Journal of Social History* (winter): 229–263.

Azevédo, Thales de. 1953. *Les élites de couleur dans une ville brasilienne*. Paris: UNESCO.

———. 1975. *Democracia Racial: Ideologia e Realidade*. Petrópolis: Vozes.

Baiocchi, Mari de Nasare. 1983. *Negros de Cedro: Estudo Antropológico de um Bairro Rural de Negros em Goias*. São Paulo: Editora Ática.

Bakhtin, M. M. 1981. *The Dialogic Imagination*. Austin: University of Texas Press.

Bandeira, Maria de Lourdes. 1988. *Territorio Negro em Espaço Branco*. São Paulo: Editora Brasilense.

Barbosa, Irene Maria F. 1983. *Socialização e Relações Raciais: Um Estudo de Familia Negra em Campinas*. São Paulo: FFLCH/Universidade de São Paulo.

Basso, Keith. 1970. "To Give up on Words": Silence in Western Apache Culture. In *Language and Social Context*. ed. Pier Paolo Giglioli, 67–86. New York: Penguin Books.

———. 1979 *Portraits of "The Whiteman": Linguistic Play and Cultural Symbols among the Western Apache*. Cambridge, U.K.: University of Cambridge Press.

Bastide, Roger, and Florestan Fernandes, eds. 1951. *Brancos e Negros em São Paulo*. São Paulo: Companhia Editora Nacional.

———. 1955. *Relações Raciais Entre Negros e Brancos em São Paulo*. São Paulo: Editora Anhembi.

Bastide, Roger, and Pierre van den Berghe. 1957. Stereotypes, Norms, and Interracial Behavior in São Paulo, Brazil. *American Sociological Review* 22 (6): 689–694.

Behar, Ruth, and Deborah A. Gordon. 1995. *Women Writing Culture*. Berkeley: University of California Press.

Billig, M. 1988. The Notion of "Prejudice": Some Rhetorical and Ideological Aspects. *Text* 8: 91–110.

Birman, Patricia. 1980. *Feitiço, Carreco e Olho Grande, Os Males do Brasil: Estudo de um Centro Umbandista numa Favela do Rio de Janeiro*. Masters thesis, Museo Nacional, Rio de Janeiro.

Borges, Dain. 1993. "Puffy, Ugly, Slothful, and Inert": Degeneration in Brazilian Social Thought, 1880–1940. *Journal of Latin American Studies* 25: 235–256.

Bourdieu, Pierre. 1991. *Language and Symbolic Power*. Cambridge, Mass.: Harvard University Press.

Brown, Diana DeG. 1994. *Umbanda: Religion and Politics in Urban Brazil*. New York: Columbia University Press.

Burdick, John. 1993. *Looking for God in Brazil: The Progressive Catholic Church in Urban Brazil's Religious Arena*. Berkeley: University of California Press.

———. 1998. *Blessed Anastácia: Women, Race, and Popular Christianity in Brazil*. New York: Routledge.

Butler, Kim. 1998. *Freedoms Given, Freedoms Won: Afro-Brazilians in Post-Abolition São Paulo and Salavador*. New Brunswick, N. J.: Rutgers University Press.

Cardoso, Fernando Henrique, and Octavio Ianni. 1960. *Cor e Mobilidade Social em Florianópolis*. São Paulo: Companhia Editora Nacional.

Carneiro, José Fernando. 1971. *Psicologia do Brasileiro e Outros Estudos*. Rio de Janeiro: Livraria Agir Editora.

Chalhoub, Sidney. 1990. *Visão da Liberdade: Uma Historia das Últimas Decadas da Escravidão na Corte*. São Paulo: Companhia das Letras.

Clark, Kenneth. 1939. Segregation as a Factor in the Racial Identification of Negro Pre-School Children: A Preliminary Report. *Journal of Experimental Education* 8 (2): 161–163.

———. 1940. Skin Color as a Factor in Racial Identification of Negro Pre-School Children. *Journal of Social Psychology* 11: 159–169.

———. 1947. Racial Identification and Preference in Negro Children. In *Readings in Social Psychology*, ed. T. M. Newcomb and E. L. Hertley, 169–178. New York: Holt.

———. 1950. Emotional Factors in Racial Identification and Preference in Negro Children. *Journal of Negro Education* 19: 341–350.

Clifford, James. 1983. On Ethnographic Authority. *Representations* 1 (2): 118–146.

Clifford, James, and George E. Marcus. 1986. *Writing Culture: The Poetics and Politics of Ethnography*. Berkeley: University of California Press.

Conrad, Robert. 1972. *The Destruction of Brazilian Slavery, 1850–1888*. Berkeley: University of California Press.

———. 1986. *World of Sorrow: The African Slave Trade to Brazil*. Baton Rouge: Louisiana State University Press.

Costa, Haroldo. 1982. *Fala Crioulo: Depoimentos*. Rio de Janeiro: Editora Record.

Costa Pinto, Luis A. 1953. *O Negro no Rio de Janeiro: Relações de Raça numa Sociedade em Mudança*. São Paulo: Companhia Editora Nacional.

Crapanzano, Vincent. 1977. The Writing of Ethnography. *Dialectical Anthropology* 2: 69–73.

———. 1986. *Waiting: The Whites of South Africa*. New York: Vintage Books.

———. 1992. *Herme's Dilemma and Hamlet's Desire: On the Epistemology of Interpretation*. Cambridge, Mass.: Harvard University Press.

Cross, William E. 1991. *Shades of Black: Diversity in African-American Identity*. Philadelphia: Temple University Press.

Curtin, Philip. 1969. *The Atlantic Slave Trade: A Census*. Madison: University of Wisconsin Press.

DaMatta, Roberto. 1984. *Relativizando*. 4th ed. Petrópolis: Vozes.

————.1985. On Carnaval, Informality, and Magic: A Point of View from Brazil. In *Text, Play, and Story: The Construction and Reconstruction of Self and Society*, ed. Edward M. Bruner, 230–246. Washington, D. C.: American Ethnological Society.

Dantas, Beatriz Gois. 1988. *Vovô Nago, Papai Branco: Usos e Abusos da África no Brasil*. Rio de Janeiro: Edições Graal, Ltda.

Degler, Carl. 1971. *Neither Black nor White: Slavery and Race Relations in Brazil and the United States*. New York: Macmillan.

Delgado, Richard, and Jean Stephancic. 1997. *Critical White Studies: Looking behind the Mirror*. Philadelphia: Temple University Press.

Dominguez, Virginia. 1986. *White by Definition*. New Brunswick, N. J.: Rutgers University Press.

Du Bois, W.E.B. 1961. *The Souls of Black Folk*. New York: Fawcett.

Dwyer, Kevin. 1977. The Dialogic of Anthropology. *Dialectical Anthropology* 2: 143–151.

Dzidzienyo, Anani. 1971. *The Position of Blacks in Brazilian Society*. London: Minority Rights Group.

Essed, Philomena. 1988. Understanding Accounts of Everyday Racism. *Text* 8: 5–40.

————. 1990. *Everyday Racism*. Claremont, Calif.: Hunter House.

————. 1991. *Understanding Everyday Racism: An Interdisciplinary Theory*. London: Sage.

Etter-Lewis, Gwendolyn. 1991. Standing up and Speaking Out: African American Women's Narrative Legacy. *Discourse and Society* 2 (4): 425–437.

Ewbank, Thomas. 1856. *Life in Brazil: or, A Journal of a Visit to the Land of Cocao and the Palm*. New York: Harper & Brothers.

Fanon, Frantz. 1967. *Black Skin, White Masks*. New York: Grove Press.

Fernandes, Florestan. 1965. *A Integração do Negro na Sociedade de Classes*. São Paulo: Dominus Editora.

————. 1969. *The Negro in Brazilian Society*. New York: Columbia University Press.

————. 1972. *O Negro no Mundo dos Brancos*. São Paulo: Difusão Europeia do Livro.

————. 1979. The Negro in Brazilian Society: Twenty-Five Years Later. In *Brazil: Anthropological Perspectives*, ed. Maxine L. Margolis and William E. Carter. New York: Columbia University Press.

Flory, Thomas. 1977. Race and Social Control in Independent Brazil. *Journal of Latin American Studies* 9 (2): 199–224.

Fontaine, Pierre-Michele. 1980. Research in the Political Economy of Afro-Latin America. *Latin American Research Review* 15 (2): 111–141.

————. 1981. Transnational Relations and Racial Mobilization: Emerging Black Movements in Brazil. In *Ethnic Identities in a Transnational World*, ed. John F. Stack Jr., 141–162. Westport, Conn.: Greenwood Press.

————. 1985a. Blacks and the Search for Power in Brazil. In *Race, Class and Power in Brazil*, ed. Pierre-Michel Fontaine, 56–72. Los Angeles: Center for Afro-American Studies/University of California.

————, ed. 1985b. *Race, Class, and Power in Brazil*. Los Angeles: Center for Afro-American Studies/University of California.

Forbes, Jack. 1988. *Black Africans and Native Americans: Color, Race, and Caste in the Evolution of Red-Black Peoples*. Oxford, U.K.: Basil Blackwell.

Foucault, Michel. 1972. *The Discourse on Language*. New York: Pantheon Books.

————. 1980. *The History of Sexuality*. New York: Vintage Books.

Fowler, Roger. 1985. Power. In *Handbook of Discourse Analysis*, ed. T. A. van Dijk, 4:61–82. New York: Academic Press.

Fowler, Roger, Bob Hodge, Gunther Kress, and Tony Trew, eds. 1979. *Language and Control*. London: Routledge & Kegan Paul.

Frankenberg, Ruth. 1993. *White Women, Race Matters: The Social Construction of Whiteness*. Minneapolis: University of Minnesota Press.

———, ed. 1997. *Displacing Whiteness: Essays in Social and Cultural Criticism*. Durham: Duke University Press.

Freyre, Gilberto. 1986. *The Masters and the Slaves: A Study in the Development of Brazilian Civilization*. Trans. Samuel Putnam. 2nd English-language ed., rev. Berkeley: University of California Press.

Fry, Peter. 1982. *Para Ingles Ver: Identidade e Politica na Cultura Brasileira*. Rio de Janeiro: Zahar Edições.

Gardner, George. 1970. *Travels in the Interior of Brazil, Principally through the Northern Provinces and the Gold and Diamond Districts, during the Years 1836–1841*. 1846. Reprint, New York: AMS Press.

Gay, Robert. 1994. *Popular Organization and Democracy in Rio de Janeiro: A Tale of Two Favelas*. Philadelphia: Temple University Press.

Godreau, Isar. 1994. "Y Tu Abuela Donde Está?": Racism, Identity, and Puerto Rican Nationality. Paper presented at the annual meeting of the American Ethnological Society, Santa Monica, Calif., April 14.

———. 1995. Where Is "Race" in This Gumbo? The Public Uses of Slippery Semantics or of Semantica Fugitiva in Puerto Rican Race and Color Talk. Paper presented at the annual meeting of the American Anthropological Association, Washington, D.C., November 17.

Goldberg, David Theo, ed. 1990. *Anatomy of Racism*. Minneapolis: University of Minnesota Press.

Goldstein, Donna. 1999. "Interracial" Sex and Racial Democracy in Brazil: Twin Concepts? *American Anthropologist* 101 (3): 563–578.

Gonzalez, Lelia. 1985. The Unified Black Movement: A New Stage in Black Political Mobilization. In *Race, Class, and Power in Brazil*, ed. Pierre-Michel Fontaine, 120–134. Los Angeles: Center for Afro-American Studies/University of California.

Graham, Maria. 1824. *Journal of a Voyage to Brazil, and Residence There, during Part of the Years 1821, 1822, 1823*. London: Longman, Hurst, Rees, Orme.

Graham, Richard. 1970. Brazilian Slavery Re-examined: A Review Article. *Journal of Social History* 3 (4): 431–453.

Graham, Sandra L. 1988. *House and Street: The Domestic World of Servants and Masters in Nineteenth-Century Rio de Janeiro*. New York: Cambridge University Press.

Guillermoprieto, Alma. 1990. *Samba*. New York: Alfred A. Knopf.

Gwaltney, John L. 1975. *Drylongso: A Self-Portrait of Black America*. New York: Random House.

Hale, Lindsay. 1995. *Hot Breath, Cold Spirits: The Poetics of the Sacred in a Brazilian Spirit Religion*. Ph.D. diss., University of Texas, Austin.

Hanchard, George Michael. 1993. Culturalism Versus Cultural Politics: Movimento Negro in Rio de Janeiro and São Paulo, Brazil. In *The Violence Within: Cultural and Political Opposition in Divided Nations*, ed. Kay Warren. Boulder: Westview Press.

———. 1994a. *Orpheus and Power: The Movimento Negro of Rio de Janeiro and São Paulo, Brazil, 1945–1988*. Princeton, N. J.: Princeton University Press.

———. 1994b. Black Cinderella? Race and the Public Sphere in Brazil. *Public Culture* 7: 165–185.

———, ed. 1999. *Racial Politics in Contemporary Brazil*. Durham: Duke University Press.

Harding, Susan. 1975. Women and Words in a Spanish Village. In *Toward an Anthropology of Women*, ed. Rayna Reiter, 283–308. New York: Monthly Review Press.

Harris, Marvin. 1956. *Town and Country in Brazil*. New York: Columbia University Press.

———. 1964. *Patterns of Race in the Americas*. New York: Walker.

———. 1970. Referential Ambiguity in the Calculous of Brazilian Racial Identity. *Southwestern Journal of Anthropology* 26: 1–14.

Harris, Marvin, and Conrad Kottak. 1963. The Structural Significance of Brazilian Racial Categories. *Sociologia* 25: 203–208.

Harris, Marvin, Bryan Byrne, Josildeth Gomes Consorte, and Joseph Lang. 1995a. Who Are the Whites? Imposed Census Categories and the Racial Demography of Brazil. *Social Forces* 72 (2): 451–462.

———. 1995b. What's in a Name? The Consequences of Violating Brazilian Emic Color-Race Categories in Estimates of Well-Being. *Journal of Anthropological Research* 51: 389–397.

———. 1995c. A Reply to Telles. *Social Forces* 73 (4): 1613–1614.

Hasenbalg, Carlos A. 1979. *Discriminações e Desigualdades Raciais no Brasil*. Rio de Janeiro: Edições Graal Ltda.

———. 1985. Race and Socioeconomic Inequalities in Brazil. In *Race, Class, and Power in Brazil*, ed. Pierre-Michel Fontaine, 25–41. Los Angeles: University of California.

———. 1994. Entre Mitos e Fatos: Racismo e Relações Raciais no Brasil. IV Congresso Afro-Brasileiro, Recife, April 17–20.

Hasenbalg, Carlos A., and Nelson do Valle Silva. 1990. Raça e Opportunidades Educacionais no Brasil. *Estudos Afro-Asiáticos* 18: 73–91.

———. 1993. Notas Sobre Desigualdade Racial e Politica no Brasil. *Estudos Afro-Asiáticos* 25.

Hellwig, David J., ed. 1992. *African-American Reflections on Brazil's Racial Paradise*. Philadelphia: Temple University Press.

Hill, Mike. 1997. *Whiteness: A Critical Reader*. New York: New York University Press.

Holloway, Thomas. 1993. *Policing Rio de Janeiro: Repression and Resistance in a Nineteenth-Century City*. Stanford, Calif.: Stanford University Press.

Houston, M., and Cheris Kramarae. 1991. Speaking and Silence: Methods of Silencing and of Resistance. *Discourse and Society* 2 (4): 387–399.

Hutchinson, Harry W. 1957. *Village and Plantation Life in Northeastern Brazil*. Seattle: University of Washington Press.

———. 1963. Race Relations in a Rural Community of the Bahian Reconcavo. In *Race and Class in Rural Brazil*, ed. Charles Wagley, 16–46. New York: UNESCO/Columbia University Press.

Ianni, Octavio. 1966. *Raças e Classes Sociais no Brasil*. Rio de Janeiro: Editora Civilização Brasileira.

———. 1978. *Escravidão e Racismo*. São Paulo: Editora Hucitec.

Iplan-Rio. 1993. *Favelas cariocas: Alguns dados estatísticos*. Rio de Janeiro: Iplan-Rio/Prefeitura da cidade de Rio de Janeiro.

Irwin-Zareka, Iwona. 1994. *Frames of Remembrance: The Dynamics of Collective Memory*. New Brunswick, N. J.: Transaction Publishers.

Istoé. 1992. O Preço da Conferencia. June 3: 46–47.

Jakubs, Deborah L. 1977. Police Violence in Times of Political Tension: The Case of Brazil. In *Police and Society*, ed. David H. Baylay. Beverly Hills and London: Sage.

Jaworski, Adam. 1993. *The Power of Silence: Social and Pragmatic Perspectives*. Newbury Park, Calif.: Sage Publications.

Joseph, Galen. 1994. "Plane Trees and Sparrows from France": Creating Argentine Race, Nation, and Civilization. Paper presented at the annual meeting of the American Ethnological Society, Santa Monica, Calif., April 14.

Khan, Aisha. 1993. What Is "a Spanish": Ambiguity and "Mixed" Ethnicity in

Trinidad. In *Trinidad Ethnicity*, ed. Kevin A. Yelvington, 180–207. Knoxville: University of Tennessee Press.

Kirmayer, Laurence. 1996. Landscapes of Memory: Trauma, Narrative, and Dissociation. In *Tense Past: Cultural Essays in Trauma and Memory*, ed. Paul Antze and Michael Lambek, 173–198. New York: Routledge.

Klein, Herbert S. 1969. The Colored Freedmen in Brazilian Slave Society. *Journal of Social History* 3 (1): 30–52.

———. 1971. The Internal Slave Trade in Nineteenth-Century Brazil: A Study of Slave Importations into Rio de Janeiro in 1852. *The Hispanic American Historical Review* 51 (4): 567–585.

Koike, Dale April. 1992. *Language and Social Relationship in Brazilian Portuguese: The Pragmatics of Politeness*. Austin: University of Texas Press.

Koster, Henry. 1817. *Travels in Brazil*. Philadelphia: M. Carey & Son.

Kottak, Conrad. 1967. Race Relations in a Bahian Fishing Village. *Luso-Brazilian Review* 4 (2): 35–52.

———. 1992. "Emics and Etics of Racial Classification in Brazil, Based on a Recent National Survey." Paper presented at the annual meeting of the American Anthropological Association, San Francisco, December 4.

Kovel, Joel. 1970. *White Racism: A Psychohistory*. New York: Pantheon Books.

Kulick, Don. 1997. *Travestí: Sex, Gender, and Culture among Brazilian Transgendered Prostitutes*. Chicago: University of Chicago Press.

Lakoff, Robin. 1975. *Language and Women's Place*. New York: Harper & Row.

Lancaster, Roger. 1991. Skin Color, Race, and Racism in Nicaragua. *Ethnology* 30 (4): 339–353.

Leeds, Anthony, and Elizabeth Leeds. 1970. Brazil and the Myth of Urban Rurality: Urban Experience, Work, and Values in "Squatments" of Rio de Janeiro and Lima. In *City and Country in the Third World: Issues in Modernization in Latin America*, ed. Arthur J. Fiel, 229–285. Cambridge, Mass.: Schenkman Publishing Co.

Lott, Bernice, and Diane Maluso, eds. 1995. *The Social Psychology of Interpersonal Discrimination*. New York: Guilford Press.

Louw-Potgeiter, J. 1988. *It Wasn't Because of Me. It Was Because of Me Being Black: A Study of Covert Racism at Natal University, Durban*. Durban, South Africa: University of Natal.

———. 1989. Covert Racism: An Application of Essed's Analysis in a South African Context. *Journal of Language and Social Psychology* 8: 307–319.

Lovell, Peggy A. 1989. *Racial Inequality and the Brazilian Labor Market*. Ph.D. diss., University of Florida, Gainesville.

Lovell, Peggy Webster, and Jeffrey W. Dwyer. 1988. The Cost of Being Nonwhite in Brazil. *Sociology and Social Research* 72 (2): 136–138.

Lucy, John. 1993. *Reflexive Language, Reported Speech, and Metapragmatics*. New York: Cambridge University Press.

Lutz, Catherine, and Lila Abu-Lughod. 1990. *Language and the Politics of Emotion*. Cambridge, U. K.: Cambridge University Press.

Maggie, Yvonne. 1991. *Medo do Feitiço: Relações entre Magia e Poder no Brasil*. Rio de Janeiro: Arquivo Nacional de Pesquisa.

———. 1992. Aqueles a Quem Foi Negada a Cor do Dia: As Categorias Cor e Raça na Cultura Brasileira. Seminario Internacional sobre Racismo e Relações Raciais nos Piaises da Diaspora Africana. Rio de Janeiro: Centro de Estudos Afro-Asiáticos.

Mansfield, C. B. 1956. *Paraguay, Brazil and the Platt: Letters Written in 1952–1953*. Cambridge, U. K.: Macmillan & Co.

Marcus, George E., and Michael M. J. Fischer. 1986. *Anthropology as Cultural Critique:*

An Experimental Moment in the Human Sciences. Chicago: University of Chicago Press.

Martinez, Alier V. 1974. *Marriage, Class, and Colour in Nineteenth-Century Cuba*. Cambridge, U. K.: Cambridge University Press.

McConnell-Ginet, Sally, Ruth Borker, and Nelly Furman, eds. 1980. *Women and Language in Literature and Society*. New York: Praeger.

Mitchell, Michael. 1985. Blacks and the Abertura Democratica. In *Race, Class, and Power in Brazil*, ed. Pierre-Michel Fontaine, 95–119. Los Angeles: Center for Afro-American Studies/University of California.

Morrison, Toni. 1992. *Playing in the Dark: Whiteness and the Literary Imagination*. Cambridge, Mass.: Harvard University Press.

Moura, Clovis. 1981. *Os Quilombos e a Rebelião Negra*. São Paulo: Brasiliense.

Mullen, Harryette. 1994. Optic White: Blackness and the Production of Whiteness. *Diacritics* 24 (2–3): 71–89.

Nader, Laura. 1974. Up the Anthropologist—Perpectives Gained from Studying Up. In *Reinventing Anthropology*, ed. Dell Hymes, 284–311. New York: Random House.

Nascimento, Abdias do. 1979. *Mixture or Massacre: Essays in the Genocide of a Black People*. Buffalo, N. Y.: Afrodiaspora.

Novo Dicionario Aurelio. 1975. São Paulo: Editora Nova Fronteira S. A.

Nogueira, Oracy. 1955. Relações Raciais no Municipio de Itapeteninga. In *Relações Raciais Entre Negros e Brancos em São Paulo*, ed. Roger Bastide and Florestan Fernandes, 164–179. São Paulo: Editora Anhembi.

Nunes, Guida. 1976. *Rio, Metropole de 300 Favelas*. Petrópolis: Vozes.

O'Dougherty, Maureen. 1997. *Middle-Classes, Ltd.: Consumption and Middle-Class Idenity during Brazil's Inflation Crisis*. PhD. diss., City University of New York.

Oliveira, Alvarus de. 1947. *Rio que Ama, Odeia, Goza e Sofre*. Rio de Janeiro: Grafica Editora Souza.

Omi, Michael, and Howard Winant. 1994. *Racial Formation in the United States: From the 1960s to the 1990s*. New York: Routledge.

Pacheco, Moema de Poli Teixeira. 1986. *Familia e Identidade Racial: Os Limites de Cor nas Relações e Representações de um Grupo de Baixa Renda*. Masters thesis, Museo Nacional da Universidade Federal do Rio de Janeiro.

Parker, Richard. 1991. *Bodies, Pleasures, and Passions: Sexual Culture in Contemporary Brazil*. Boston: Beacon Press.

Pearse, Andrew. 1961. Some Characteristics of Urbanization in the City of Rio de Janeiro. In *Urbanization in Latin America*, ed. Philip M. Hauser. New York: International Documents Service/Columbia University Press.

Pedrosa, Fernanda, Francisco Luis Noel, Luarlindo Ernesto, and Sergio Pugliese. 1990. *A Violença que Occulta a Favela*. Porto Alegre: L & PM. Pereira, Armando. 1984. *Bandidos e Favelas: Uma Contribuição ao Estudo do Meio Marginal Carioca*. Rio de Janeiro: Livraria Eu e Você Editora Ltda.

Pereira, João Baptista Borges. 1967. *Cor, Profissão e Mobilidade: O Negro no Radio de São Paulo*. São Paulo: Livraria Pioneira Editora.

Perlman, Janice R. 1976. *The Myth of Marginality: Urban Poverty and Politics in Rio de Janeiro*. Berkeley: University of California Press.

Pierson, Donald. 1942. *Negroes in Brazil: A Study of Race Contact in Bahia*. Chicago: University of Chicago Press. Reprint, 1967, Carbondale, Illinois University Press.

Porcaro, Rosa Maria. 1988. Desigualdade Racial e Segmentação do Mercado de Trabalho. *Estudos Afro-Asiáticos* 15: 171–207.

Prefeitura da Cidade do Rio de Janeiro. 1990. *Santa Teresa: A Cidade na Montanha*. Rio de Janeiro: Departamento Geral de Patrimonio Cultural.

Rahier, Jean Muteba. 2000. Body Politics in Black and White: Señoras, Mujeres, Blanqueamiento, and Miss Esmeraldas, 1997–1998, Ecuador. *Women and Performance: A Journal of Feminist Theory* 21, 11 (1): 102–119.

Reeves, F. 1983. *British Racial Discourse.* Cambridge, U. K.: Cambridge University Press.

Reis, Joao Jose. 1988. Um Balanço dos Estudos sobre as Revoltas Escravas na Bahia. In *Escravidão e Invenção da Liberdade: Estudos sobre o Negro no Brasil*, 87–142. São Paulo: Editora Brasilense.

Reis, Joao José, and Eduardo Silva. 1989. *Negociação e Conflito: A Resistência Negra no Brasil Escravista.* São Paulo: Companhia das Letras.

Rodrigues, José Honorio. 1967. *The Brazilians: Their Character and Aspirations.* Austin: University of Texas Press.

Roediger, David R. 1991. *The Wages of Whiteness: Race and the Making of the American Working Class.* New York: Verso.

————. 1998. *Black on White: Black Writers on What It Means to Be White.* New York: Schocken Books.

Roth Gordon, Jennifer. 1999. Hip-Hop Brasileiro: Brazilian Youth and Alternative Black Consciousness Movements. Paper presented at the annual meeting of the American Anthropological Association, Chicago, November.

Russell-Wood, A.J.R. 1982. *The Black Man in Slavery and Freedom.* London: Macmillan Press Ltd./ Oxford: St. Anthony's College.

Sacks, Karen. 1992. How Did Jews Become White Folks? In *Race*, ed. S. Gregory and Roger Sanjek, 78–102. New Brunswick, N. J.: Rutgers University Press.

Sanjek, Roger. 1971. Brazilian Racial Terms: Some Aspects of Meaning and Learning. *American Anthropologist* 73 (5): 1126–1143.

Sansone, Livio. 1992. Cor, Classe e Modernidade em Duas Areas da Bahia. *Estudos Afro-Asiáticos* 23: 143–173.

————. 1993. Pai Preto, Filho Negro: Trabalho, Cor e Diferenças de Geração. *Estudos Afro-Asiáticos* 25: 73–98.

————. 1994. The Local and the Global in Today's Afro-Bahia (English-language version). Paper presented at the Encontro Anual do ANPOCS, Caxambu, M. G., November 23–27.

Saunders, George. 1985. Silence and Noise as Emotion Management Styles: An Italian Case. In *Perspectives on Silence*, ed. Deborah Tannen and Muriel Saville-Troike, 165–184. Norwood, N. J.: Ablex Publishing Corp.

Saunders, John. 1972. Class, Color, and Prejudice: A Brazilian Counterpoint. In *Racial Tensions and National Identity*, ed. Ernest Q. Cambell. Nashville, Tenn.: Vanderbilt University Press.

Saville-Troike, Muriel. 1985. The Place of Silence in an Integrated Theory of Communication. In *Perspectives on Silence*, ed. Deborah Tannen and Muriel Saville-Troike, 3–18. Norwood, N. J.: Ablex Publishing Corp.

Scott, James. 1990. *Domination and the Arts of Resistance: Hidden Transcripts.* New Haven, Conn.: Yale University Press.

Segal, Daniel A. 1993. "Race" and "Colour" in Pre-Independence Trinidad and Tobago. In *Trinidad Ethnicity*, ed. Kevin A. Yelvington, 81–115. Knoxville: University of Tennessee Press.

Seyferth, Giralda. 1985. Antropólogia e a Teoria do Branqueamento no Brasil: A Tese de João Batista de Lacerda. *Revista do Museo Paulista* 30: 81–98.

————. 1989. As Ciencias Sociais no Brasil e a Questão Racial. In *Cativeiro e Liberdade*, ed. Jaime da Silva, Patricia Birman, and Regina Wanderley, 11–31. Rio de Janeiro: UERJ.

Shapiro, Delores. 1996. "A Barriga Limpa": Metaphors of Race and Strategies of Class

Mobility in Northeastern Brazil. Paper presented at the annual meeting of the American Anthropological Association, San Francisco, November 22.

Sheriff, Robin E. 1999. The Theft of Carnaval: National Spectacle and Racial Politics in Rio de Janeiro. *Cultural Anthropology* 14 (1): 3–28.

———. 2000. Exposing Silence as Cultural Censorship: A Brazilian Case. *American Anthropologist* 102 (1): 114–132.

Sider, Gerald. 1997. Against Experience: The Struggles for History, Tradition, and Hope among a Native American People. In *Between History and Histories: The Making of Silences and Commemorations*, eds. Gerald Sider and Gavin Smith, 62–79. Toronto: University of Toronto Press.

Silva, Denise Ferreira da. 1989. Revisitando a "Democracia Racial": Raça e Identidade Nacional no Pensamento Brasileiro. *Estudos Afro-Asiáticos* 16: 157–170.

Silva, Nelson do Valle. 1985. Updating the Cost of Not Being White in Brazil. In *Race, Class, and Power in Brazil*, ed. Pierre-Michel Fontaine, 42–55. Los Angeles: University of California.

———. 1996. Morenidade: Modo de Usar. *Estudos Afro-Asiáticos* 30: 79–96.

Silva, Nelso de Valle, and Carlos A. Hasenbalg. 1993. *Relações Raciais no Brasil Contemporâneo*. Rio de Janeiro: Rio Fundo Editora.

Silverstein, Michael. 1976. Shifters, Linguistic Categories, and Cultural Description. In *Meaning in Anthropology*, ed. Keith Basso and Henry A. Selby, 11–55. Albuquerque: University of New Mexico Press/School of American Research.

———. 1979. Language Structure and Linguistic Ideology. In *The Elements: A Parasession on Linguistic Units and Levels*, ed. P. Clyne, W. Hanks, and C. Hofbauer, 193–247. Chicago: Chicago Linguistic Society.

Simpson, Amelia. 1993. *Xuxa: The Mega-Marketing of Gender, Race, and Modernity*. Philadelphia: Temple University Press.

Skidmore, Thomas. 1990. Racial Ideas and Social Policy in Brazil, 1870–1940. In *The Idea of Race in Latin America*, ed. Richard Graham, 7–36. Austin: University of Texas Press.

———. 1992. Fact and Myth: Discovering a Racial Problem in Brazil. Working paper no. 173, Helen Kellogg Institute for International Studies, University of Notre Dame, Notre Dame, Ind.

———. 1993a. *Black into White: Race and Nationality in Brazilian Thought*. 1974. Reprint, Durham: Duke University Press.

———. 1993b. Bi-racial U.S.A. vs. Multi-racial Brazil: Is the Contrast Still Valid? *Journal of Latin American Studies* 25: 373–386.

Smitherman-Donaldson, Geneva, and Teun A. van Dijk, eds. 1988. *Discourse and Discrimination*. Detroit, Mich.: Wayne State University Press.

Sniderman, Paul M., and Thomas Piazza. 1993. *The Scar of Race*. Cambridge, Mass.: Belknap Press of the Harvard University Press.

Souza, Neusa Santos. 1983. *Tornar-se Negro*. Rio de Janeiro: Graal.

Stein, Stanley. 1957. *Vassouras: A Brazilian Coffee County, 1859–1900*. Cambridge, Mass.: Harvard University Press.

Stepan, Nancy. 1991. *The Hour of Eugenics: Gender and Nation in Latin America*. Ithaca, N. Y.: Cornell University Press.

Stewart, C. S. 1856. *Brazil and La Plata: The Personal Record of a Cruise*. New York: G. P. Putnam & Co.

Stutzman, R. 1981. El Mestizaje: An All-Inclusive Ideology of Exclusion. In *Cultural Transformations and Ethnicity in Modern Ecuador*, 45–93. New York: Harper and Row.

Telles, Edward. 1992. Residential Segregation by Skin Color in Brazil. *American Sociological Review* 57: 186–197.

———. 1995. Who Are the Morenas? *Social Forces* 73 (4): 1609–1611.

Terkel, Studs. 1992. *Race: How Blacks and Whites Think and Feel about the American Obsession*. New York: Anchor Books.

Thorne, Barrie, and Nancy Henley. 1975. *Language and Sex: Difference and Dominance*. Rowley, Mass.: Newbury House.

Toplin, Robert Brent. 1975. *The Abolition of Slavery in Brazil*. New York: Atheneum.

Turner, J. Michael. 1985. Brown into Black: Changing Racial Attitudes of Afro-Brazilian University Students. In *Race, Class, and Power in Brazil*, ed. Pierre-Michel Fontaine, 73–94. Los Angeles: Center for Afro-American Studies/University of California.

Twine, France Winddance. 1995. Towards an Engendered Analysis of Encounters with Racism: The Case of Upwardly Mobile Afro-Brazilians. Paper presented at the annual meeting of the American Anthropological Association, Washington, D.C.

———. 1996. O Hiato de Genero nas Percepcoes de Racismo: O Caso dos Afro-Brasileiros Socialmente Ascendentes. *Estudos Afro-Asiáticos* 29: 37–54.

———. 1998. *Racism in a Racial Democracy: The Maintenance of White Supremacy in Brazil*. New Brunswick, N. J.: Rutgers University Press.

Valladares, Licia do Prado. 1978. *Passa-se uma Casa: Análise do Programa de Remoção de Favelas do Rio de Janeiro*. Rio de Janeiro: Zahar Edições.

van Dijk, Teun A. 1984. *Prejudice in Discourse*. Amsterdam: Benjamins.

———. 1992. Discourse and the Denial of Racism. *Discourse and Society* 3: 87–118.

———. 1993. *Elite Discourse and Racism*. Newberry Park, Calif.: Sage Publications.

Veja. 1988. Centenario de um Mau Seculo. Editora Abril, Ano 20, No. 19, May 11.

Vogt, Carlos, and Peter Fry. 1996. *Cafundó: A Africa no Brasil*. São Paulo: Editora da Unicamp/Companhia das Letras.

Volosinov, V. N. 1973. *Marxism and the Philosophy of Language*. Cambridge, Mass.: Harvard University Press.

Wade, Peter. 1993. *Blackness and Race Mixture: The Dynamics of Racial Identity in Columbia*. Baltimore: Johns Hopkins University Press.

———. 1997. *Race and Ethnicity in Latin America*. London: Pluto Press.

Wafer, Jim. 1991. *The Taste of Blood: Spirit Possession in Brazilian Candomblé*. Philadelphia: University of Pennsylvania Press.

Wagley, Charles. 1963a. Race Relations in an Amazon Community. In *Race and Class in Rural Brazil*, ed. Charles Wagley, 116–141. New York: UNESCO/Columbia University Press.

———. 1971. *An Introduction to Brazil*. Rev. ed. New York: Columbia University Press.

———, ed. 1963b. *Race and Class in Rural Brazil*. 2nd ed. 1952. Reprint, New York: UNESCO/Columbia University Press.

Ware, Vron. 1992. *Beyond the Pale: White Women, Racism, and History*. London: Verso.

Wellman, D. T. 1977. *Portraits of White Racism*. Cambridge, U.K.: Cambridge University Press.

Wetherell, Margaret, and Jonathan Potter. 1993. *Mapping the Language of Racism: Discourse and Legitimation of Exploitation*. New York: Columbia University Press.

Willis, Paul E. 1977. *Learning to Labor: How Working-Class Kids Get Working-Class Jobs*. New York: Columbia University Press.

Winant, Howard. 1992. Rethinking Race in Brazil. *Journal of Latin American Studies* 24 (1): 173–192.

———. 1994. *Racial Conditions*. Minneapolis: University of Minnesota Press.

———. 1999. Racial Democracy and Racial Identity: Comparing the United States and Brazil. In *Racial Politics in Contemporary Brazil*, ed. George Michael Hanchard, 98–115. Durham, N.C.: Duke University Press.

Wood, Charles. 1990. Census Categories and Subjective Classifications of Race in Brazil: An Empirical Assessment. Paper presented at the Seminario Internacional sobre Desigualdade Racial no Brasil Contemporaneo, CEDEPLAR/UFMG, Belo Horizonte, March 6–9.

Wood, Charles H., and Jose Alberto M. de Carvalho. 1988. *The Demography of Inequality in Brazil*. Cambridge, U.K.: Cambridge University Press.

Wood, Charles H., and Peggy A. Lovell. 1992. Racial Inequality and Child Mortality in Brazil. *Social Forces* 70 (3): 703–724.

Wright, W. 1990. *Café con Leche: Race, Class, and National Image in Venezuela*. Austin: University of Texas Press.

Zaluar, Alba. 1985. *A Machina e a Revolta: As Organizações Populares e o Significado da Pobreza*. São Paulo: Editora Brasilense.

Zimmerman, Ben. 1963. Race Relations in the Arid Sertão. In *Race and Class in Rural Brazil*, ed. Charles Wagley, 82–115. New York: UNESCO/Columbia University Press.

Index

accommodation: politics of, 73–74, 202; racism and, 200; silence as public form of, 83

activism, antiracist, 187–189. *See also* black movement, Brazil's

activists, black: conversion experience of, 207–209, 210; movement critiqued by, 214–217. *See also* black movement, Brazil's

adoption (*criacão*), 239–240n.2

Africa: and cultural reappropriation, 190; ethnic groups in, 13

Anastácia, Escrava, 10; image of, 76; legend of, 75, 81–82; miniseries about, 77–78; rejection by authorities of, 76; submissive qualities of, 81; symbolic meaning and silence of, 81–82

ancestors, and role of color, 144–145

Andrews, George Reid, 38, 186

anger, containment of, 74. *See also* raiva

anthropology, ethnographic encounters in, 153

appearance: and discourse of color description in, 45, 51; and pragmatic discourse, 50–54; and racialized discrimination, 72–73

Arago, M. J., 76

"Aryan race," use of term, 163

asphalt: racism on, 86; world of, 119; use of term, 10

Assembly of God, 230

avoidance, and racial discourse, 206

Azevédo, Thales de, 219

beauty pageants, 236n.4

betrayal, narratives of, 119, 149

birth control, 236n.3, 242n.2

Black Brazilian Front (Frente Negra Brasileira), 187

black consciousness, 8, 126, 186, 189–191, 200–206; and politics of identity, 213

black men: and encounters with racism, 98, 106–111, 240n.4; occupations of, 96–97, 105; police harassment of 71, 94, 108–109, 110, 111, 124; prejudice against, 108, 113–114. *See also* gender differences

black movement, Brazil's, 8, 10, 30, 126, 173, 186; attitudes toward, 192–194; broader base for, 215–216; disagreements within, 189–190, 200; discourse of, 38, 196–197, 198; dominance of men in, 189; following of, 190–191; goal of, 217; internal criticism of, 214–214; routes to participation in, 209; white perception of, 163, 180, 181, 194

blackness: construction of, 58; devaluation of, 48–49, 50; euphemisms for, 31, 51–54; notions of, 48

black organizations: in contemporary Rio de Janeiro, 189–190; of 1946–1964, 187

black race: and whitening, 119–122; concept of, 30–31, 135; discourse about, 37–46; pride associated with, 45

Boas, Franz, 4
Bourdieu, Pierre, 60
"brainwashing," 202
brancazeda/brancoazedo, meaning of,
    241n.4
branca/branco, identification as, 39, 50.
    See also whiteness; whites
branqueamento (whitening), 119–122,
    142, 204, 219
branquelo, 85
Brazil: and idelology of racial democracy,
    4–8, 218–224; compared with South
    Africa, 242n.5; culture of, 4, 236n.1;
    national character of, 222–224
brincadeira (joking), 35, 51, 56, 134;
    within family, 143–144; racialized, 36;
    racist, 93
bumdum, 163, 176
Burdick, John, 80, 186, 237n.5, 239n.6
bureaucratization, and class
    consolidation, 14–15
Butler, Kim, 186

cab drivers, morro feared by, 110–111,
    240n.3
Campinas, research in, 150
Candomblé, 13, 76, 189, 210
canela (cinnamon), 146
capitalism: and class consolidation,
    14–15; globalized, 197; racism
    supported by, 149, 188, 195–196
Cardoso, Fernando Henrique, 187, 188
Carneiro, José Fernando, 223
carnival parades, 24
carnival performance groups, 190
Casa Grande e Senzala (Freyre), 4
cemetery, slave, 4
censorship, cultural, 60; and black
    movement, 191; as protection
    stratgegy, 83; rejection of, 197; silence
    of, 62. See also silence
censorship, government, 188
census interviews, 32, 237n.2
children: homeless, 226; of interracial
    marriages, 143; and racism,
    238–239n.2; racist discourse of,
    128–129; white, 241n.3

clareando a família (lightening the
    family), 135, 142, 219
clarinha, 143
Clark, Kenneth B., 127
claro, identification as, 34
class: and correlation with racial
    identity, 6, 8, 18, 30, 85, 86, 90,
    92–93, 104, 108, 122, 164, 198,
    199, 200; and courtship, 137; and
    social boundaries, 92, 95, 115; as
    explanation for prejudice, 27, 179,
    180, 181, 194, 198, 199
"cleaning the color," 142
"cleaning the family," 211–212
coffee plantations, 14
Collar government, 241n.1
color: Brazilian perceptions of, 118; and
    class structure, 30; in courtship and
    marriage, 135–143; description of, 31,
    36, 56, 57; and familial relations, 118,
    143–149; hierarchy of, 50, 122, 142;
    linguistic play associated with, 54–56;
    in pragmatic discourse, 31, 50–54; vs.
    race, 37, 43–45, 237n.5; and racial
    classification, 30, 33, 39, 56–57; in
    romantic relationships, 240–241n.4;
    and sexual politics, 240n.3; and
    socioeconomic status, 37–38, 122;
    terms used in survey, 34–35
color, people of: exclusion of, 181; free,
    14; issue of self-esteem among, 202,
    213; jokes about, 150; narratives of
    racism of, 154; poor, 200; in Rio's
    favelas, 18; silence of, 215
"color-blindness," for whites, 159
color identification, in census interview,
    32
color line, crossing, 170–174
community: and neighborly ethos, 9,
    130, 131, 133; racism in, 130–135;
    and violence, 3, 27–28, 226–233. See
    also Morro do Sangue Bom
competence, linguistic, 60–61
conformity, racism and, 200
confrontation: avoidance of, 133; futility
    of, 71
consciência negra, 207, 214, 216;

discursive nature of, 212–213. *See also*
black consciousness
consciousness: black, 189; fractured,
206, 207; of poor Brazilians of African
descent, 206; wounded, 204
contamination, fears of racial, 102
conversion: discourse of, 207–214;
racial, 210–211
courtship: color differences in, 135–143;
cross-class, 137; racially bounded
contexts for, 168
criacão (adoption), 239–240n.2
crime: and drug trafficking in Morro do
Sangue Bom, 22–23, 226, 228,
229–230; and favela stereotypes, 3,
17; racism as, 182
crioulo: as epithet, 49; identification as,
55; in racist context, 94; use of term,
177
culture: Brazilian, 4, 7, 236n.1; concept
of, 4; and concept of race, 12; and
silence, 62; and social structure, 7, 8.
See also censorship, cultural

DaMatta, Roberto, 121
dating, racially bounded contexts for,
168
death squads, 3, 27
Degler, Carl, 37
democracia racial, 4–9, 57, 58; Brazilian
discourses on, 155, 200–206; Brazilian
dream of, 223; contradictions of,
149; and cultural censorship, 60;
and discourses on race, 218; ideology
of, 219; meanings for, 8; and
miscegenation, 121, 141; mystificatory
character of, 11; as national hypocrisy,
117; and racist name-calling, 95;
silence and, 82–83, 116; utopianism
of, 184; victims of racism silenced by,
224
demonstrations, attending, 192–193
demystification, need for, 200
denial, discourse of, 64, 67
diminutives, function of, 52–53
discourse: of black movement, 186,
196–197, 198; of conversion,

207–214; of democracia racial, 201,
202, 218; of denial, 64, 67;
descriptive, 31, 36; devaluing
blackness, 134; and discrimination,
115, 155; dominant, 154–157, 186;
false, 200–206; manipulation of, 201;
metadiscourse, 9, 32, 45, 46, 57, 58,
62, 186; national, 222; pragmatic, 32,
50–54, 57; on racism, 194–200; racist,
88, 128; as unit of analysis, 8. *See also*
public discourse
discourse analysis, 155
discriminação social, 179
discrimination: awareness of, 68,
207–208; and black movement, 216;
discourse and, 155; job, 105, 106–107;
lack of recognition of, 205; by middle-
class whites, 165–168; perception of,
212; racial, 6, 72, 108, 196–197, 201,
238n.12; in racial discourse, 115;
white justification of, 103
dissimulation, and racial discourse, 206
domestic service, 97; and class
differences, 104; girls in, 98–99; and
middle class, 241n.1; work in, 239n.1.
See also empregadas
dominant, the: characteristics of, 154;
discourse of, 154–157
domination: critique of, 119; language
of, 47, 60–61; silence and, 82
dreaming: and moral doubt, 224;
rhetoric of, 222
drug traffickers, of Morro do Sangue
Bom, 22–23
drug use, in Morro do Sangue Bom, 233

Eco 92 (Internation Earth Summit),
225–226
economy: Brazilian, 6; moral, 114. *See
also* capitalism; wage labor
education: discrepancies in, 6; racism
and, 112
elites, Brazilian: as minority, 196; on
miscegenation, 120–121; racist
discourse of, 150, vs. middle class, 7
elites, negro, 214
emotions, silence and, 61, 70–74, 74–75

employer-empregada relationship, 104, 165

employment: denial of, 208–209; and discrimination, 105; and racism, 104–105; unemployment, 97, 105. *See also* wage labor

empregadas, 99, 103; food eaten by, 241n.2; white perceptions of, 166–167; work of, 239n.1

entrapment, 206; of dominated, 204; racialized basis of, 117; racism as form of, 172

equality, claims of, 220

escravo (slave), 238n.10. *See also* slavery

escuro, 34; identification as, 33

Essed, Philomena, 88

essentialism, 216; and politics of identity, 213

ethnography: discourse in, 9; narratives about racism in, 89; silence in, 62; UNESCO-sponsored, 154

eugenics movement, 120

euphemism: in pragmatic discourse, 36, 52, 53–54, 57–58; and racial discourse, 206

Eurocentrism, 195

evasion, of racism, 212

evil eye (*mau olhado*), 91

Ewbank, Thomas, 1, 2

exclusion: discriminatory, 93; racialized hierarchy of, 148; and racist discourse, 129

exploitation, economic, 5–6, 195

false consciousness, Marxist notion of, 202, 204

family: "cleaning," 211–212; as race criterion, 238n.7; racism in, 143–145

Fanon, Frantz, 127, 204, 205, 242n.4

favelas: associations with blackness, 18; criminal activity in, 17, 22, 23; housing in, 15; percent of population living in, 15, 16; in Rio de Janeiro, 15, 16; social networks in, 9; stereotypes of, 17–18; use of term, 15, 236n.2; video of, 240n.1; whites in, 200

feminism: antiracist politics and, 242n.3; sociolinguistics of, 61. *See also* women

Fernandes, Florestan, 47, 187

Fontaine, Pierre-Michel, 186

force, state-sanctioned, 71. *See also* police

fracturing, of consciousness, 206

Frankenberg, Ruth, 156

Frazier, E. Franklin, 59, 75, 183

Free people of color, 14

Frente Negra Brasileira (Black Brazilian Front), 187

Freyre, Gilberto, 4, 5, 121, 122, 147

Fry, Peter, 236n.1

fula, identification as, 146

gangs, of Morro do Sangue Bom, 22, 23

gender differences: in employment expectations, 104–105; in experiencing racism, 98, 111–113, 175–176, 240n.4. *See also* men; women

Goldstein, Donna, 240n.4

"good appearance," 101

Guerra, Yolando, 76

Guillermoprieto, Alma, 80

hair, in racial identification, 33, 42, 43

hairstyles, and racism, 72–73

Hanchard, George Michael, 186

Harris, Marvin, 29, 33, 54, 55, 237n.2, 238n.12

Hasenbalg, Carlos, 6, 38

Hausa, 13

Hegel, Georg Wilhelm Friedrich, 204

help-wanted ads, 101

hierarchy: color, 50, 122, 142; in empregada-patroa relationships, 104; and racism, 87

history: and black families, 144–148; of Brazillian black movement, 187–189; and Gilberto Freyre, 4–5; lack of negro heroes in, 205; and miscegenation, 119–122; of Morro do Sangre Bom, 15–17; national rhetoric of, 222; and silence, 61–62; of slavery and post-abolition era, 13–14

hopelessness, sense of, 108, 183

hotels, exclusion of people of color from, 181
hypodescent, 43

Ianni, Octavio, 187
identity: bipolar visions of, 30–31, 38–46, 57–58; and black consciousness, 207–214; color vs. race, 37, 43–45, 237n.5; and local survey data, 32, 34–35; role of race in, 7, 29–30; and system of racial classification, 33, 54; transnational conceptions of, 45; and whiteness, 154–157
ideology: ambiguity of, 135, 143, 148, 223; and *branqueamento* (whitening), 120–122, 204; and *democracia racial*, 5–6, 7, 46, 58, 59, 183, 218; and derogation of blackness, 47–50, 57, 87, 88, 89, 95, 119, 194, 195, 196, 205; and gender, 113–114; and internalized racism, 126–127, 129–130, 197; and nationalism, 7, 119, 219, 222; and silence, 82–83
"improving the race" (*melhorando a raça*), 119–122, 142
indifference, culturally produced, 184
industrialization, and class consolidation, 14–15
informants: activist, 200, 214–215; on black racism, 123–126; defensiveness of, 158, 159; and democracia racial, 116–117; exposure to news media of, 157–158; and stories about slavery, 65–66; white middle-class, 150–154, 158–170, 161, 241n.1
International Earth Summit (Eco 92), 225
interracial relationships: and *branqueamento* (whitening), 119–122, 142; among middle-class white informants, 170–174; in Morro do Sangue Bom, 118–119, 135–143; whites' attitudes toward, 174–178. *See also* miscegenation

Jackson, Michael, 122–123, 125, 126, 240n.1

jambo: identification as, 44; in pragmatic discourse, 52
job application process, 105–106, 208–209
job discrimination, 105, 106–108, 208–209. *See also* employment
jokes, racist, 93, 150
joking relationships, 35–36. *See also brincadeira*
Joseph, Galen, 157

Kottak, Conrad, 33, 34

labor, for free people of color, 15. *See also* wage labor
language: of domination, 47, 60–61; "hard words," 93–95; of race and color, 54–55; of racial identity, 9–10, 30, 34–35; of racialized discrimination, 38; and racialized traits, 49–50; to reach masses, 215. *See also* discourse
Lee, Spike, 240n.1
legitimacy, linguistic, 60–61
leisure activities: gendered nature of, 113; racism encountered in, 110
lightening the family (*clareando a família*), 135, 142, 219. *See also branqueamento*
limpeza (cleansing), 226, 227

macaco, as epithet, 49
Mandela, Nelson, 45
Mansfield, C. B., 185–186
marginality, 8; identity of, 129, 153, 170–171, 196
marriages: color differences in, 135; interracial, 174; mixed, 118–119. *See also* interracial relationships
Marxism: false consciousness of, 202; of MNU, 188
masked racism, 188
masters, study of, 156, 157
The Masters and the Slaves (Freyre), 4
mau olhado (evil eye), 91
media: author's portrayal in, 26–27; middle-class whites' exposure to, 157–158; racism of, 196, 202

melhorando a raça (improving the race), 119–122, 142

memory, and encounters with racism, 68–69, 75, 85–86; historical production of, 61–62, 201

men, encounters with racism of, 240n.4. *See also* black men; gender differences

mestiça/mestiço, identification as, 44, 103

middle class: aspirations for, 212; and black movement, 194; characteristics of, 241n.1; and drug trafficking, 22; favelas viewed by, 17–18; housing and, 16; identity articulated by, 152; indifference of, 184; and racism, 10, 204. *See also* whiteness; whites

militants, black, 18, 59, 185–186; accusations against, 205; imprisonment of, 187; linguistic reappropriation of, 238n.9; and notion of culture, 213; TV coverage of, 27. *See also* black movement

military coup of 1964, 187, 201

miscegenation, 5; celebration of, 29, 118, 140, 141; historical view of, 119–120; and racial categories, 29–30; in rhetoric, 222; and whitening of population, 120. *See also* marriages

mobility, upward: and denigration of blackness, 127; and "improving the race," 122; and racial discrimination, 6, 113

moral economy, racism in, 114

mordaça (muzzle), of Escrava Anastácia, 78–79

morena/moreno: as euphemism, 41; identification as, 33, 35, 38, 42, 44, 45, 50, 51; in polite register, 238n.12; in pragmatic discourse, 52, 53

moreninha, 143

Morrison, Toni, 156, 157

morro, 3; cleansing of, 226–227; and prejudice, 90; use of term, 15. *See also* favelas

Morro do Sangue Bom: and black activism, 191–194; children of, 95–96; drug trafficking in, 22; drug use in, 233; and Eco 92, 225–226; exodus

from, 230; history of, 3, 15, 16, 28; in international news, 229; ironic perspective of, 222; name of, 235n.1; police shakedowns in, 25; population of, 16; racism in, 119, 130–135; silence in, 62–68; social networks in, 9; transportation to, 18–19; understandings about oppression in, 114; work patterns of inhabitants of, 95–114

Movimento Negro Unificado (MNU), 188

mulata/mulato: identification as, 33, 34, 36, 37, 38, 41, 42, 44; in marriage market, 136; use of term, 237n.3

"mulato press," 237n.4

muzzle (*mordaça*), of Escrava Anastácua, 78–79

myth: of democracia racial, 218–219, 221; of "friendly master," 239n.4

Nader, Laura, 152, 157

Nago, 13

name-calling: in encounters with racism, 94–95; and racist epithets, 46–47, 48–49

narratives: about courtship, 137–140; abrupt recall in, 85–86; of betrayal, 119, 131; metadiscursive, 57–58; of race mixture, 146; women's, 100

narratives of racism: and cultural continuities, 149; definition of, 87; and definition of racism, 89–91; and dominant groups, 87–88; in family and community, 87, 119, 126, 130, 140; and family history, 145; and gender differences, 95–114; and informants critiques of racism, 114–117; published, 88; and racist name-calling, 93–95; and surveillance, 91–92; theoretical analysis of, 88–89

national identity, 119

nationalism, 5, 7, 119, 218, 219, 222

negão: identification as, 35, 51

nego, 47

negra/negro, 34; discrimination against,

115; identification as, 33, 40, 41, 42, 43, 44, 45, 50, 55; job market for, 106; negative associations with term, 39, 47–48

negritude, transnational discourses on, 213

negro, use of term, 238n.8

negro assumido, becoming, 207–214

negrophobia, codification of, 197

negros de ganho (hired slaves), 14

neguinha/neguinho, 124; colonial etymology of, 53; identification as, 41; in pragmatic discourse, 52

news media: racism covered by, 157–158; role in Brazil of, 202

nightclubs, exclusion of people of color from, 181

Nova Època, 22, 23, 226, 228, 229, 240n.3

nursemaids, 99, 166, 171, 241n.3

objectification, racialized, 171

occupations: men's, 96–97; womens, 96. *See also* employment

odd-jobbing, 96

oppressed, psychology of, 60, 127

oppression: political accommodation to, 75; racialized nature of, 10, 30, 58, 112, 114, 116, 130, 205–206, 214; and silence, 82

paixao, interracial, 192

Pão de Azucar, 21

parda/pardo, 32; identification as, 33, 42, 43, 44, 45; in pragmatic discourse, 52, 53

patriotism, Brazilian, 222

Patrocínio, José, 192

Pelé, 123, 126, 240n.2

police: black, 124; force used by, 71; military, 230, 231; morro feared by, 240n.3; racial epithets used by, 52, 94, 109; working poor and, 236n.5

police harassment: arbitrary, 71; of men, 71, 94, 108–109, 110, 111, 124; as racism, 201, 239n.5

police informers, 27

polite register, 35, 46, 50, 51, 52, 55, 57, 207. *See also* euphemism; pragmatic discourse

political repression, 71, 187–188, 200, 212; and censorshp, 60; and psychology, 75

politics, sexual, 240n.3

poor, definition of, 96

Portuguese, 5, 13, 146, 180

Portuguese language, Carioca or Rio, 11. *See also* language

poverty: in Brazilian society, 4, 6, 15, 18, 196; and community, 131; race and 235n.4; and racism, 4, 6, 28, 91, 122, 147, 148, 179, 196, 199–200. *See also* class

power: acquisitive, 5, 125; and dominant ideology, 7, 83, 122, 155, 157; and language-discourse, 9, 155; of racist epithets, 47, 141; and social boundaries, 153, 154

powerlessness: confrontation with, 72; racialized basis of, 117

pragmatic discourse, 31, 46, 50–54, 205, 206; definition and function of, 52–55, 56–57

prejudice: boundary-maintaining forms of, 93; class, 90; class vs. color, 27, 91; color, 89, 90; and job opportunities, 107; racialized, 6, 67, 108; regional, 90; studies of, 88; white justification of, 103

preta/preto, 34; identification as, 38, 39, 40, 41–42, 42, 44, 45, 55; negative connotation of, 48; use of term, 238n.8

pretinha/pretinho, 143; identification as, 35; in pragmatic discourse, 52, 54

privacy, for middle class, 152

protest, futility of, 71

psychology: Fanonian, 205; of racism, 74–75

public discourse: democracia racial in, 7; limited access to, 61; miscegenation in, 102; on racism, 188, 202. *See also* discourse

purchasing power, discrepancies in, 5

quilombolas (escaped slaves), 3

race: bipolar concept of, 27, 30–31, 34, 38, 45–46, 57, 237n.5, 237n.6; vs. color, 37, 44–45, 237n.5; concept of, 12; in courtship and marriage, 135–143; discourse on, 31, 37–46; dominant narratives of, 116; explicit talk about, 36; and hypodescent, 43; linguistic play associated with, 54–56; and sexual politics, 240n.3; use of term, 12, 235n.3

race-color terms: contextual meaning of, 30, 31–32, 34; in everyday discourse, 35–36; in pragmatic discourse, 31, 51, 52, 56, 57; and racial classification, 33, 34, 54–55, 56

race relations, Brazilian model of, 30, 237n.1

racial classification: system of, 33, 54–58

racial identity, 210, 235n.2; bipolar concept of, 45, 46, 238n.12; Brazil's history of, 29; and color hierarchy, 50; hair in, 33, 42, 43; language of, 9–10, 30, 34–35; subjectivity of, 37; and transnational discourse, 213

racial inferiority, concept of, 130

racial slurs, of police, 36, 52, 94, 109

racism, 183; accounting for, 114–117; acknowledgment of, 179; awareness of, 160, 178, 179–181; black, 120, 124, 125–126; Brazilian-style, 4, 8, 121, 149, 217; and carnival parades, 24; childhood experiences with, 64–65; during commute, 108–109; concealment of forms of, 82; construction of, 87; and cultural censorship, 10, 60; defining, 89–91, 119, 126–127, 128; denial of, 63, 64, 67, 101, 195, 203; destructive power of, 85; of dominant (white) groups, 155; and employment, 104; evil eye of, 91–93; in family, 143–149; forms of overt, 103; gender differences in perception of, 111–113; government recognition of, 189; history of, 194–195, 197; internalization of, 85,

126–130, 129; on job, 98; masked, 188; men's encounters with, 240n.4; in morro, 130–135; motivation for, 95; of negro, 119; obfuscated, 184; perceptions of, 66–67, 133; pervasiveness of, 142–143; of police, 109; political economy of, 114; poverty and, 198–199; reality of, 81; reverse, 216; silence surrounding, 69–70, 74, 188, 190; systemic, 27, 89–90, 112; and unemployment, 107; "veiled" forms of, 202–203; victims of, 224; and wage labor, 116

racism, discourse on, 194–200; academic challenge, 4–5; conversations, 84; discourse analysis in, 155; as explanation of last resort, 100; gender differences in, 100–102; lack of, 59, 62, 63, 64, 98, 182, 209, 211–212; narratives, 10, 86, 87, 89–91, 103; representing, 87–89; secondhand stories about, 67; white perspectives, 163, 171–172

racismo mascarado, 188

rage. *See* raiva

raiva, concept of, 127, 172

Red Command, 23, 25, 228, 229–230

religion, in Brazil, 13, 239n.6; Candomblé, 13, 76, 189, 210; and black movement, 191; and conversion, 230, 233; and legend of Escrava Anastàcia, 75–77, 82, 239n.6; Protestant, 76, 230; Umbanda, 13

repression: communal form of, 201; physical, 200. *See also* political repression

residents' association, of Morro do Sangue Bom, 17, 19

resignation, forms of, 215

resistance: and race-color discourses, 56–57; silence as form of, 83

restaurants: Brazilian, 242n.5; exclusion of people of color from, 181

reveillon, of 1991, 23

rich, definition of, 96

Rio de Janeiro: black movement organizations in, 189; carnival of, 24;

history of, 1–2, 14–15; and
  International Earth Summit, 225–226;
  shantytowns of, 15–18
Rodrigues, José Honorio, 222, 224

sainthood: and silence, 75–83. *See also*
  Anastácia, Escrava
Samba music, 23–24, 108, 137
samba schools, 189
sangue bom, term defined, 235n.1
Sanjek, Roger, 55; 54
Sansone, Livio, 238n.11
Santa Teresa, escaped slaves in, 3;
  middle-class residents of, 152;
  shantytowns of, 3–4; wealth and
  poverty in, 5
sarará, identification as, 39, 146
Saunders, George, 61
segregation, 188; de facto, 92;
  residential, 15, 18, 195, 197; of white
  middle-class life, 169. *See also*
  discrimination
self-alienation, and racist discourse, 129
self-censorship, 82
self-hatred, black, 127
self-identification, 32
self-presentation, to avoid racism, 73
servants. *See* domestic service;
  empregadas
sexual partners, and stereotypes, 137
shame: of blackness, 206; racism and,
  72, 148
shantytowns, 236n.2; Rio's hillside,
  15–18; of Santa Teresa, 3–4; violence
  and, 28. *See also* favelas
Sider, Gerald, 62
silence, 58; about racism, 116;
  accounting for, 68–75; forced, 81;
  government-enforced, 188; in Morro
  do Sangue Bom, 62–68; paradox of,
  75; between parents and children, 60,
  64, 65, 66–68, 239n.3; and power, 69;
  as protection, 68; and sainthood, 75;
  speaking against, 115; theoretical
  treatments of, 60–62
Silva, Nelson do Valle, 37–38
Silverstein, Michael, 56

Skidmore, Thomas, 38, 120, 121
slavery: abolition of, 14; and association
  with term negro, 39, 47, 239n.10; in
  Brazil, 84, 195, 197; compared to
  contemporary racism, 4, 65–66, 84;
  ending of, 191–192; and Escrava
  Anastácia, 76, 77, 81; racism "rooted"
  in, 114; stories about, 65–66, 146,
  149; in 19th century, 2–3, 13–14
slaves: study of, 156; white middle class
  perception of, 168
slave trade, Brazilian, 13
social behavior, and racist discourses,
  134–135
social memory, production of, 61
society, Brazilian, 199; as explanation for
  racism, 111, 112, 113, 129, 130
socioeconomic status, 6. *See also* class
solidarity: black, 126, 189; racialized, 43;
  and racist discourse, 129
stereotypes: awareness of, 136; sexual, 137
sterilization, forced, 242n.2
street vending, 96
suicide, among 19th-century slaves, 2–3,
  239n.7
survival, racism and, 64
syncretistic traditions, Brazilian, 13

talk: cultural significance of, 9; inability
  to, 82; ineffectiveness of, 69–70. *See
  also* discourse; silence
talking back: danger of, 71; vs. talking
  about (racism), 69, 70, 72
Teatro Experimental do Negro (TEN),
  187
television, sensationalism of, 26–27. *See
  also* news media
terminology, race-color, 30, 54–55. *See
  also* race-color terms
terror, 200
Third Command, 230
Twine, France Winddance, 97–98, 114,
  239n.2, 241n.5, 241n.6

Umbanda, 13
understanding, unexpressed, 75, 183
unemployment, 97, 105

UNESCO studies, 134
Unified Black Movement (MNU), 188.
    See also black movement, Brazil's
unity, racial, 223
urbanization, and class consolidation,
    14–15

values: and racism, 87; universal human,
    220
van Dijk, Teun A., 87, 155
Vargas, Getulio, 16
Vargas regime, 187
Veríssimo, José, 121, 142
victimization, silence and, 75
video, of Rio's favelas, 240n.1
vocabulary, race-color, 30, 54–55. *See
    also* language

wage labor: attitudes toward, 97;
    gendered nature of, 113; housing and,
    15; and racism, 86, 116
Wagley, Charles, 29, 219, 235n.2
water, in Morro do Sangue Bom, 16
wealth, unequal distribution of, 5–6
well-being, measures of economic, 6
whiteness: attitudes toward, 131;
    construction of, 10, 155–156; defined,
    156; dominant discourse and,
    154–157; as genetic resource, 177;
    hyper-valuation of, 142; positive

valuation of, 49; and racial
    transgression, 174–178; social
    geography of, 170
"whitening" (*branqueamento*), 120, 121,
    122, 142, 204, 219
whites: and black movement, 194;
    identification as, 33, 42, 51, 152;
    indifference of, 184; poor, 200; racism
    of, 103, 112; racist discourse of, 165;
    and silence about racism, 182–183
white superiority, presumption of, 132
women: in domestic service, 81, 97,
    98–100; professional African-
    American, 88; racism defined by, 90;
    reproductive patterns of, 236n.3; work
    of, 96. *See also* empregadas; gender
    differences
women, black, 113; and white men, 80;
    as workhorses, 136
women of color, urban, 15. *See also*
    color, people of
women's groups, African Brazilian,
    242n.1
workers, daily commute of, 95–96

X-Nines, 228

Yoruba, 13

Zimmerman, Ben, 238n.7

About the Author

Robin E. Sheriff is an assisstant professor of anthropology at Florida International University.